Animal Ethics

Animal Ethics

Robert Garner

polity

First published in 2005 by Polity Press

Polity Press
65 Bridge Street
Cambridge CB2 1UR, UK.

Polity Press
350 Main Street
Malden, MA 02148, USA

ISBN: 0-7456-3078-2
ISBN: 0-7456-3079-0 (pb)

A catalogue record for this book is available from the British Library.

Typeset in 10.5 on 12 pt Sabon
by SNP Best-set Typesetter Ltd, Hong Kong
Printed and bound in Great Britain by
TJ International Ltd, Padstow, Cornwall

The publisher has used its best endeavours to ensure that the URLs for external websites referred to in this book are correct and active at the time of going to press. However, the publisher has no responsibility for the websites and can make no guarantee that a site will remain live or that the content is or will remain appropriate.

Every effort has been made to trace all copyright holders, but if any have been inadvertently overlooked the publishers will be pleased to include any necessary credits in any subsequent reprint or edition.

For further information on Polity, visit our website: www.polity.co.uk

Contents

Preface

This book is the culmination of many years' study of the politics and philosophy of the animal rights movement. John Thompson at Polity suggested to me that I write a more general text on animal ethics than I had originally intended, and I'm grateful to him for that advice. What has resulted, I hope, is a text that is more comprehensive and rounded than other introductory volumes on animal rights, which tend to promote a particular way of looking at animal ethics. My approach is more eclectic, but having said that I am convinced of the case for according to animals a higher moral status than the current orthodoxy allows, a position which would change radically what it is morally permissible to do to animals.

As always with a project such as this I have cause to thank those people who have helped in a variety of ways. I would like to thank two anonymous referees who provided many useful comments on the first draft. I have been privileged to meet some of the key activists and thinkers in the animal protection movement and I hope that some of their knowledge and enthusiasm has rubbed off on me. Many cohorts of students have had to put up with attempts by me to try out ideas on them, as have my academic colleagues in research seminars. Other people have, with some justification, felt a little neglected by my all-too-often decision to seek out the company of a word processor rather than theirs.

Last but not least, the book is dedicated to Henry Spira, with whom I had the great privilege of meeting and communicating over a period of years. In his all-too-short lifetime he achieved more for the well-being of animals than I could ever hope to do.

Robert Garner
Leicester

1

Introduction

Why another book on animal ethics? Aren't there enough accounts of the moral relationships between humans and nonhuman animals? Well, in one sense, yes, there are. Numerous accounts exist, referred to in the course of this book, trying to tell us how we should treat animals and, in most cases, showing that there is a gap between how we ought to treat them and how we actually do treat them. However, there is, I believe, room for at least one more text on the moral status of animals.

This is partly because this volume serves a slightly different function from most of the existing animal ethics literature. This literature tends either to focus on one particular area of the debate or tries to develop a distinctive position, paying only a passing and sometimes grudging interest to alternative views. By contrast, this volume takes a much more comprehensive approach, describing and evaluating a wide variety of different positions in the animal ethics debate and applying them to different ways in which animals are treated. In addition, despite the ink spilt in trying to articulate how we should regard animals not of our species, in practice there still appears to be not only enormous confusion – some would say schizophrenia – about our relationship with animals, but also extremely divergent views. For example, how do we referee between someone who holds the view that we are morally entitled to confine highly intelligent and social mammals in barren environments, in order to fatten them so we can slaughter them to eat their flesh and wear their skin, and someone who regards it as a moral imperative not to eat animals or wear their skins irrespective of the character of their rearing? The fact that people can hold such polar opposite views illustrates the need for continuing reflection on this issue.

Describing what humans do to animals is not only morally confusing, but also elicits a variety of different emotions. A number of examples will illustrate this. Take this description of a scene filmed by a video camera in the kitchen of a Chinese restaurant, where a cat is being prepared for customers (Regan, 2004: 1):

> While the cat claws and screeches, the cook hits her several times with an iron bar. Clawing and screeching more now, she is abruptly submerged in a tub of scalding water for about ten seconds. Once removed, and while still alive, the cook skins her, from head to tail, in one swift pull. He then throws the traumatized animal into a large stone vat where . . . we watch her gulp slowly . . . her eyes glazed, until . . . she drowns. The whole episode . . . takes several minutes. When the meal is served, the diners eat heartily, offering thanks and praise to the cook.

At this stage, it might be useful to think what it is about this scene that you find, to say the least, morally problematic (assuming, of course, that you do find it morally problematic). Is it the fact that it is a cat being killed and cooked? Would you feel the same if it was a rat, or, indeed, a lobster? Or is it the fact that the cat was not killed humanely? If the latter, it should be noted that, according to Regan (2004: 199–200), the world's best-known animal rights philosopher, compared to many other animals – the billions of animals raised in factory farms and killed for food in the developed world, those confined in circuses or zoos, or being experimented on in the laboratory – the cat may have been 'one of the lucky ones'. While not necessarily wishing to endorse Regan's conclusion, his comment does, of course, raise questions both about the treatment of animals in these other arenas and about the constituent elements of an animal's life that need to be identified by the animal ethicist.

Take another example. The green sea turtle is said to be a 250-million-year-old species. It is now an endangered species, supposedly protected by international agreement. In parts of the world, however, the treaty is not enforced and an illegal trade in the meat of the creature flourishes. A journalist comments on the trade (Aglionby, 2000):

> Barbaric is too gentle a word for the slaughtering process I witness: apparently it would ruin the meat to kill them before skinning them. The turtle, which can live more than 200 years, is one of the few animals that cries, and on more than one occasion I see tears running down these animals' faces.

Again, the reader is invited to think about what, if anything, is particularly disturbing about this situation. There are a number of candidates. One might be that the sea turtle is endangered, or the fact that it can live up to 200 years. Alternatively, it could be the fact that a wild animal is confined or that it is not humanely killed. Finally, it might be the comment about the turtle's ability to cry that is particularly disturbing. If so, an interesting contrast is with the laboratory rabbit. Rabbits are particularly useful as testers for the toxicity of cosmetics and household products, precisely because they do not have any tear ducts and therefore cannot flush out substances that are put in their eyes. Again, the reader is asked to think about which is worse, the treatment of the green sea turtle or that of the laboratory rabbit?

The final example is from closer to home. In 1998, the British and international media went into a feeding frenzy covering the story of two pigs that had escaped on their way to an abattoir in Wiltshire. The story was even dramatized later for television. The press and the public pleaded with the owners not to have the animals slaughtered once caught and, sure enough, they were reprieved. But while the public response to this event was understandable, it still remains an odd reaction in the context of the brutal reality of the way pigs are raised and killed for food, a practice which the vast majority of people implicitly accept by eating them. Sympathetic responses to the plight of animals for whom we would usually not give two hoots are not uncommon, however, revealing our schizophrenic attitude to them in all its glory. There was, for instance, the case of Phoenix the calf, so named because she somehow survived a Ministry of Agriculture cull of healthy animals during the British foot-and-mouth crisis in 2001. Under sentence of death a second time, a massive media campaign, which brought the issue into the general election campaign, resulted in a reprieve from no less a place than 10 Downing Street. Put in the context of the way that calves are normally treated, then, there is no doubt that Phoenix, like the cat earlier, would have been one of the lucky ones even had she been humanely killed.

Perhaps one can understand the sympathetic reaction to a cute two-week-old calf. Less understandable was the discomfort that many felt at the policy of slaughtering animals as part of the campaign against foot and mouth. Many journalists waxed eloquently about how terrible it was that the British countryside was littered with the burning corpses of dead animals. However, those journalists who eat meat – the vast majority – cannot, with any consistency at least, complain about this on animal welfare grounds. Yes, the slaughter was an appalling indictment of our strongly anthropocentric – or human-centred – attitude to nonhuman animals, but then so is the industrialized way in which we raise and slaughter animals for food. Indeed, there is a strong case for saying that, for the most part, the animals slaughtered on farms as a result of foot-and-mouth were the lucky ones in the sense that they avoided the stress of a lengthy and often painful trip to the abattoir, and the terror of the slaughterhouse itself.

As a result of the cases described above, and there are many more I could have included, a large number of readers will have experienced a range of emotions, perhaps including confusion, anger, pity, sadness, resignation and maybe even nausea. As a species we don't seem to be clear at all how we should treat nonhuman animals. What we do to them would appear to encompass the extremes of cruelty, indifference and sentimentality. Animal rights advocates seek to add another element, currently in short supply, that of respect. The goal of this book is to reduce or even eliminate the collective scratching of heads by explaining and evaluating the behaviour described above in the context of competing moral theories.

Contexts

While the act of philosophizing about the moral status of animals is as old as philosophy itself, more has been written on animal ethics in the past three decades or so than in the previous 2,000 years. Much of this more contemporary literature has challenged the view, long enshrined in mainstream moral philosophy, that animals have an inferior moral status to humans. As Benton (1993: 75) points out: 'Modern Western moral philosophy has been almost exclusively centred on the moral character of the actions of human individuals, the moral status of persons, and the ethical legitimacy of human social institutions.'

Richard Ryder (1989; 1998), the best-known historian of the animal protection movement (as well as being an important political activist), chronicles the challenge to the previously dominant anthropocentrism. The emergence of a revitalized and radicalized animal rights movement has been accompanied by a body of ideas seeking to justify a higher moral status for animals. The best-known philosophical accounts are Singer's (1990) utilitarian case for a higher moral status for animals, and Regan's (1984) rights-based study, but there are many other worthy contributors to this debate.[1] Since then, a 'second wave' of animal ethics has emerged, at least in part as a response to the philosophical backlash to the original pro-animal works.[2]

This book is different from much of the existing animal ethics literature in the sense that, rather than adopting one particular position which is applied to the treatment of animals and defended against challenges, it tries to provide a comprehensive account of animal ethics and the implications of different positions for the way in which animals are treated and what we are entitled to do to defend them from human exploitation. That is not to say, of course, that I have no ethical position of my own. I strongly believe, as I will indicate here – and have indicated elsewhere – that animals are worthy of a higher moral status than the one currently given in developed countries and that, as a consequence, much of what we do to animals is unjustified.

Beyond this, I make no apologies for my eclectic disposition. I admit to being undecided about what exactly it is that animals are due and how this is to be justified, and to that extent researching and writing this book has continued the voyage of discovery for its author, much as I hope it sets the reader on his/her own. Equally, I am also conscious, not surprisingly perhaps, that because of my background as a political scientist it is extremely unlikely, in the near future at least, that Western societies will avail themselves of a new paradigm regarding their relationships with animals. As a result, it is important to ask whether what we do to animals is consistent with the mainstream or orthodox moral view about them.

Moral blindspot?

From the start it should be recorded with emphasis that, irrespective of the apparent acts of kindness recorded at the start of this chapter, animals *are* exploited mercilessly at the hands of humans, and *do* suffer enormously for our benefit. We kill billions of animals every year for a wide variety of purposes, primarily for food, but also in the pursuit of scientific knowledge, to ensure that the products we use are safe, and to use parts of their bodies such as their fur or skin, and merely for sport. Arguably more to the point, we also subject them to every imaginable atrocity, disposing of them when we no longer require their company, confining them in zoos and circuses, and deliberately inflicting suffering on them in the laboratory and in industrialized agriculture. Crucially, the animals debate is not now, if it ever was, concerned about individual acts of cruelty to animals, but is about their institutional exploitation as sources of our food, clothes, entertainment or good health. Inflicting suffering on animals is big business.

In this context, those who are uncomfortable, if not downright hostile, regarding current practices might wonder what kind of moral malaise humans have got themselves into here. It is this moral incomprehension that J. M. Coetzee's character Elizabeth Costello expresses so eloquently in his work of fiction *The Lives of Animals* (1999). Costello says in the course of a public lecture to a university audience:

> Let me say it openly, we are surrounded by an enterprise of degrada-tion, cruelty, and killing which rivals anything that the Third Reich was capable of, indeed dwarfs it, in that ours is an enterprise without end, self-regenerating, bringing rabbits, rats, poultry, livestock cease-lessly into the world for the purpose of killing them.

Talking later to her son, after a largely negative reaction to her lecture, Costello tries to grapple – as many animal rights advocates do – with her involvement in a world where the vast majority par-ticipate in the exploitation of animals without any moral qualms:

> I seem to move around perfectly easily among people, to have perfectly normal relations with them. Is it possible, I ask myself, that all of them are participants in a crime of stupefying proportions? Am I fantasiz-ing it all? I must be mad! Yet every day I see the evidences. The very people I suspect produce the evidence, exhibit it, offer it to me. Corpses. Fragments of corpses that they have bought for money. It is as if I were to visit friends, and to make some polite remark about the lamp in their living room, and they were to say, 'Yes, it's nice, isn't it? Polish-Jewish skin it's made of, we find that's best, the skins of young Polish-Jewish virgins.'

Of course, such a comparison can only be made if one thinks that the moral status of animals is identical to that of humans. The aim of this book is to submit that position to critical scrutiny. For the record, unlike Costello, I do not hold that position to be true, and neither, incidentally, does Singer, who wrote a response to Coetzee in an edition of his book (Coetzee, 1999: 85–91). Nevertheless, I do think that animals have a much higher moral status than is commonly believed to be the case, and that many of the ways animals are cur-rently treated are morally illegitimate. Because of this, I sympathize greatly with Costello's alienation from this aspect of human thought and behaviour. If Gandhi's famous statement, that 'the greatness of a nation and its moral progress can be judged by how its animals are treated', has any merit then there are few, if any, countries in the world which deserve the epithet.

Structure of the book

The most profitable way of determining the moral status of animals – or, in other words, how they ought to be treated by us humans – involves an attempt to identify morally relevant differences. A failure to identify any morally relevant differences would result in a valid claim for moral equality. We would not then be morally entitled to treat animals any differently from humans. For example, if we do not eat humans or experiment on them in laboratories then we are not entitled to use animals in this way either. Obviously, humans differ from animals in a variety of ways, just as much as there are major differences between different humans as well as members of different non-human animal species. To have any impact on the moral worth of animals and humans, however, these differences have to be *morally* relevant.

It is widely accepted now, although it was not in the past, that racial or gender differences are morally insignificant. A question pertinent to animal ethics is whether the fact of species difference, without any additional argument, has any moral significance. Those who argue that it has not, stating that species membership alone is a reason for justifying moral superiority, are guilty of speciesism, just as those who make similar statements regarding race or gender are guilty of racism or sexism respectively (Ryder 1975: 16). Indeed, for the pro-animal philosophers, as we might call them, the 'liberation' of animals represents an expansion of the circle of moral consider-ability. As Singer (1981: 120) points out:

> The circle of altruism has broadened from the family and tribe to the nation and race, and we are beginning to recognize that our obliga-tions extend to all human beings. The process should not stop there . . . The only justifiable stopping place for the expansion of altruism is the point at which all whose welfare can be affected by our actions are included within the circle of altruism.

This, of course, includes animals by virtue of their ability to appre-ciate pleasure and suffer pain.

The problem of according moral weight to species membership is considered in more detail in chapter 2. It is argued that, as many pro-animal philosophers have pointed out, a more appropriate guide to the moral significance of animals is the principle of the equal consideration of interests. This enables us to jettison mere species membership as a criterion of moral worth since both humans and animals can have interests. Before we can hope to establish what moral weight ought to be applied to animals, of course, we have to discover exactly what interests are possessed by humans and animals. This task is undertaken in chapters 3–5.

It might be suggested that animals have no interests at all, or none that we need to worry about furthering. If this is accepted then we have no direct duties to animals at all. This does not mean that we can necessarily do what we like to animals, since we may have indirect duties to them as a result of direct duties we owe to other humans. The case for according no direct moral worth to animals, and the degree to which animals can still be protected as a result of indirect duties we might owe them, is the subject matter of chapter 3.

If we do owe some direct moral duties to animals then we have to ask how much do we owe and why? Put another way, if we establish that animals are morally worthy, then what is to stop us from according moral equality to them so that they are as morally worthy as human beings? This is the subject matter of chapters 4 and 5. In chapter 4, we consider various reasons for according moral superiority to humans. These include the fact that humans are moral agents, and that, it is alleged, they have souls, but the most sustained claim has been based around the mental complexity of humans, often characterized in shorthand as personhood. The rest of chapter 4 and all of chapter 5 are concerned with assessing this claim.

There are three main responses we could make to the claim that those who have the characteristics of personhood are deserving of moral superiority over those who do not. The first is to deny that all animals lack personhood. The second is to explore the implications of the fact, say, that not all humans are persons – to be achieved through an examination of the so-called 'argument from marginal cases'. The third, considered in chapter 5, is the argument that, in any case, personhood does not do what is claimed for it, or at least not as much. In other words, those who are not persons, or who do not have all of the characteristics of personhood – or not to the same degree – may still have considerable moral worth. This latter response takes us, in particular, into issues of life and death. Is it a greater wrong to kill a person than a non-person and, if so, does this mean that human life is more morally significant than animal life?

Chapters 6–10 take us in different directions. Most of chapter 6 provides a critical evaluation of the various theories – primarily rights and utilitarianism – designed to tell us how we should treat humans and animals once we have established their moral worth. As we will see from chapters 2–5, establishing the moral worth of animals is fraught with difficulties, not least because of the apparent contestability of many of the arguments (see below for more on this). Chapter 6 begins with an examination of attempts to apply the contractarian approach to animals. This approach claims to avoid these problems of contestability by defending, ultimately unsuccessfully in this author's view, what it sees as an objective means of establishing a high degree of moral worth for animals without needing to engage in the philosophical niceties explored in chapters 2–5.

Chapters 7–9 seek to apply the theories developed in the preceding chapters to the actual ways in which animals are treated. We will ask whether we should eat animals (the subject matter of chapter 7), whether we should use them as our testers in laboratories (the subject matter of chapter 8) and whether we should keep animals as our companions, in circuses or in zoos, and whether we should utilize them as our prey by hunting them (the subject matter of chapter 9). Chapter 10, finally, focuses on issues of agency. It asks what particular social and political framework is most appropriate for the protection of animal interests, whether there is a particular social grouping more likely to be instrumental in bringing about change in the way animals are treated, and what methods of bringing about this change are justified.

The issue of agency is an important but much-neglected aspect of animal ethics. Put simply, given that animals – George Orwell notwithstanding – are not going to effect their own liberation, who is best placed to do it for them? This issue of agency might be regarded by some as a separate, political or sociological dimension and therefore not the subject of ethics, however 'applied' they are. This is mistaken in two ways. In the first place, animal liberation strategies are informed from, and ought to be judged by, moral theories of what we are entitled to do to animals. Put simply, how urgently we regard the need to improve the way in which animals are treated – and what we are entitled to do in order to effect this improvement – will depend largely upon how badly we judge the present treatment of animals to be from a moral viewpoint. Second, ethical theories which tell us – as animal rights/liberation theories do – that so much is wrong with our current treatment of animals are renegeing on their responsibility by then refusing to get involved in a discussion of political praxis. This unity of theory and practice, derived originally from Marx – described simply as 'reflective living' – is essential for those who want to improve the way in which animals are treated (Lodge, 1951: 1). As Warnock (1998: 107) has emphasized: 'The subject-matter of ethics demands that one becomes emotionally as well as theoretically and philosophically committed to one's beliefs.'

One feature of the political praxis of animal liberation is, as indicated above, the relationship between moral theory and the strategies animal advocates are morally obliged or permitted to use. Here, in particular, it can be asked to what degree direct action in pursuit of animal liberation is justified, particularly when it involves an element of violence. Another feature of political praxis is the relationship between political ideologies and the moral status of animals. Here, a little-commented upon feature of animal ethics is that the predominant approaches derive from the liberal tradition, and yet, as we will see, liberalism is problematic as an appropriate ideological location for animal protection. As an alternative, it might be more appropriate to adopt feminist or socialist analyses if we are to have any chance of making progress in improving the way animals are regarded and treated, should we, of course, wish to see such an improvement.

Animals and ethics

Before we begin our exploration of the animal ethics debate it is worthwhile noting that this debate is subject to the same contestability problem affecting all ethical issues. This involves the question: to what extent are moral statements knowable in the sense, at the very least, of being able to be defended effectively against alternative views, or are we condemned to a moral relativism where anything goes? There has been a long-standing metaethical debate about the purpose and relevance of moral statements. For much of the twentieth century, moral philosophy in general, and political philosophy in particular, had something of a bad press. This was partly to do with the influence of logical positivism, an early twentieth-century school of thought that recognized only definitional statements and those capable of empirical verification as meaningful (Ayer, 1936). Statements of norms, then, were regarded as literally meaningless. The 'emotivist' school of ethics, similarly, regards moral statements as 'nothing but expressions and attempted elicitations of emotion', which are 'incapable of truth and cannot embody knowledge' (Thomas, 1993: 51).

While moral statements are not meaningless in the sense of being gibberish, it is important to confirm that they do differ from statements of fact. This is not to say that empirical facts cannot play an invaluable role in ethics, but they cannot, in deference to 'Hume's Law' (the denial that we can generate an 'ought' from an 'is') be the ultimate arbiters in ethical questions. This is one reason why moral philosophers often invoke intuitions – defined by Holland (2003: 4) as 'the typical, not particularly-philosophical responses and judgments that we tend to have and make' – to reinforce their case.

Moral pluralism, if not moral relativism (the latter denying that it is possible to choose intellectually between competing moral positions) has been one of the central features of modern liberal thought. For this reason, liberals advocate a neutral state which does not impose one particular version of the good life on to civil society, but rather facilitates the prospering of a wide range of moral beliefs and practices. This approach is advocated partly on the grounds that it will help to maintain social stability in an increasingly multicultural environment, a view particularly associated with Rawls (1993). In addition, it also reflects an intellectual recognition of the difficulty in determining the preferability of one moral position over another. As will be shown in more detail in chapter 10, the liberal ideology of moral pluralism impacts upon animals in the sense that what we do to them becomes an element of choice rather than moral, and even legal, compunction.

Are we resigned then to accepting, at the very least, a certain degree of moral relativism? It is not the occasion for a full rehearsal of the arguments that might be employed here, but a number of observations are appropriate. First, it might be suggested that it is possible to exaggerate the degree to which judgements on the validity of competing belief systems are not possible. A 'strong subjectivist thesis', then, is 'plainly false' (Carruthers, 1992: 4). As Nagel (1987: 232) remarks, it may well be possible to dismiss the espousal of a belief 'in terms of errors in their evidence, or identifiable errors in drawing conclusions from it, or in argument, judgement, and so forth' and that while 'conflicts of religious faith fail this test . . . most empirical and many moral disagreements do not'. Moreover, there are surely some conceptions of the good – health, bodily integrity, wealth, even liberty – to which everyone might aspire (Waldron, 1989: 74–5), as well as 'conceptions of the good which are manifestly unreasonable' (Arneson, 2000: 71). Brandt's checklist for an 'acceptable normative moral theory' cannot be bettered (1992: 112–13):

> The theory must contain no unintelligible concepts or internal consistencies; it must not be inconsistent with known facts; it must be capable of precise formulation so that its implications for action can

be determined; and – most important – its implications must be acceptable to thoughtful persons who have had reasonably wide experience.

Tooley (1983: 6) is right to suggest that most people's beliefs are
unexamined, the product of socialization and norms of behaviour
accepted on trust. The purpose of ethics is to use the elements of a
viable normative theory described above to evaluate these unexamined beliefs and values to see if there is a valid justification for holding
them. Animal ethics seeks to examine beliefs that are held about the
moral status of nonhuman animals. Despite raising the possibility of
judging between different moral beliefs, Nagel (1987: 233) rather lets
the side down by then arguing that we cannot make such a judgement on the killing of animals for food (along with abortion and
sexual conduct). I would suggest, however, that it is possible to make
some statements about the morality of killing animals for food that
would meet with widespread approval, at least in the West.

The starting point is that, partly at least because of the fact that it
is known that animals are sentient, we owe direct duties to them and
that inflicting unnecessary suffering on them is wrong. As a result we
can say with a great deal of assent that the *way* in which animals are
raised and killed for food matters; that it is right to ensure as far as
possible that the most humane methods are used for rearing and
killing animals. As chapter 7 reveals, it does not require that animals
be regarded as our moral equals for many of the practices in modern
so-called 'factory' farming to be condemned as illegitimate. I would
want to go further than this and suggest that it is difficult to justify
morally many, if not most, of the elements of modern animal agriculture. By the end of this book I would hope that readers share this
assertion.

Brian Barry (1995: 169), a leading liberal political theorist, has
said that 'no conception of the good can justifiably be held with a
degree of certainty that warrants its imposition on those who reject
it'. It is certainly difficult to be certain about the value of competing
ethical positions. But, as Arneson (2000: 77) points out, 'if one sets
the threshold of supporting reasons for public policy at the level of
certainty, it is doubtful that any proposed policy can pass'. As he
astutely continues, at the very least a limited non-neutral approach –
one which aims to 'root out weeds while acknowledging that there
are many flowers any of which might be favoured' is eminently justified. By contrast, outright moral scepticism, in the words of Goodin
and Reeve (1989: 2): ' masks vacillation, the absence of intellectual
or political courage, an unwillingness to make hard decisions and difficult choices, an abdication of responsibility, and an indifference to

the actual fate of the individuals whom it makes a formal claim to flourish'.

A related point here is that to entertain the notion of moral relativism is to belittle the many who hold values of one kind or another. As Harrison (1979: 285–7) points out, no participant in normative ethics with a moral view of his own could make the case for toleration of competing moral positions. He continues:

> It is true that we could understand a man who said, 'All moralities apart from mine are equally good' . . . But if he said, 'All moralities including mine are equally good' we should be at a loss. Could, for example, a Christian who admitted that other religious/moral positions were just as good as Christianity still be regarded as a Christian?

In this context, neutrality and toleration of competing conceptions of the good amounts to 'betraying your own values' (Nagel, 1987: 222). This present author strongly affirms the assertion that much is wrong with our treatment of animals and whatever else the reader thinks of the pages that follow, the worse indictment would be a suspicion that this value has been betrayed.

2

Animals and the Equal Consideration of Interests

It is easy to become bemused very quickly by the variety and complexity of the moral arguments employed in the animal ethics debate. In order to make things a little easier, an important task in this first substantive chapter is to clear away the weeds in the intellectual garden so that we can pursue, with some confidence, the key dimensions of the debate. We start by outlining the positions in the debate before describing and evaluating an important initial principle, the so-called 'equal consideration of interests'. It is suggested that while this principle is vital in minimizing the illegitimate use of species alone as a way of distinguishing between the moral worth of humans and animals, it can only take us so far without further identification and evaluation of the moral worth of the interests which humans and animals actually have. This is a task that will preoccupy us in three subsequent chapters.

Positions in the debate

So what might we owe to animals morally? What I have described, elsewhere (Garner, 2004), as the 'continuum of recognition' looks, diagrammatically, something like this:

1 Completely lacking moral status. Only indirect duties owed to animals.
   (a) Animals lack sentiency (Descartes, Carruthers).
   (b) Animals are sentient but lack any morally significant interests (Kant, Frey).

2   Moral orthodoxy/animal welfare/humane treatment – some moral status but inferior to humans.

   (a)   Animals have an interest in not suffering but this can be overridden to promote the greater good of humans who are autonomous agents (common view held by many contemporary moral and political philosophers).

   (b)   Even if moral orthodoxy is accepted there are few uses of animals which are necessary (Francione).

3   Challenges to the moral orthodoxy.

   (a)   Animals have rights:

      (i)   based on animals having inherent value (Regan).

      (ii)   based on sentiency (Rollin, Ryder).

   (b)   Utilitarianism (Singer).

   (c)   Contractarianism (Rowlands).

From this continuum, it will have become apparent that there are three key positions we could adopt. It might be, unlikely though it sounds, that we owe nothing to animals; that, for whatever reason, they have no moral worth and our treatment of them, however extreme, does not register on the scales of morality. Or, we might recognize that animals have some moral worth; that what we do to them does matter morally, but human beings are more important, and in the event of a conflict between the interests of humans and animals, it is humans who ought to win out. From this second position it will be evident that there is a very important difference between moral standing, by which I mean that an entity has a worth morally as opposed to being worthless, and moral status, by which I take to mean the degree of moral worth an entity has. Thus, it is possible to have moral standing but not to have as much moral status as another entity. Finally, we might adopt a position, still regarded as radical, that humans and animals ought to be regarded as moral equals, so that, all things being equal, what we regard as morally unacceptable to do to humans ought to have a similar status when we consider doing it to animals.

At the risk of confusing the reader even further, the animal ethics debate – which focuses on which of the above positions one should adopt – tends to be organized around a number of sub-arguments, and this book is no exception in seeking to cover them. Four arguments are particularly worthy of note. These are:

1   *The lack of sentiency argument.* This is the suggestion that animals have no moral standing because they are not sentient or conscious.

2   *The personhood argument.* This is the justification for the moral
    orthodoxy. It represents a claim that because humans have greater
    cognitive abilities, constituting personhood, than animals, then
    humans are morally superior and their interests should always
    take precedence.
3   *The marginal cases argument.* This is the argument that the
    attempt to distinguish between humans and animals on the
    grounds that the former, unlike the latter, are persons (the per-
    sonhood argument, in other words) is illegitimate because not all
    humans are persons.
4   *The sentiency argument.* This is the argument that according sen-
    tiency, or the capacity to experience pleasure and pain, to animals
    makes them more morally considerable than the personhood
    argument will allow, although the sentiency argument agrees with
    the personhood argument that a human life is worth more than
    an animal life.

Opponents of moral equality between humans and animals tend
to start from the assumption of inequality, that humans are morally
superior to animals, and then ask those who disagree to justify equality. For proponents of equality, the position is reversed. A presump-
tion is made in favour of equality and opponents are asked to justify
inequality. The end result is the same in the sense that similar arguments tend to be employed eventually. There is some advantage,
however, in forcing your opponents to come up with the arguments
to defeat your position, and this is a particularly attractive approach
to proponents of equality who have traditionally found themselves
on the back-foot, having to attack the orthodox inequality view.

For it is, in reality, widely accepted in virtually all societies that
animals are morally inferior to humans and this, in turn, has been
used to legitimize a huge amount of well-documented animal
exploitation and suffering, the details of which will be reviewed in
the course of this book. On occasions, the degree of suffering inflicted
on animals in any particular practice is disputed, but by and large
advocates of inequality do concur with cross-species egalitarians that
humans do cause animals to suffer. The difference between them is
not primarily then about the degree of suffering but on the degree to
which this suffering is justified.

Any attempt to argue for equality between humans and animals
requires the adoption of a set of general moral rules that we can apply
to the animals debate. As I suggested, however, most people do not
appear to accept the validity of the principle of equality between
humans and animals. The obvious response is that in order for them

to be accepted people will have to be persuaded of their worth. The problem with this is it becomes more difficult to invoke 'intuition' – an important element in the moral philosopher's armoury – on the side of the pro-animal position. An alternative approach, which enables us to involve intuitions, is to accept societal norms and seek to show that logical consistency demands that a particular desired outcome – in this case the end of most, if not all, animal exploitation – be followed (see Rowlands, 2002: 28–31). One way of applying this principle in the animals debate is to seek to show that most, if not all, of the ways in which animals are currently treated are unnecessary in the sense that they do not produce human benefits or that such benefits can be achieved in other ways.

The animal protection movement has made considerable use of this strategy, particularly in the field of animal experimentation where it is argued, not that animals are morally equal to humans and therefore should not be used in such experiments because it infringes their rights or whatever, but that they are not justified because they do not produce the human benefits claimed for them (see chapter 8). If it can be shown that this is the case, at least in particular instances, then the suffering inflicted on animals becomes unnecessary and, providing we hold that animals have some moral worth, however little, then it becomes morally illegitimate too. Francione (2000), for instance – although in reality a committed advocate of moral equality – adopts this approach in his book-length text on animal rights. We can all accept, he suggests, what he calls the 'humane treatment principle', which prohibits the infliction of unnecessary suffering on animals. But, he continues, we do not practise what we preach because 'the overwhelming portion of our animal use can be justified *only* by habit, convention, amusement, convenience or pleasure'. As a result, 'most of the suffering that we impose on animals is completely unnecessary *however* we interpret that notion' (ibid.: xxiii–xxiv).

To some extent it is possible to empirically assess Francione's claim, and later chapters in this book will seek to do just that. Of course, there is a possibility, or – many would say – probability, that we will still find that some animal exploitation is necessary in the sense that it serves significant human benefits. If this is the case then the moral orthodoxy demands that it be permitted. To avoid this outcome, it is necessary to show that animals and humans are morally equal, or at least that their interests are comparable in most, if not all, ways. Only then can we say that, even if animal experimentation, for example, produces beneficial results for humans, such benefits are morally illegitimate because we gained them by treating animals as unequals.

But what exactly do we mean by moral equality? Quite often, equality in animal ethics is equated with the granting of rights to animals. So, if we were to give the right not to suffer, and especially the right to life, to animals, then – persisting with the animal experimentation example a little longer – while there may be gains to be had from inflicting suffering on animals in the laboratory, these would be morally illegitimate because they involved the infringing of animal rights. It is important to note here, though, that the granting of rights to animals is not the only, or even the most appropriate, means of applying a moral status to animals that is equivalent to that of humans. For example, we would still be treating humans and animals as equals if we were prepared to experiment on them both, an outcome which would not be acceptable for a rights-based theory but which might, as we shall see, be justified by a utilitarian approach to animal ethics. Peter Singer (1990, 1993) is the most notable exponent of a utilitarian approach to animal ethics, although I hasten to add that he does not advocate experimenting on humans! Yet another approach to animal ethics is the so-called 'contractarian' model associated with Rowlands (1998), who claims advantages for it over rights and utilitarian accounts.

Feting the equal consideration of interests

Partly in order to avoid coming down on one side or another in this debate about the exact moral theory to be applied to animal ethics, it is increasingly common for those sympathetic to equality between humans and animals to use the *equal consideration of interests* principle to denote their position. As DeGrazia (2002: 19) explains: 'This claim entails that whenever a human and an animal have a comparable interest, we should regard the animal's interest and the human's interest as equally morally important.' Those, such as DeGrazia, Francione, Rowlands and Singer, who invoke the equal consideration of interests principle tend to conclude from it that, although the interests of humans and animals may differ in some respects, the interests of the latter are morally significant, and because of this many of the ways in which we currently use animals are illegitimate. Therefore, it is suggested by all of the authors mentioned above that unless we are prepared to countenance the use of humans for food or scientific experimentation or whatever, then we should not use animals either.

To avoid confusion here, it is important to explore exactly what is meant by the equal consideration of interests principle in order to identify its explanatory limits. It is, in some ways, an essential formulation for those who want to argue for moral equality between humans and animals. It is also, I would suggest, intellectually convincing. In particular, by focusing on interests rather than species, it provides an opportunity for moral equality across the species boundary. If correct, then, the principle of the equal consideration of interests allows us to dispose of an alternative view that what matters morally is species. This is the view that humans should be accorded greater moral worth than animals merely by dint of the fact that they *are* human. By contrast, basing moral judgements on the equal consideration of *interests* has the effect of minimizing the moral importance of species. What matters is not what species one belongs to but whether there are any morally relevant differences between individuals, whether human or non-human.

This is an important corrective to what is a widely accepted social convention, in the developed world at least, that membership of the human species is an entitlement to moral equality, whereas membership of a non-human species has been regarded as sufficient reason for moral inequality between humans and other animals. There is little justification for prioritizing species in this way, and to do so has been labelled as 'speciesism', a term first invoked by Ryder (1975: 16) and used since by most pro-animal philosophers. Leahy (1991: 22) – not a pro-animal philosopher himself it should be added – provides a good definition here. He writes:

> A speciesist is someone who gives preference to their own interests and those of other human beings over those of other species even when the latter are as peremptory as the former and, if called upon to justify it, they do so simply in terms of the primacy of human concerns.

The common retort to the importance attached to species is to imagine the arrival on Earth of extraterrestrial beings who are better than humans in all kinds of ways: intellectually, culturally and physically (DeGrazia, 2002: 24–5; Rowlands, 2002: 39–40). The question to ponder here is whether we would still want to say that because they are not human we can therefore discount their interests? To do so would, intuitively, seem arbitrary and unjust.

A related justification for maintaining the importance of species is the position, most associated with Midgley (1983), that moral status is dependent on relationships rather than on interests or characteristics. The strongest obligations we have are therefore to our closest kin and the weakest are to strangers. It follows, it is suggested, that we are most likely to be closer to other humans, as members of our own species, than we are to animals. A number of objections can be made to this view. In the first place, this claim is, in part, subject to empirical confirmation that may not be forthcoming. In particular, it is evident that humans do form very close bonds with animals, particularly those that are companion animals. Second, although it is true that we have stronger obligations to those who are closest to us, and not least our children, it is difficult to see how advocates of this approach could deny that we still have strong negative obligations to those who are not part of our social group. Yes, we may well prioritize members of our close social circle in the event of a conflict, but this is very different from deliberately seeking to harm those who are not part of this circle.

The application of the equal consideration of interests principle not only challenges moral inequality between humans and animals, but also challenges moral equality *within* the human species. There is a moral consensus that we should treat humans equally, in the sense that for the most part it is accepted that there are no morally relevant differences between humans that justify fundamentally unequal treatment. In particular, human life, despite its great differences of quality, continues to be regarded as sacred. For Singer (1993: 88) this view derives from the coming of Christianity, and the emphasis on an eternal fate, coupled with the 'ownership' of humans by God which meant that 'to kill a human being is to usurp God's right to decide when we shall live and when we shall die'.

Human equality and the sanctity of human life is not necessarily consistent with the application of the principle of the equal consideration of interests. If we were to apply it a number of interesting, and disturbing, questions would present themselves, questions which Singer (1993; 1994), for one, has not shied away from. For instance, does the severely mentally retarded, or physically disabled, human have the same interests as a healthy human? Do children have the same interests as adults? Are all human lives, to put it bluntly, of the same value? Arguably, in a more secular age, this consideration of interests is a more appropriate method of determining very difficult ethical questions than species membership.

Another advantage of utilizing the equal consideration of interests principle is that it avoids equating moral equality between humans and animals with equal treatment. Opponents of moral equality between the species have often ridiculed the idea by translating it into a demand for giving the vote or the right of free speech to animals or even, as Rowlands (2002: 54) wryly observes, 'Pigs being taken to school. Subsidized visits to the opera for dogs.' By defining equality in terms of considering the *interests* of humans and animals equally, this problem is avoided. Animals do not have an interest in voting or in free speech (or being taken to school or the opera!); therefore such demands are irrelevant.[1] Moreover, emphasizing the equal consideration of interests avoids the clearly preposterous conclusion that equality necessitates according as much moral status to an insect as to a human being. The interests of an insect will be very different, and presumably less demanding, than those of higher species. Above all, it is extremely doubtful if insects can feel pain and therefore they cannot be harmed in ways that animals, both human and non-human, can.

Begging the question

The strength of the equal consideration of interests principle as an appropriate operational definition of equality between humans and animals is also, however, its weakness. It would be wrong to assume that we can, as is sometimes implied, move directly from an acceptance of the equal consideration of interests principle to the conclusions reached by the pro-animal philosophers without additional arguments. The major limitation here is that the principle provides no content to the term 'interests'. It merely tells us to treat like cases alike. It does not tell us what these like cases are. As a consequence, it could be a principle consistent with a wide variety of positions. Singer (1993: 22) confirms this when he writes that: 'It is true that we cannot know where equal consideration of interests will lead us until we know what interests people have.' And, to embellish the point, Rowlands (2002: 33) rightly points out that: 'Identifying exactly what is involved in giving due weight and consideration to the interests of everyone is, in fact, where the hard work really starts. Philosophers have been arguing about this for a long time, and different moral theories give very different accounts of what is involved here.'

The use of the principle of equal consideration in the animal ethics debate has been confusing precisely because it is sometimes used as a substantive rather than a formal principle. In other words, it is sometimes equated with moral equality, rather than being a means by which the degree of moral equality between humans and animals can be judged. Francione (2000), for instance, despite seemingly understanding the correct formal nature of equal consideration earlier in his book, then subsequently uses it in a substantive way. Thus, he legitimately considers a number of reasons put forward to deny that animals have an equivalent moral status to humans but then rules them out, without any further examination, on the grounds that they are inconsistent with the equal consideration of interests principle (ibid.: 103–29). But, of course, these reasons may be consistent with the principle if it can be shown that differential interests justify unequal treatment.

Singer, too, although not so blatantly as Francione, comes close to using the equal consideration of interests in a substantive way. He says (1993: 56) that the principle means that the fact 'that other animals are less intelligent than we are does not mean that their interests may be disregarded'. Two responses can be made to this. First, this assumes animals have interests, a judgement yet to be sustained. Moreover, it is possible that after taking the interests of animals into account we might decide that the nature of human interests are such that they should override the interests of animals.

For instance, imagine we discover that human beings have a much greater interest in being alive than animals (a position Singer accepts: see chapter 5). Now Singer might argue in response that accepting this does not mean we should regard an animal's interest in avoiding pain as any less worthy than a human's interest in avoiding pain. The problem here, though – and this is far from being an academic debate – arises if we can preserve many human lives, say by finding a cure for cancer, only if a certain degree of pain is inflicted on some animals? Are we not obliged to accept this outcome as morally legitimate? To sum up, we could recognize that animals have an interest in avoiding pain but still conclude that this interest ought to be overridden in order to protect a human interest in living. And all of this could be justified by invoking the equal consideration of interests.

We have established that whether or not animals and humans are morally equal (and, indeed, whether or not all humans are to be regarded as morally equal) will depend on the interests they have. And we can only consider these interests once we know what they are. It might be, then, that animals have no interests, or it could mean that animals have interests in not suffering but humans can suffer in a greater variety of ways and more intensively, or it could mean that a human interest in life overrides an animal interest in avoiding pain. In other words, everything is up for grabs.

Warnock (1998: 49) provides an example of the principle we have established drawn from the field of reproductive ethics. In an examination of the ethics of in vitro fertilization, Warnock reveals that the general consensus on embryos is that they are sufficiently unlike a human being before fourteen days not to count morally. Therefore, an embryo less than fourteen days old, it is said, has no interests at all to be considered, and we can therefore not morally wrong it directly. In another example, Singer himself (1993: 24) applies the equal consideration of interests principle to non-sentient parts of nature and concludes that because trees and plants and rocks and mountains cannot feel anything they have no interests. So, he argues: 'We need not deliberately exclude nonsentient things from the scope of the principle of equal consideration of interests: it is just that including them within the scope of this principle leads to results identical with excluding them, since they have no preferences – and therefore no interests . . . to be considered' (see chapter 3).

But, of course, we have yet to establish that animals have any interests to be considered either. Conversely, there are some – so-called 'ecocentric' thinkers – who want to claim that being sentient is not a necessary characteristic for an entity to be accorded moral standing. According to the formulation developed in the preceding few paragraphs, then, what we are entitled to do to animals will vary depending on the interests identified. So, if we argue that animals have no interests at all then we cannot harm them and therefore we cannot wrong them directly. This is equivalent to the first of the three key moral positions we identified earlier. By contrast, if we think that animals can suffer from pain, and even death, but humans can suffer more, then, in the event of a conflict of interests, we would be justified in choosing to sacrifice the interests of animals. Significantly, neither of these attempts to provide content to the equal consideration of interests principle amount to any meaningful notion of equality between humans and animals. At the very least, both would seem to justify, for instance, continuing to use animals in scientific experiments where the end result is likely to reduce human suffering or save human lives.

Conclusion

The aim of this chapter has been to show that the equal consideration of interests is a valid principle within which we can debate the moral worth of animals. I hope it has also been established that the problem with the principle is that it begs the question of what animal and human interests are. By itself, therefore, it does not automatically lead to moral equality between humans and animals. Instead, we have to fill in the gaps and ask whether there are any morally relevant differences between humans and animals that justify the unequal treatment of the latter. The next three chapters will attempt to answer this question.

3

Are Animals Worth Anything?

It may seem odd to suggest that animals are worth nothing morally, yet some philosophers have held, and do hold, this to be the case. If animals are worth nothing then we owe no moral obligations to them and therefore what we do to them does not matter to them directly. What I do to an animal may matter to other humans and this may restrict what I am permitted to do, but once we have examined the extent of our indirect obligations to animals our task is completed. The fact that there are a number of following chapters in this book would indicate that, for this author at least, animals do matter morally. This chapter explores the extent of our indirect obligations to animals and critically examines the views of those who have suggested that animals lack any moral worth.

The view that we have no direct moral duties to animals may not hold much weight these days, although, as we shall see below, there are still philosophical defenders of it. In earlier times, though, it was a common position. In the nineteenth century, the slaughter of African game, usually at the behest of the British colonists, is perhaps the best example of human disregard for animals. Midgley (1983: 14–15) quotes an example of this from a memoir written in 1850 by a British hunter, and it is so evocative it is worth quoting at length. The author writes:

> The elephant stood broadside to me, at upwards of one hundred yards, and his attention at the moment was occupied with the dogs . . . I fired at his shoulder, and secured him with a single shot. The ball caught him high on the shoulder-blade, rendering him instantly dead lame; and before the echo of the bullet could reach my ear, I plainly saw the

elephant was mine . . . I resolved to devote a short time to the con-
templation of this noble elephant before laying him low; accordingly
. . . I quickly kindled a fire and put on the kettle, and in a very few
minutes my coffee was prepared. There I sat in my forest home, coolly
sipping my coffee, with one of the finest elephants in Africa awaiting
my pleasure beside a neighbouring tree . . . Having admired the elephant for a considerable time, I resolved to make experiments for vulnerable points . . . (He bungles this again and again; eventually, after
even he had become a little worried, he succeeds in wounding the elephant fatally.) Large tears now trickled from his eyes, which he slowly
shut and opened, his colossal frame quivered convulsively, and, falling
on his side, he expired.

The fact that most of us regard this passage as shocking is because
of the total disregard for the elephant's interest in not suffering, which
we, intuitively, regard as morally unacceptable. This disregard,
however, is not an historical anachronism. Indeed, until relatively
recently, at least some in the scientific community in the United States
– supposedly a highly civilized society – appeared to doubt the moral
significance of animal suffering or even its existence (Rollin, 1989:
191–6).

Animals and sentiency

The easiest way to show that animals are worth nothing morally is
to deny that they are sentient. This is the lack of sentiency argument
described in the previous chapter. If we can establish that they cannot
experience pleasure and pain, the argument goes, then it is tantamount to saying that what we do to them has no bearing on their
well-being. We can define pain here, following DeGrazia (1996: 107)
as 'an unpleasant or aversive sensory experience typically associated
with actual or potential tissue damage'. The value of sentiency is held
by many pro-animal philosophers as much as it tends to be by their
opponents. Singer (1993: 123) is clear about this. He writes:

I believe that the boundary of sentience . . . is not a morally arbitrary
boundary in the way that the boundaries of race or species are arbitrary. There is a genuine difficulty in understanding how chopping
down a tree can matter *to the tree* if the tree can feel nothing.

And again (1993: 57):

The capacity for suffering and enjoying things is a prerequisite for
having interests at all, a condition that must be satisfied before we can

speak of interests in any meaningful way. It would be nonsense to say that it was not in the interests of a stone to be kicked along the road by a schoolboy. A stone does not have interests because it cannot suffer.

Many pro-animal philosophers, and many of their opponents, agree then that sentiency is a necessary condition for moral standing, and that those entities without it have no moral worth. It is, in DeGrazia's (1996: 3) words, 'the admission ticket to the moral arena'.

The use of sentiency as a benchmark for moral standing sounds eminently reasonable. Interestingly, however, at least when applied to humans, sentiency is not always the criteria adopted in practice. Largely as a result of the conclusions reached by the Committee of Enquiry into Human Fertilisation and Embryology chaired by Mary Warnock in the early 1980s, for instance, the law in Britain (and elsewhere) allows human embryos to be kept alive in the laboratory for up to fourteen days, after which, it is argued, the first vestiges of a distinct human being can be discerned (Warnock, 1998: 48). The fourteen-day cut-off point is not, however, based on sentiency. Rather, at about fourteen days the so-called 'primitive streak' (a piling up of cells as they reproduce themselves) appears, and this is associated with the emergence of the spinal cord and the central nervous system (Warnock, 1998: 43). As Singer (1993: 137) remarks: 'At this point the embryo could not possibly be conscious or feel pain.' In this case, then, it is the emergence of a distinct human being and not the sentiency of a being that is regarded as morally important. For Singer (1993: 157), because the embryo is not sentient, this fourteen-day cut-off point 'is still an unnecessarily restrictive limit'.

In the abortion debate too, sentiency is not the only, or even the most important, consideration. In their campaigns, anti-abortionists have invoked the possibility that the foetus can feel pain, but their case is not dependent on the validity of this claim. Rather, the anti-abortion case is built on the fact that the foetus is a distinct human individual, whether or not it is capable of feeling when aborted. Indeed, for the purest anti-abortionist, there is no morally important difference between the fertilized egg and the child, and yet it is estimated that the point at which the foetus is capable of feeling pain is between eighteen and twenty-five weeks. As Singer (1993: 148) confirms: 'Opponents of abortion really want to uphold the right to life of the human being from conception, irrespective of whether it is conscious or not.'

As we suggested in chapter 2, the emphasis put upon sentiency by pro-animal philosophers such as Singer has the intention of morally dethroning humans. Thus, for Singer (1993: 150), the human foetus (and the embryo after fourteen days) may be a human being (or a potential one) but it clearly lacks the characteristics – of rationality, autonomy and so on – of a person. As a consequence, not all human life is regarded by philosophers such as Singer as of equal value, not all of it is therefore necessarily sacred, and not all of it should be regarded as morally superior to animals. As we have seen, the practice has not yet, for the most part, caught up with his theory. This is not least, of course, because many deny the validity of the theory that human babies should not be regarded as persons. What is clear is that the assumption that humans are very different (and superior) from animals – a difference of kind rather than degree – has been under intellectual attack at least since the time of Darwin (Rachels, 1990). Darwin continued to emphasize the moral superiority of humans, but by stressing the animal origins of humans he contributed to a decline in the belief that humans are somehow separate from, and morally superior to, animals. Singer's philosophy is merely the culmination of this new paradigm.

As was pointed out in the previous chapter, prioritizing sentiency also rules out the possibility of what has been described as a genuine environmental ethic, one which accords moral worth to non-sentient and, in some cases, non-living parts of nature (see Attfield, 2003: 15–17). For environmental philosophers who want to go the whole way and attach moral worth to living and inanimate parts of nature, such as Fox (1984), and for those who want to attach moral worth to living things (in a so-called biocentric ethic), such as Taylor (1986), sentiency is a sufficient condition for moral standing. It is not, however, a necessary condition, and environmental ethicists use a variety of arguments to justify attaching moral worth to non-sentient parts of nature.[1]

More to the point here, there are some who would deny that animals are sentient and – if they are right – this would, at the very least, raise serious doubts as to whether animals have moral standing. Traditionally, the view that animals lack sentiency was associated with the seventeenth-century French philosopher Rene Descartes – although whether or not he held this view in reality is a matter of some dispute (see Guerrini, 2002). The conventional interpretation of Descartes' view on animal cognition is that he held that animals are mere automata, such that their apparent aversive reaction to negative stimuli is a mechanical response with no conscious intent. Whether or not this was his intention, his theory did provide a justification for those who would experiment on animals that most of us now accept are conscious. As one contemporary observer wrote:

The scientists administered beatings to dogs with perfect indifference and made fun of those who pitied the creatures as if they felt pain. They said the animals were clocks; that the cries they emitted when struck were only the sound of a little spring that had been touched, but that the whole body was without feeling. They nailed the poor animals up on boards by their four paws to vivisect them to see the circulation of the blood which was a great subject of controversy. (Quoted in Regan, 1984: 5)

Descartes derived his conclusion that animals are not conscious and feel no pain from his claim that animals are not rational. Rationality, then, was regarded as necessary for thought *and* feeling. As a corollary, because animals cannot tell us, there is no reason to believe they have rational souls. Trying to link the absence of a soul with moral worthiness has little credibility in our more secular age. For one thing, if it is true that animals lack a soul one might argue that this is a reason why we should treat them well, because they, unlike humans who have the eternal afterlife to look forward to, only go round once. The relationship between rationality, sentiency and moral standing, however, still has some philosophical purchase and will be considered below.

We can never know for certain that other humans, let alone animals, can feel pain. As Singer (1990: 10) points out:

It is conceivable that one of our close friends is really a cleverly constructed robot, controlled by a brilliant scientist so as to give all the signs of feeling pain, but really no more sensitive than any other machine. We can never know, with absolute certainty, that this is not the case.

Nevertheless, there is strong evidence that animals, like humans, do feel pain. Voltaire, writing a century after Descartes, commented that:

What a pitiful thing, what poor stuff it is to say that animals are machines deprived of knowledge and feeling . . . Barbarians seize this dog who so prodigiously surpasses man in friendship. They nail him to a table and dissect him alive to show you the mesenteric veins. You discover in him all the same organs of feeling that you possess. Answer me, mechanist, has nature arranged all the springs of feeling in this animal in order that he should not feel? Does he have nerves to be impassive? Do not assume that nature presents this impertinent contradiction. (Quoted in Leahy, 1991: 91–2)

We can invoke behavioural, physiological and evolutionary factors here as evidence for the 'springs of feeling' possessed by animals, with only some invertebrates – such as amoebas – completely excluded.[2] In behavioural terms, animals give a strong impression that they feel pain, for example when they seek to avoid or escape situations – such as intense heat – which would cause humans pain, where they cry out in distress, and where they – as in limping – are affected by an injured body part. Moreover, humans and animals share similar physiological responses to pain, such as sweating and increased respiration. The brains of vertebrates possess similar physiological features that we associate with a human capacity to experience pain. The release of endogenous opiates – the body's natural pain-killing substances – have been exhibited in all mammals, birds, reptiles and even fish. Why should animals produce these if they cannot feel pain? In addition, pain in all vertebrates seems to be controlled, as it is for humans, by the use of anaesthetics and analgesia. The similarity between humans and animals in this regard is reflected in the fact that animals are often used as models for the study of pain in humans.

Finally, pain has an evolutionary function for humans whereby it acts as a warning of danger, those with an inability to feel pain having less chance of survival, at least without taking considerable steps to compensate for the lack. It would seem that pain serves the same function for animals. Support for this assertion can be found in the theory of natural selection whereby 'conscious awareness of suffering . . . helps the animal to avoid further damage to the injured site and avoid the source of pain in the future' (Webster, 1994: 27). As DeGrazia (1996: 111) points out then, given the evidence described above, 'it is parsimonious to attribute pain, and consciousness generally, to most or all vertebrate species and probably at least some invertebrates such as cephalopods' (squids, cuttlefish, and octopuses).

Carruthers: bucking the trend

For Lynch (1994: 1, 4), as for many others, the evidence noted above is 'sufficiently persuasive to remove all reasonable doubt with regard to the conscious pain of animals'. As a result, 'it takes much philosophical resolve to deny that animals feel their pains'. Despite this apparently overwhelming evidence, there are still philosophic accounts denying that animals have moral standing on the grounds that they are not able to feel pain. The most notable recent account has been provided by Carruthers (1989; 1992). Carruthers' doubts about the capacity of animals to suffer are based upon the distinction he makes between conscious and non-conscious mental states. The former is a mental state 'that is available to conscious thought', so that 'when we think things consciously to ourselves, the events that express our thoughts are themselves available to be objects of further thoughts' (Carruthers, 1989: 262–3). By contrast, non-conscious mental states, Carruthers argues, are not available to be thought about, in the sense that we have no recollection of them. They are not subject to conscious reflexive thinking, and it therefore 'feels like nothing' (1989: 259) to have such a non-conscious experience. A useful way of understanding what he means by this is to imagine when we absent-mindedly drive a car or, more benignly, do the washing up. Think of the last journey you made by car. Rather worryingly, it is likely that you will not remember stopping at every red light or turning every corner. 'It is common in such cases', Carruthers (1989: 258) comments, 'that one may suddenly "come to", returning one's attention to the task at hand with a startled realization that one has not the faintest idea what one has been doing or seeing for some minutes past.'

For Carruthers, only humans have conscious mental states – mental states, that is, which are available to be thought about. Animals, by contrast, have non-conscious mental states, which are not available to be thought about. In other words, only humans have the ability to think reflectively about their conscious experiences. Since pain is also a mental state it follows that it too must come in conscious and non-conscious varieties. For Carruthers, only humans have a conscious awareness of pain whereas animals do not. As a result:

> the fact that a creature has sense organs, and can be observed to display sensitivity in its behaviour to the salient features of its surrounding environment, is insufficient to establish that it feels like anything to be that thing. It may be that the experiences of brutes . . . are wholly of the nonconscious variety. It is an open question whether there is anything that it feels like to be a bat or a dog or a monkey. If consciousness is like the turning on of a light, then it may be that their lives are nothing but darkness. (Carruthers, 1989: 259)

There is no disagreement between Carruthers and many of the pro-animal philosophers on the moral importance of sentiency; that the capacity to feel pain is a necessary condition for moral standing. Where they differ, of course, is that Carruthers denies that animals have conscious awareness of their pain. As a result, the non-conscious mental states possessed by animals are not 'an appropriate object of sympathy and moral concern' (Carruthers, 1989: 266). To demonstrate this, Carruthers (1989: 267) asks us to imagine an individual, Mary, who has no feeling in her legs, although they perform normally in all other respects. If we try to injure her legs she claims to feel nothing. While we might feel sympathy for Mary's condition, injuries to her legs by themselves are not an object of moral concern, precisely because she does not suffer from them (although if they impact on her life in general they will have to be taken into account morally). Such a case might seem fanciful, but examples do exist of those who have concentrated so hard on something else that they have reported not feeling pain despite being severely injured, the paradigmatic example being a soldier caught up in a ferocious battle.

The implications for animals of the above example are obvious, and Carruthers (1989: 268–9) does not shirk from drawing them. Imagine a situation where we are faced with an accident where a number of people, including Mary, have been badly injured. In this situation, even if Mary is screaming the loudest, because we know that she can't feel anything we should leave her until last behind those who are in pain. Logic demands that we treat animals in the same way because 'since their pains are nonconscious (as are all their mental states), they ought not to be allowed to get in the way of any morally-serious objective'. Thus Carruthers (1989: 268), noting how much time and money is spent on campaigns to reduce the suffering of animals in factory farms and laboratories, regards such activities as 'not only morally unsupportable but morally objectionable'.

There have been a number of criticisms of the Carruthers view. DeGrazia (1996: 113) states the obvious point that, armed with the evidence of animal sentiency described above, common sense makes it 'extremely hard to believe that all mental states of all nonhuman animals – including dogs and dolphins, elephants and monkeys – are unconscious'. Warren (1997: 58) concurs by noting the 'empirical implausibility of the claim that animals do not feel their pains'. Lynch (1994: 5) suggests that pain cannot have survival value for animals if they cannot feel it. It is understandable, perhaps, why Descartes could think that animals were not sentient. Now, armed with Darwin, it is much more difficult to hold this view seriously. As Rachels (1990: 131) points out, 'Darwin stressed that, in an important sense, their [animal] nervous systems, their behaviours, their cries *are* our nervous systems, our behaviours, and our cries, with only a little modification.'

Here, it is important to note that there is a difference between being conscious of something and 'not paying attention to something of which one is already conscious'. Thus, the car driver who is apparently not conscious for part of the journey is nothing of the sort. Rather, it is 'a case of intelligent cognitive economy within the stream of conscious experiences' involving 'diverting one's attention from certain conscious experiences and focusing on others'. Reiterating the point, Duran (1994: 8) makes it clear that: 'One cannot be said to be driving "unconsciously". An unconscious individual cannot drive.' In any case, there is little evidence that humans are the only species that have 'real' consciousness. As DeGrazia (1996: 114) convincingly argues: 'At the very least, Carruthers owes us some reason to think that there is a specific, exclusively human brain part underlying consciousness.' Yet he fails to offer us one.

For Holland (2003: 36–7) the strongest objection to the Carruthers view is that his key, albeit implicit, premise is extremely debatable but is never supported by relevant arguments. This is the assumption that being available to be thought about is a necessary condition for a mental state to be conscious. Lynch (1994: 4) sets out this position succinctly:

> it is the capacity for thought that provides the sole basis for a crea-
> ture's falling within the scope of morality: a creature counts morally
> only if it is conscious, and it is conscious only if it can engage in
> thought. And animals cannot think. Since they cannot think, their pain
> must be of the unconscious variety.

We can agree with the claim that only conscious creatures count morally without accepting that consciousness is dependent upon thought. Now, Carruthers may be right to say that humans can be distinguished from animals by their ability to think about their mental experiences. And the ability to think reflectively about their conscious experiences is likely to mean that humans have the capacity to suffer in ways which animals do not. But it does not necessarily follow, without further argument at least, that an inability to think about mental experiences is equivalent to a non-conscious mental state. As DeGrazia (1996: 114) remarks, 'Carruthers gives the impression of conflating basic consciousness with something more intellectual, either thinking or self-consciousness.' If animals are unable to think about mental states, then, it does not rule out the possibility that they are conscious nevertheless. And, of course, if animals are conscious then there is no reason to think they are unable to experience pain and pleasure. If this is so, then even Carruthers has to admit that animals must be objects of moral concern.

Rather paradoxically, Carruthers himself, in his book-length study published three years later than his original article, accepts that in all probability at least some animals are sentient. He writes: 'It seems safe to assume that all mammals, at least, are genuinely sentient, given the variety and flexibility of mammalian behaviours, and given the close similarities in brain structure and function between even the lower mammals and ourselves' (Carruthers, 1992: 58). His earlier views, which he clearly now thinks are unacceptable for most people, are relegated to a final chapter. There, he slightly dilutes the position stated in his article. Rather than the certainty of the non-conscious nature of animal experience, this only now 'may be' the case (Carruthers, 1992: 171).

In his book, Carruthers still holds to the view that we have only indirect duties to animals but this is argued for, not on the grounds that animals lack sentiency, but on the grounds that animals are not moral agents and therefore cannot be part of a social contract allocating duties and responsibilities (on which see below). He is forced to recognize that these contractarian arguments become redundant if the non-conscious nature of animals is accepted, but since this position is 'controversial and speculative, and may well turn out to be mistaken . . . it may well be wiser to continue to respond to animals as if their mental states were conscious ones' (Carruthers, 1992: 192–3).

Moral agency, interests and animals

In his earlier work at least, Carruthers wants to deny that animals have conscious pain experiences. Other philosophers want to deny the moral standing of animals, while accepting that they are sentient. Frey (1980), for instance, offers a sustained attempt to deny that animals have interests that should be considered despite their sentiency, a position which Francione (2000: 105) describes as 'a regurgitation of the Cartesian position minus God'. Frey distinguishes between having an interest in something and something being in the interests of something. This latter sense of interests can be attached to anything 'having a good or well-being which can be harmed or benefited' (Frey, 1980: 79). As Leahy (1991: 44) points out: 'This form of words is more inclusive in that it applies not only to unicellular organisms and the vegetable world but to man-made artefacts such as paintings and machines.' Therefore: 'Just as it is not good to deprive a dog of warmth so it is bad to expose a valuable oil-painting to strong sunlight.' In other words, inanimate objects such as paintings and machines can have needs if a need is defined in a way which does not require the recipient to be aware of them.

For an entity to be of direct moral significance it must have interests in the sense of being interested in something as opposed to something merely being in its interests. Frey argues that for animals to have morally relevant interests they must have desires. Having desires, a necessary component of an entity being interested in something, presupposes beliefs which, Frey continues, animals cannot have because they have no language.[3] Without language it is impossible for animals to believe that any particular statement (for example, that the purpose of food is to satisfy hunger) is true or false. The animal may want the food in the same way that an engine wants fuel, but without the belief that the food will satisfy hunger the animal cannot desire the food.

We can readily agree that desires, and therefore morally relevant interests, are dependent upon beliefs. The question is whether animals can have beliefs. One way to demonstrate this is to show that at least some animals can use a language. We leave this until chapter 4, but for now it should be said that such a proposition is doubtful. This leaves us with the question of whether language is necessary for beliefs. Here, critics of Frey have argued that he has failed to show that non-linguistic beliefs are not possible. As Leahy (1991: 54) has argued, there is a difference between saying that animals do not have beliefs and that we do not know whether animals have beliefs because they cannot tell us. It might be argued, then, that non-linguistic behaviour in animals, in Leahy's words: 'is too imprecise to provide the tight connection necessary to establish whether a belief *is present* in the animal and, if so, what its content is'. We might want to go further than this, of course, and claim that we have every reason to believe that beliefs are possible for those not possessing language.

Such a claim can be based partly on the non-linguistic performance of adults. Regan, for instance, asks us to imagine a non-English speaker who is startled by a boy threatening him with a rubber snake. Despite his inability to state it in English, it would be odd to deny that this person has a belief that the snake might harm him. Given this, for Regan (1984: 41), 'it is very unclear what sense it can make to persist in claiming that what is believed is that *a* sentence is true'. It might also be claimed, as Regan (1984: 45) does, that the existence of beliefs is necessary for children to learn a language in the first place. By definition, then, beliefs are prior to a language. Finally, it might also be suggested that animal behaviour too is difficult to explain without the assumption that they have beliefs. DeGrazia (1996: 149), for instance, asks us to imagine a ball being thrown for a dog countless times before the thrower just pretends to throw it. The dog's reaction, of apparent surprise and bewilderment that the ball has not been thrown this time, is surely indicative of the dog's belief that the ball should have been thrown. This is part of considerable empirical evidence that animals have beliefs (reviewed in DeGrazia, 1996: 158–63). As Midgley (1983: 59) remarks, then, 'Neither with dog nor human do we need words to reveal to us what expressive and interpretative capacities far older and far deeper than words make clear immediately.'

The claim that animals have complex belief systems has been disputed (see, for instance, Leahy, 1991: 62–7). For our present purposes, though, it is important to note that we do not have to dispute the importance of language, nor, for that matter, that those who possess it have greater moral significance. Rather, this chapter is concerned with assessing the claim that animals have no moral standing or worth at all. To deny animals *any* moral standing on the grounds that they do not have language, as opposed to granting them less moral significance than humans, is surely to illegitimately deny the moral importance of sentiency. Sentiency enables us to distinguish between animals on the one hand and machines and plants on the other. The use of language may well enrich the lives of those who possess it. DeGrazia (1996:157) for one describes it as a 'conceptual rocket' in the sense that 'linguistic beings are capable of a system of beliefs that is enormously richer than the conceptual worlds of non-linguistic beings'. However, language does not seem to have much bearing on the ability of an animal to experience pain, a capacity which, as we have seen, animals are well capable of expressing. It makes perfect sense then to say that animals desire not to suffer pain and this is clearly an interest we must take into account. As Lynch (1994: 6) bluntly puts it, 'the writhing and screams of a one-year-old child, or a lamb, is evidence only a philosopher could ignore'.

Another attempt to exclude animals as beings worthy of direct moral concern is based upon their lack of moral agency. Thus, Kant (1965), and, more recently, Narveson (1987), among others, want to hold that only moral agents – those capable of recognizing right from wrong and participating in moral agreements – can be directly morally wronged. A version of this approach is suggested by Carruthers (1992) in his book-length study. Dismissing his earlier attempt to deny moral standing to animals on the grounds that they cannot feel, Carruthers still denies that we have direct duties to them. He bases this claim on the adoption of a contractarian approach – exemplified by the work of two modern political philosophers, Rawls (1972) and Scanlon (1982) – which he suggests is most in accord with our intuition as to how duties and responsibilities ought to be allocated. Since animals are not moral agents they cannot participate in the deliberations in the social contract and are therefore unable to be direct beneficiaries from it.

The use of moral agency as a morally relevant characteristic is based upon the ability of the agent to understand what it is to make a moral claim and what it is to have moral obligations. As a general criticism, it should be said that the implications of adopting moral agency in this way are that there are many humans – young children and mentally defective adults – who are not moral agents either. Carruthers seeks to defend his contractarian position against this so-called argument from marginal cases, and, since it is an issue that has a significant bearing on the animal ethics debate in general, we will discuss it in some detail in chapter 4. For now, it is important to note that there is a strong case (explored in chapter 6) for incorporating animal interests within the kind of contract promoted by Carruthers (as well as Rawls and Scanlon). By so doing, the interests of animals become objects of direct moral concern. One of the strongest arguments in favour of incorporating animals as beneficiaries of a contract, and against the moral significance of moral agency, is the argument from marginal cases, that excluding animals from direct moral worth on the grounds that they are not moral agents condemns us to excluding young children and mentally enfeebled adults from direct moral concern too. This latter consequence, which is clearly counter-intuitive, is a position which is difficult for Carruthers, very aware of the importance of intuition in moral deliberations, to hold.

There are at least two further weaknesses of Carruthers' position. The first one relates to a misreading of Rawls, a contractarian thinker Carruthers invokes in defence of his own position. Carruthers is right to say that Rawls excludes animals as possible beneficiaries of his social contract since they lack what he calls 'moral personality', which is another way to describe moral agency. However, despite the fact that Rawls concludes from this that animals cannot be incorporated within his theory of justice, he explicitly states that this does not mean that we can do what we like to animals. This is because Rawls distinguishes between a narrow theory of justice, which excludes animals, and a wider sphere of morality where animals are included. From this, it is apparent that Rawls does think that, despite being morally inferior to humans, we do owe direct duties to them. As he writes (1972: 512):

> While I have not maintained that the capacity for a sense of justice is necessary in order to be owed the duties of justice, it does seem that we are not required to give strict justice anyway to creatures lacking this capacity. But it does not follow that there are no requirements at all in regard to them . . . Certainly it is wrong to be cruel to animals

... The capacity for feelings of pleasure and pain and for the forms of life of which animals are capable clearly impose duties of compassion and humanity in their case.

The third weakness of the Carruthers position is that it is clearly counter-intuitive to deny that animals are worthy of direct moral concern. This would not be so much of a problem if Carruthers himself did not claim throughout his book that intuition is one of the most important guides to the validity of moral positions. Moreover, he is well aware that the moral orthodoxy, 'that animals have *partial* moral standing – their lives and experiences having direct moral significance, but much less than that of human beings' (Carruthers, 1992: 8–9), appears to be at odds with the view that we have no direct duties to animals. In order to get round this discrepancy, between his denial that direct duties are owed to animals and the moral orthodoxy which insists that they are, Carruthers suggests that some restrictions on what can be done to them are justified by the indirect duties to animals that derive from the contractarian position. The next section will argue, however, that the specific indirect duties suggested by Carruthers, and indeed all indirect duty views, offer little genuine protection for animals. Consequently, his contractarian position remains strongly counter-intuitive.

Indirect duties

If we accept the argument that animals have no moral standing it does not mean that they have no value. The question about the moral standing of animals, then, is distinct from the question whether animals matter. After all, inanimate objects such as buildings and works of art may matter to us but they don't have moral standing (Carruthers, 1992: 1). If animals cannot be harmed directly, however, then the value they have must – like buildings or works of art – be indirect, of benefit to those (i.e. humans) who do have moral standing. In other words, we may have indirect duties to animals based on our direct duties to humans. Many of the key names in the history of Western thought have adopted this position.[4]

There are good reasons, already explored, for thinking that animals can be harmed directly, and therefore we are not dependent on justifying a case for animal protection on the basis of indirect duties. Leaving this aside for a moment, it is worth asking what mileage there is in indirect justifications for protecting animals. At the most obvious level, hurting an animal may be deemed morally wrong because she is the property of another human. The law in many countries reflects this in the sense that the compensation for the unwanted death of an animal is based on its property value, whereas damages for the emotional loss the death of a loved animal can cause are not usually granted.

On closer examination, the property justification for protecting animals is not a particularly fruitful area. This is partly because animals in the wild have no owners and therefore cannot be protected by property rights. In this context, it is interesting to note the example of the British League Against Cruel Sports who have adopted the tactic of buying land in hunting areas in order to protect the fox when it strays on to this land. More significantly, though, the property justification for protecting animals is weak because it is more often than not those who own animals who are primarily responsible for inflicting suffering on them. Indeed, one view is that the private property status of animals is the main reason for the failure of animal welfare. For, despite proposing – as we saw in chapter 2 – that the interests of animals, although inferior to humans, should be weighed against human interests, the unwillingness of the legal system to intervene in property rights means that fundamental animal interests are sacrificed even for trivial human ones (Francione, 1995).

A second possibility of an indirect reason for protecting animals is where 'causing suffering to an animal would violate the right of animal lovers to have their concerns respected and taken seriously' (Carruthers, 1992: 107). However, this principle does not offer much protection for animals. This is because the concerns of 'animal lovers', as Carruthers rightly points out, are no match for what many would regard as more fundamental human interests involving economic benefits or, indeed, those relating to physical well-being or even life itself. This is because, of course, we are here weighing human benefits from animal exploitation, not against animal suffering but against the concerns of animal lovers.

Another interesting facet of this debate, which raises further doubts on the validity of rejecting direct duties to animals, is the claim, endorsed by Carruthers, that only those acts of animal exploitation carried out in public are subject to possible prohibition on the grounds that 'animal lovers' will only be affected by those activities they can see. Since the vast majority of animal exploitation takes place in windowless factory farms and laboratories, not much animal suffering is left for public gaze (although this principle would provide great incentives for animal rights activists to get, by one means or another, detailed information on what happens to animals away from the public gaze). I'm not convinced that this public clause is justified. After all, those concerned about the welfare of animals can imagine, on the basis of evidence that already exists, what happens to animals in private, and as a result the mental torment engendered remains significant. Interestingly, Carruthers (1992: 108) recognizes it does not really make sense to regard, say, the beating of a dog in the street as more morally reprehensible than doing it in private. But our intuition that it does not matter *where* the dog is beaten derives from a strong suspicion that what we are doing to the dog matters to the dog directly and not just, if at all, to the sensitivities of those who might be offended by it. And if we accept this intuition then this, of course, means that we are not reliant on indirect duty views to justify the moral condemnation of inflicting suffering on animals.

Sometimes, protecting animals undoubtedly benefits humans. For example, many human lives are enriched by the presence and well-being of companion animals, although this should not disguise the very many acts of cruelty inflicted on such animals (see chapter 9). In the case of wild animals, likewise, much of the practical case for conservation is based on the benefits to humans of the continued existence of animals. These benefits, for example, might be aesthetic (we get pleasure out of seeing majestic creatures such as elephants and whales), economic or medicinal. The problem in this latter case, as chapter 9 will explore in more detail, is that such benefits do not depend upon the protection of individual animals as opposed to the maintenance of the species. The conservation of a species, furthermore, is not inconsistent with the dismissal of the interests of individual animals. The economic value of whales, for instance, depends upon the maintenance of sufficient whale stocks, but once whale stocks are deemed sufficient then hunting them to produce the economic gain (which involves firing a harpoon with an explosive device into the body of a whale and then detonating it) is morally justified.

A common indirect reason for justifying the protection of animals, held by Locke and Kant among the key figures in the history of moral thought, is that those who are cruel to animals are likely to be inclined to treat humans in the same way. This alleged link, it has been suggested, was the rationale for much of the early nineteenth-century animal protection law. Cruel practices such as bear-baiting, for instance, were prohibited, not only because of the suffering inflicted on the animal, but primarily because it despoiled the moral character of the working classes, encouraging cruelty, as well as gambling, drunkenness and absence from work (Ritvo, 1987). The view that cruelty to animals has a negative impact on human character remains a popular standpoint. In the contemporary British debate about fox-hunting, for instance, much is made of the effects that hunting has on those who participate in it, particularly if they are children (see letter from the astronomer and long-time anti-hunt campaigner Patrick Moore in the *Guardian*, 17 January 2001).

Although there are some dissenting voices (see Piper, 2003), the research consensus is that those who are violent towards animals are more likely to be violent towards their partners and children, and that abused children are more likely to abuse animals (Bell, 2001). One study, funded by the RSPCA, found that no less than 82 per cent of twenty-three families investigated by the RSPCA for animal cruelty had been identified by social services as having children at risk of abuse (Hutton, 1981). There is a strong case for saying, therefore, that 'animal abuse is often a part of a constellation of family violence, which includes child abuse and domestic violence' (Bell, 2001: 226). It can be seen then that it is particularly important to identify children who are cruel to animals since this 'may be an important symptom of negative experiences and/or predictor of future aggressive behaviour and that cruelty to animals should be included in assessments of vulnerable children' (Bell, 2001: 223).

This connection between the protection of children and animals is reflected in the fact that there are some organizations which combine both functions. Most notably, the American Humane Association has both animal protection and child protection wings. In Britain, the NSPCC and the RSPCA are working increasingly closely together in recognition of the link between animal and child abuse (*Guardian*, 13 February 2001; 5 March 2003). Historically, too, the development of the animal protection movement in the nineteenth century was linked with social reform movements designed to improve the lot of disadvantaged humans, and particularly children. For example, leading figures in the RSPCA – such as William Wilberforce and Fowell Buxton – were also heavily involved in the campaign against slavery. Similarly, Lord Shaftesbury, an animal protection campaigner, was the author of the Factory Acts, which attempted to protect children from unscrupulous employers, and also played a leading role in the setting up of the National Society for the Prevention of Cruelty to Children. In the United States, the New York Society for the Prevention of Cruelty to Children began life in the offices of the American Society for the Prevention of Cruelty to Animals, and prior to this the ASPCA had prosecuted a child cruelty case by using a statute designed to protect animals (Turner, 1964: 129; Singer, 1990: 221–2).

There is a considerable difference, however, between identifying a link between animal and human abuse and demonstrating that the former causes the latter. Those who cite this possible indirect duty tend to be unclear about the claim they are making, oscillating between the causal claim that cruelty to animals is likely to *lead* to cruelty to humans, and the much weaker claim that those who are violent towards animals are likely also to be violent towards humans. For example, Kant famously wrote that: 'If man is not to stifle his human feelings, he must practise kindness towards animals, for he who is cruel to animals becomes hard also in his dealings with men. We can judge the heart of a man by his treatment of animals', and again, 'we have duties towards the animals because thus we cultivate the corresponding duties towards human beings' (quoted in Leahy, 1991: 181–2). Carruthers (1992: 153–4), to give a contemporary example, writes that being cruel to animals betrays 'an indifference to suffering that may manifest itself . . . in that person's dealings with other rational agents'. The phrase 'may manifest' here would not seem to mean that cruelty to animals causes cruelty to humans, as Kant at times seems to think, and Carruthers (1992: 160) himself seems to rule out a causal link when he suggests that being desensitized to human and animal suffering is 'surely, psychologically separable'.

There would seem to be little empirical evidence for the causal claim. Without empirical evidence to the contrary it is just as plausible to propose the opposite relationship, that cruelty to animals might *lessen* the prospects of cruelty to humans. As DeGrazia (2002: 18) points out: 'Perhaps kicking his sheep around will allow the shepherd to blow off some steam, making him less likely to rough up his wife and kids.' In actual fact, as we saw, there is empirical evidence suggesting that those who are cruel to animals are likely to be cruel to humans. This weaker claim, however, while more likely to be true than the causal claim, does not provide grounds for indirect duties to animals. Scrutinizing those who are cruel to animals – maybe when they are children – might be an effective way of identifying the potential human abusers of the future, but stamping out animal cruelty is no guarantee that human abuse will be prevented. As a consequence, although greater attention is likely to be paid to animal cruelty, there is no great incentive to protect animals from their human abusers. Indeed, in order to discover those who are likely to abuse humans in the future, there may be a case for actually encouraging cruelty to animals precisely so we can find out who is likely to be a danger to humans.

One final point to make here is the common critique that the very exercise of trying to equate animal abuse with human abuse raises further doubts about the validity of the indirect duty view. Really, it only makes sense to say that cruelty to animals impacts negatively on the character of the human who commits it, and is likely to lead the perpetrator to be cruel to humans too, if we make the added assumption that there is something wrong with abusing animals and that the two acts – of cruelty to humans and animals – are broadly similar. And yet, for those who hold the indirect duty view it is not possible to directly wrong an animal. DeGrazia (2002: 26) sets this critique out nicely when he writes that:

> Animals, on this view, lack moral status and cannot be directly wronged. So why should pulverizing cows for fun reveal a defective moral character any more than does tearing up a newspaper for fun? The only plausible account of why cruelty is a vice acknowledges the moral status of its victims. (See also Midgley, 1983: 16–17)

Conclusion

This chapter has revealed that the claims of those who persist in arguing that we owe no direct duties to animals are weak. While empirical evidence of animal sentiency can never demonstrate conclusively that animals have moral standing, the evidence that they can suffer pain is strong grounds for suggesting that it ought to be taken into account in our moral deliberations. This position is strengthened by moral intuition, reflected in the law of all developed countries of the world, which suggests that the capacity to feel pain means that we owe moral duties to animals directly. To see this is so, imagine, as Francione (2000: 4) does, the unpleasant thought of Simon using a blowtorch on a rabbit. Why, if at all, might we object to what Simon is doing?

We might object to Simon's use of the blowtorch on four grounds. We might say that we object to it because it upsets other humans. This does not cover our intuitive concern about what Simon is doing because we would still feel uncomfortable about it even if it was done in secret. Likewise, the fact that the animal might belong to someone else would not end our discomfort because we would still have moral qualms even if the animal is a stray. Third, the fact that stopping Simon might prevent him from using the blowtorch on a human in future is an equally insufficient explanation for our concern, since we would still be troubled by Simon's actions even if his behaviour towards humans was impeccable. It is the fourth objection which appears most convincing. This time, we feel uncomfortable about the use of the blowtorch because, without the use of anaesthetic at any rate, it will cause barely imaginable agony for the animal. Therefore, because the rabbit is sentient it would appear to have an interest in not being blowtorched, and therefore we have a duty to take this interest into account in our moral deliberations.

Taking this into account is the operative need at this stage. Because what we have said so far does not mean that using a blowtorch on a rabbit is never justified. For example, it might be, and indeed has been, argued that such an activity is justified because of the human benefits that accrue from it – in terms, for instance, of investigating ways of treating burns. We might suspect that blowtorching a rabbit for fun is morally unjustified. At this stage, however, all I am trying to show is that a rabbit, unlike an inanimate object, has an interest in not being blowtorched.

The need to demonstrate that we have direct duties towards animals might not be so acute if they can be protected to a high degree through the carrying out of indirect duties. Relying on indirect duties, however, is a poor substitute, since the degree to which animals are protected by indirect duty views is always contingent upon its benefit to humans. Once human benefit is not furthered then protecting animals ceases to be an object of moral concern. It therefore provides a very fragile basis for animal protection. Indeed, it is more often the case that human benefit is secured by exploiting animals, whether for food, scientific research or merely for entertainment. Since we strongly suspect that moral duties are owed to animals directly, the purpose of the next two chapters is to try to work out what kind of direct duties we do owe to animals.

4

Why Shouldn't Animals Be Equal?

We established in the previous chapter that there are strong grounds for the claim that animals count for something morally, and that what we do to them matters to them directly, and therefore has to be taken into account in our moral deliberations. We move on in this chapter and the next to consider exactly what moral worth or status animals have. In particular, what, if anything, can stop us from treating humans and animals as morally equal? As we saw in chapter 2, moral equality in this sense does not mean that we are always obliged to treat humans and animals in the same way. It would not, for instance, make sense to grant animals the right to vote or the right to free speech. What moral equality does mean in this context is that we have to treat morally relevant animal and human interests in the same way, so that, for instance, we should not entertain the idea of inflicting pain on an animal if we are not prepared to consider inflicting the same degree of pain on a human.

The stakes here are high because translating moral equality between humans and animals into public policy would mean, as chapters 7–9 will reveal, fundamental changes to what we are, at present, allowed to do to animals. So why shouldn't we regard humans and animals as morally equal? What enables us to discriminate morally between them? Well, the usual candidate here is a collection of mental characteristics which, it is said, humans possess and animals do not. These characteristics constitute personhood, in the sense that they enable us to label an entity that has them as a person. As we shall see in chapter 5, there are those who want to use this alleged difference between humans and animals to justify the moral dominance of the former (this approach is referred to from now on as the 'personhood argument').

It will be left until chapter 5 to try to determine whether personhood can carry the weight of expectations placed upon it. In other words, what is the difference between the moral obligations owed to persons and non-persons respectively? In this chapter, we will engage in something a little different. Here it will be asked how far personhood *enables* us to distinguish between humans and animals. In other words, is it correct to describe humans as persons and animals as non-persons? Two challenges to its utility will be explored. The first focuses on the claim that not all animals lack personhood, and the second on the implications of the fact that not all humans are persons.

Personhood

Personhood is a difficult concept to define. This is at least partly because the term person is associated with full moral status, and is thereby a label attached to any entity that the proposer thinks deserves full moral status. Thus, for Poole (1996: 38) 'it is in virtue of our identity as persons that philosophers ascribe to us special moral privileges and responsibilities'. Hegel (1942: part one, para, 35) even went as far as to say that being a person is 'the highest achievement of a human being'. For most scholars, then, the term person is regarded as pivotal in modern philosophy and it is no wonder that ethical debate is more often than not structured around it. In the abortion debate, to give one example, opponents tend to argue that human embryos are persons while defenders of abortion suggest they are not. Because of these definitional difficulties, some philosophers, such as Tooley (1972), have concluded that the term person has an ethical content, denoting full moral status, but no descriptive content. As Warren (1997: 91) points out, 'the claim that something is a person implies that it has a strong moral status, but not that it has any empirically observable property, such as life, sentience, or rationality'.

Even Tooley, in a later work (1983), however, concedes that 'person' does have some objective meaning, however clouded it is with moral judgements. Indeed, there is a tendency amongst pro-animal philosophers to use 'person' in a descriptive sense, equating it with mental capacities. As we shall see, Regan bases his theory of animal rights on the intellectual capacities of some animals, therefore excluding those who do not have these capacities from moral consideration. Likewise, Singer and others argue that the greater the intellectual sophistication of a being, the greater the moral value placed upon their lives, so that killing an intellectually sophisticated being is a greater wrong than killing a being with less intellectual sophistication. The emphasis placed by pro-animal philosophers such as Regan and Singer on the importance of the characteristics usually associated with personhood has led critics such as Callicott (1995) to allege that much animal rights and liberation thinking remains, to all intents and purposes, anthropocentric, in the sense that it does not reject the moral importance of personhood, but seeks to show that animals, like humans, can be persons too.

From what we have said above, the reader should have guessed what personhood, in a descriptive sense, is usually taken to mean. Probably the most revealing way of identifying the characteristics of personhood is to distinguish them from degrees of non-personhood. To this end, Pluhar (1995: 1–10) provides a useful typology. She identifies six categories. At the apex are 'fully-fledged persons'. This includes 'the highly autonomous and linguistically sophisticated, who are capable of moral agency and able to act on principle'. This group is followed by 'persons lower on the autonomy scale', 'self-conscious beings who have little or no autonomy', 'merely conscious beings', 'living beings with no capacity for consciousness' and 'natural objects or systems'.

Full-personhood, then, is usually taken to include a variety of cognitive abilities, including rationality, creativity, intelligence and language use. Beings with these characteristics are deemed to be self-conscious, recognizing themselves as distinct entities with a past and a future. They are therefore autonomous, capable of rational choice, having beliefs and preferences and able to develop and follow a life plan based upon them. Locke provides one of the best accounts of personhood, defining a person as a 'thinking intelligent being, that has reason and reflection, and can consider itself as itself, the same thinking thing, in different times and places' (quoted in Holland, 2003: 15). Kant agrees with Locke that personhood is related to cognitive abilities, but, as we saw in chapter 3, he provides a particular slant arguing that personhood is distinguished by moral agency. As Holland (2003: 16) points out: 'a paradigmatic exercise of the capabilities Kant had in mind is when an agent works out their duties, and acts out of a sense of duty. Uniquely, persons have this capacity and it ensures their moral status.' Finally, a more recent well-known definition is provided by Dennett (1976) who includes the following as the most important characteristics of personhood: rationality, behaving intentionally, being perceived as behaving rationally and intentionally, the ability to perceive others as rational and intentional, self-consciousness, and the ability to communicate verbally.

Animal personhood?

It will be noted that the first challenge to the position that personhood enables us to distinguish morally between humans and animals – that not all animals lack personhood – is framed in the form of a claim and not a fact. This is because it is by no means certain that animals can be persons. Warnock (1998: 54) is absolutely clear, for instance that 'it is generally agreed that persons have to be human'. Warnock is merely aping a long philosophical tradition dating back to Aristotle, but, conceptually, it is quite reasonable to separate 'personhood' and 'human being' and thereby leave open the possibility that not all humans might be persons and not just humans can be persons. Both Kant and Locke recognized this conceptual difference, although both, after further examination, went on to deny personhood to animals. For Locke, if a non-human animal could be found:

> that had the use of Reason, to such a degree, as to be able to understand general Signs, and to deduce Consequences about general Ideas, he would no doubt be subject to Law, and in that Sense, be a Man, how much soever he differ'd in Shape from others of that Name.

It is being increasingly recognized that animals can have extensive cognitive abilities, and a considerable body of literature now exists seeking to describe what these abilities are.[1] For some pro-animal philosophers, the case for animal personhood is less important, since they seek to accord a higher moral status for animals primarily on the grounds that animals are sentient. Singer's utilitarian analysis obviously centres on sentiency. This is also the case in some accounts of animal rights. Ryder (1989: 325–6), to name one, although disagreeing with the validity of a utilitarian aggregation of preferences, describes suffering as the 'bedrock of morality'. Rollin (1981: 55), similarly, argues that 'even though concern for pleasure and absence of pain does not capture all of our intuitions about our moral concern for people, it certainly captures a good many of them'.

Perhaps the best-known case for animal rights, provided by Regan (1984), does place a great deal of emphasis on mental capacities. Regan seeks to show that at least some animals are, what he calls 'subjects-of-a-life', possessing enough mental complexity to be morally considerable. These capabilities are:

> Beliefs and desires; perception, memory, and a sense of the future, including their own future; an emotional life together with feelings of pleasure and pain; preference – and welfare – interests; the ability to initiate action in pursuit of their desires and goals; a psychophysical identity over time; and an individual welfare in the sense that their experiential life fares well or ill for them, logically independently of their utility for others. (Regan, 1984: 243)

Because at least some animals have these capabilities, Regan argues that they have a welfare which is capable of being harmed by not only inflictions of pain and deprivation, but also by death, since it forecloses all possibilities of finding satisfaction in life.

The key question here is how far do non-human animals possess the characteristics of a subject-of-a-life and to what extent are they sufficient for the personhood label to be attached to them, or at least some of them? The first point to make is that few would dispute that many species of non-human animals have capabilities that go way beyond their ability to experience pain and basic pleasures. It is undoubtedly true that animals can experience a 'wide range of unpleasant emotional states' that may include fear, frustration, exhaustion, stress and loss of social companions, as well as physical pain, characteristics which can be incorporated under the umbrella term of suffering. Modern animal welfare science has devised effective ways – mortality, productivity, physiological changes, abnormal behaviour – of measuring such suffering (see Dawkins, 1980). Likewise, although there is less evidence for this, it 'would be extremely surprising if animals were capable of having bad mental states but not good ones' (Rowlands, 2002: 12), such as pleasure, enjoyment and happiness.

In a post-Darwinian age, where the influence of theological separatism has declined, the claim that animals have cognitive abilities not unlike those of humans should not surprise us too much. Darwin dealt a severe blow to the view that there is a qualitative difference between humans and animals. As he pointed out:

> the difference in mind between man and the higher animals, great as it is, certainly is one of degree and not of kind. We have seen that the senses and intuitions, the various emotions and faculties, such as love, memory, attention, curiosity, imitation, reason etc, of which man boasts, may be found in an incipient, or even sometimes in a well-developed condition, in the lower animals. (Quoted in Radford, 2001: 93)

More recently, it has been established that the genetic similarities between humans and the great apes are marked. Indeed, the differences between humans and chimpanzees are smaller than those between chimpanzees and gorillas. This is another nail in the coffin of those who insist on a strict moral divide, with all humans on the privileged side and all animals on the other.

Having said all of this, the ability of non-human animals to be more than just conscious recipients of pain and basic pleasure does not by itself constitute the characteristics necessary for the full-personhood label to be attached to them. For the application of this label, animals, as we saw, must exhibit self-consciousness, and a high degree of rationality enabling them to devise long-term life plans based on beliefs and desires. Even Darwin does not provide support for this. As well as the above comments, he also insists that: 'There can be no doubt that the difference between the mind of the lowest man and that of the highest animal is immense' (quoted in Radford, 2001: 93). Moreover, the differences of degree, rather than kind, are not between humans and all animals but between humans and only the higher non-human animals.

So, what of the claim that humans and animals share the characteristics of personhood? Well, first of all it should be said, Frey's arguments considered in chapter 3 notwithstanding, that few would deny that most animals – including mammals and birds – are capable of having beliefs and desires, however simplistic these beliefs and desires may be, and acting upon them. Thus, the evidence suggests that animals are capable of making choices based upon a belief that a certain action will achieve a desired outcome. At least some animals, then, would appear to exhibit autonomy at least in a weak sense of the term (see below).

In order to provide further evidence of animal capabilities, the pro-animal philosophers have focused, not surprisingly, on research on the higher mammals, and particularly non-human primates. We share much with non-human primates and it should not be forgotten that humans are apes too. Much is made, for instance, of the experiments with (non-human) apes revealing considerable cognitive abilities. Pride of place goes to the teaching of sign language to the great apes, which began in the 1960s. Here, it has been claimed that apes have considerable ability to learn and use sign language, not only in terms of their propensity to learn signs but also in terms of their ability to put signs together to make simple sentences. Singer (1993: 118–19) also speculates that whales and dolphins might 'turn out to be rational and conscious', and perhaps even cats and dogs and some farm animals too. It has even been denied that all animals lack moral agency. Evidence has been found of altruistic behaviour in animals, ranging from the use of warning calls, to threatening or attacking predators to save others, food sharing, and helping injured animals.[2]

Whether or not language is a necessary condition for full-personhood or the possession of any kind of thought is a debatable issue. As we saw in chapter 3, philosophers such as Frey and Leahy argue that it is. We could make two responses to this. One is to show that at least some animals, principally the apes, do have the capacity to learn language and, in addition, we could also make the claim that other species of animals do use language, only not ours! However, on this first response, while most animal species have clearly developed means of communicating with each other, it is doubtful if it constitutes language. Even the sign language of apes is regarded as a fairly impoverished form of communication (see Leahy, 1991: 159–64). As Carruthers (1992: 140–1) remarks there is: 'no evidence of the chimpanzees ever using their signs in thought, for solving problems or reasoning about what to do. They treat them merely as practical tools for enabling them to fulfil their immediate desires.'

The second response, as suggested in chapter 3, is that conceptual thought is not inconceivable without a language. Indeed, it is certainly true that the sometimes complex behaviour patterns of animals are difficult to explain without reference to an animal's ability to think conceptually. Singer (1993: 114–17) provides some examples to illustrate this. One such illustration was observation of chimpanzees at Amsterdam Zoo. Singer writes that observers have often seen:

> co-operating activity that requires planning. For example, the chimpanzees like to climb the trees and break off branches, so that they can eat the leaves. To prevent the rapid destruction of the small forest, the zookeepers have placed electric fencing around the trunk of the trees. The chimpanzees overcome this by breaking large branches from dead trees . . . and dragging them to the base of a live tree. One chimpanzee then holds the dead branch while another climbs up it, over the fence and into the tree. The chimpanzee who gets into the tree in this way shares the leaves thus obtained with the one holding the branch.

It seems extremely probable then that, without possessing a language capability, a significant number of non-human species exhibit quite complex and sophisticated mental capacities. As Pluhar's review of the evidence confirms (1995: 46): 'Many sentient nonhumans apparently have the ability to learn from past experience, to anticipate future events, to change their behaviour in the face of changing circumstances, to carry out short-term plans, and to solve problems in a creative fashion.'

Moreover, she continues (ibid.: 57), 'no characteristic has yet been found that is *wholly* lacking in nonhumans and wholly present in humans'. This section ends with a lengthy description of the mental capacities of a gorilla called Koko by a researcher who observed her for over twenty years (Patterson and Gordon, 1993: 58–9). The reader is left to formulate his or her own conclusions on what this reveals about the intelligence of great apes in general.

> She communicates in sign language, using a vocabulary of over 1,000 words. She also understands spoken English, and often carries on 'bilingual' conversations, responding in sign to questions asked in English . . . She demonstrates a clear self-awareness by engaging in self-directed behaviours in front of a mirror, such as making faces or examining her teeth, and by her appropriate use of self-descriptive language. She lies to avoid the consequences of her own misbehaviour, and anticipates others' responses to her actions. She engages in imaginary play, both alone and with others. She has produced paintings and drawings which are representational. She remembers and can talk about past events in her life . . .
>
> She laughs at her own jokes and those of others. She cries when hurt or left alone, screams when frightened or angered. She talks about her feelings . . . She grieves for those she has lost . . . She can talk about what happens when one dies . . . She displays a wonderful gentleness with kittens and other small animals. She has even expressed empathy for others seen only in pictures.

Reservations about animal personhood

Despite the comments by Pluhar above and the evidence of the cognitive abilities of non-human animals, there are a number of problems associated with attempting to demonstrate that not all animals lack personhood. In the first place, it is extremely difficult to establish with any precision, beyond the rather vague generalizations that were made above, what the mental capacities of animals are. This is partly because of the intellectual difficulties in establishing whether another being is self-conscious, and partly because of the disproportionate attention paid to the cognitive abilities of apes to the neglect of other species (see Nagel, 1974). As Carruthers (1992: 123) points out: 'we need to be cautious in interpreting animal behaviour in experiments that require animals to interact with human beings. For it is hard to be sure that we have not been unwittingly encouraging the animals to do what we want, by conditioning them to respond to unconscious human signals.'

There is a tendency for pro-animal philosophers to cite anecdotes illustrating what is claimed to be animal intelligence. The signing of apes is one such source as is the behaviour of apes, and other animals, in the wild and in the laboratory environment. But these are usually open to interpretation. Leahy (1991: 36–9) offers us one such reinterpretation of an observation made by the noted primatologist Jane Goodall. Observing a chimp, Figan, with designs on one remaining banana in a tree under which an older chimp, Goliath, was resting, Goodall relates what happened next:

> Figan moved away and sat on the other side of the tent so that he could no longer see the fruit. Fifteen minutes later, when Goliath got up and left, Figan without a moment's hesitation went over and collected the banana. Quite obviously he had sized up the whole situation: if he had climbed for the fruit earlier, Goliath would almost certainly have snatched it away. If he had remained close to the banana, he would probably have looked at it from time to time. Chimps are very quick to notice and interpret the eye movements of their fellows, and Goliath would possibly, therefore, have seen the fruit himself. And so Figan had not only refrained from instantly gratifying his desire but had also gone away so that he could not 'give the game away' by looking at the banana.

If this interpretation is correct then it would indeed illustrate a high degree of rationality. Leahy, however, offers an alternative interpretation:

> Figan, seeing Goliath in close proximity, was scared out of his sight and with nothing better to do just hung around more or less losing interest in the banana. He sees Goliath leaving, interest in the banana is rekindled, and he takes it; no sizing up, nor careful planning, just class-consciousness and opportunism.

Whether more research would enable us to judge between these competing interpretations is an open question. We cannot ask the animals what they are thinking.

The second reservation about relying on attempts to show that at least some animals are persons is that it creates a potential moral divide between different animal species. We can marvel at the capabilities of the great apes, whales and dolphins, thereby attaching great value to them and campaigning for legal rights to be attached to them.[3] Such a move is politically astute, not least because focusing on those non-human species which are closer to us is more likely to gain social and political acceptability. Furthermore, by recognizing the moral and therefore legal importance of apes we are making the crucial claim that according considerable moral worth does not stop at the boundary of the human species. However, by adopting this position, we are effectively then devaluing those mammals who have fewer cognitive abilities. This 'threatens to create new hierarchies in which we move some animals, such as the great apes, into a "preferred" group based on their similarity to humans, and continue to treat other animals as our property and resources' (Francione, 2000: 119).

The line of moral considerability, therefore, can be drawn beyond the human species but not too far! Thus, Steven Wise, a leading American legal scholar, bases his case for the legal rights of animals primarily on apes, arguing that: 'Whatever legal rights these apes may be entitled to spring from the complexities of their minds' (Wise, 2000: 237). Likewise, precisely because he uses mental complexity as a criterion for moral worth, Regan (1984) is then committed to attaching subject-of-a-life status, and therefore rights, only to mammals aged over one year. As a result, as Benton (1993: 87) rightly points out, 'the immense majority of animal species are offered no protection whatsoever from Regan's argument'.

For obvious reasons, Regan is uncomfortable with this and responds in two ways (1984: 365–9). He suggests first that it remains possible that an argument for including those animals who are not subjects-of-a-life might be developed at some point in the future. This clearly does not help us very much. His second, more promising – at least superficially – response is that we should exercise moral caution because the boundary between those who have the necessary characteristics to be subjects-of-a-life and those who do not is blurred. This may be the case for some species, which may or may not be included, but equally for others there is 'no reasonable doubt that they fall on the wrong side of Regan's criterion'. The most these animals – 'the teeming millions of insects and other invertebrates, amphibians, reptiles, fish, birds and mammals at the earliest stages of infancy' – can hope for is protection as a result of the indirect duty that treating them badly may affect the way those animals, and humans, with inherent value are treated (Benton, 1993: 87–8).

Sapontzis (1993: 271) is one pro-animal philosopher who urges the rejection of attempts to show that animals are sophisticated enough intellectually to be regarded as persons. As he points out:

> Overcoming speciesism requires going beyond the modest extension of our moral horizons to include intellectually sophisticated, nonhuman animals, such as chimpanzees and whales. It requires recognising not only that the origin of value does not lie in anything that is peculiarly human; it also requires recognising that the origin of value does not lie in anything that is human-like or that humans may be assured they have the most of (because they are the most intellectually sophisticated beings around).

Instead, Sapontzis (1993: 271–2) recommends focusing on feelings. For him 'values originate with feelings, such as pleasure and pain, fulfilment and frustration, joy and sorrow, excitement and depression and so forth' which 'are not peculiarly human nor peculiar to human-like animals'. Such an approach is suggested by Singer in some of his writings at least, and the implications of dispensing with the attempt to demonstrate that animals can come close to having the intellectual capabilities of humans are discussed further in chapter 5.

It is undoubtedly true that animals do exhibit varying degrees of mental capabilities, and these become considerable in the cases of the great apes and, perhaps, dolphins. However, the final argument against the animal personhood quest is that what we do know is that even the most intellectually able animals do not have the character-istics of personhood to the same degree as the average normal adult human. This comes out very strongly in Frey's critique of Regan's subject-of-a-life criterion (1987). Frey distinguishes between what he calls 'control' autonomy (possessed by human persons) and 'prefer-ence' autonomy (possessed by some species of nonhuman animals and human nonpersons). The former, for Frey, involves a much higher quality of life with a rational assessment of desires and a willingness to shed or moderate some, particularly first-order (more base), desires if they are not consistent with an individual's conception of the good life. The latter, which he equates with Regan's subject-of-a-life crite-rion, on the other hand, involves the satisfaction of 'first order' desires, and only requires that beings be able to have desires, or pref-erences, together with the ability to initiate actions with a view to satisfying them. For Frey, Regan's preference autonomy is an 'impov-erished' form of the concept, lacking all of the features of his 'control' sense of the term. What it means is that, at most, animals are only capable of dealing with a very basic set of first-order desires which denies them 'means to that rich full life of self-fulfilment and achieve-ment' which is 'quite apart from any satisfaction and fulfilment that comes through the satisfaction of our appetites'.

In conclusion to this section, then, if the full-personhood criterion is applied rigorously, it is plausible to exclude all non-human animals. In other words, adopting mental complexity as the primary determi-nant of moral status inexorably leads us to the conclusion that, as Pluhar (1995: 57) correctly recognizes, although animals 'may have lesser degrees of the relevant characteristics . . . as far as we know, none can match the capacities of the mature, normal human being. In short, only humans appear to be fully-fledged persons.' Regan is well aware that the mental capabilities of humans are greater than animals and that, without an additional argument, it would be difficult to conclude that they possessed equal inherent value. His subject-of-a-life criterion, then, is not, he himself recognizes, equivalent to personhood (Regan, 2004: 50).

As something of a digression, the above argument leads me to suggest that there is, in my judgement, a serious problem with Regan's central subject-of-a-life principle. In some of his writings, at least, the characteristics of a subject-of-a-life are not particularly difficult for a human or animal being to achieve. Thus he writes (2004: 50) that the similarities between normal humans, marginal humans and animals is that: 'we all are aware of the world and aware as well of what happens to us. Moreover, what happens to us . . . matters to us because it makes a difference to the quality and duration of our lives, as experienced by us, whether anybody else cares about this or not.'

The problem here is that Regan has chosen the characteristics constituting a subject-of-a-life precisely because they allow him to include animals and so-called marginal humans, those humans who do not have full-personhood. But isn't this the wrong way round? In other words, should we not be establishing what characteristics are essential for moral considerability *before* describing who meets the criteria we have established? Regan points out that his subject-of-a-life principle *explains* the 'moral sameness' and 'moral equality' between humans and animals. But isn't it this very moral equality that needs explaining in the first place?

In reality, recognizing the fact that animals lack personhood, Regan justifies the egalitarian implications of the subject-of-a-life criterion not by emphasizing the similarities between humans and animals but by emphasizing the differences between humans. This argument, commonly used by pro-animal philosophers, is that if non-human animals are not full persons, exhibiting, in Frey's terms, only preference autonomy, then not all humans are full persons either. Therefore, if we want to continue exploiting animals in the ways we do now on the grounds that they are not full persons then we must, consistency demands, also be willing to exploit those humans who are not full persons. It is to a consideration of this so-called 'argument from marginal cases' that we now turn.

The argument from marginal cases stated

Given the problems encountered above it may be the case that a more effective, and more widely pursued, attempt to challenge the personhood argument than denying that at least some animals lack personhood, is to deny that all humans are persons. This was framed as a fact as opposed to a claim in the sense that it is self-evident that some humans do have such severe mental disabilities that they do not have the characteristics required for personhood. There are three distinctive types of human non-persons. First, there are those – such as anencephalic infants and those born with severe learning difficulties – who have never been and can never be persons. Second, there are those – such as those in a persistent vegetative state and those with senile dementia – who are not persons but used to be. Third, it is also evident that young children do not have the characteristics of full-personhood but are potential persons. The law, of course, recognizes this in the sense that young children are regarded as moral patients (that is, lacking moral agency), not regarded as morally responsible for their actions until a certain age and required to be governed by a parent or guardian.

The identification of the fact that not all humans are persons is the basis for a much-debated dimension of animal ethics, the so-called argument from marginal cases (hereafter AMC). The AMC is an argument which, as Dombrowski (1997: 3) points out, 'has generated perhaps more light and heat than any other argument in moral philosophy over the last twenty years'. Such weight is attached to the AMC by the pro-animal philosophers that it is worthwhile examining it in some detail. It is easy to see why the AMC is invoked so regularly by the pro-animal philosophers, and particularly those who seek to pursue the personhood strategy. It enables them to maintain the moral importance of personhood but at the same time, by denying that all humans are persons, enables them to argue that we cannot morally distinguish between humans and animals on the basis of it. So, Singer (1993: 18–19), for instance, can dismiss the claim by Rawls, among others – that only those who have what he calls 'moral personality' (meaning moral agency) can be included within a theory of justice – on the grounds that not all humans can be moral agents. Likewise, Singer, somewhat provocatively, states (1993: 117–18) that: 'So it seems that killing, say, a chimpanzee is worse than the killing of a human being who, because of a congenital intellectual disability, is not and never can be a person.' Even Regan, as we have seen, although seeking to show that at least some animals have considerable cognitive capabilities, ultimately falls back on the AMC.

It is important to note that there are two versions of the AMC (Pluhar, 1995: 63–4). The 'categorical' version holds that *because* marginal humans (or human non-persons, which is a more popular term now) are deemed to have rights, or maximum moral significance, despite their lack of personhood, then consistency demands that these rights are accorded to at least some animals. By contrast, the 'biconditional' version holds that *if* marginal humans have rights or are regarded as having maximum moral significance, then so do at least some animals (Pluhar, 1995: 63–4). The difference between these two versions is that the latter could be used to justify excluding both animals *and* marginal humans from full-personhood. As a result, if we persist with the view that it is morally legitimate to inflict suffering on animals for the benefit of humans – as scientific tools or as a source of food – then consistency demands that it is morally permissible to treat marginal humans in the same way.

Singer (1993: 78) provides probably the best example of the categorical version. He writes that:

> I do not wish to suggest that intellectually disabled humans should be force-fed with food colourings until half of them die ... I would like our conviction that it would be wrong to treat intellectually disabled humans in this way to be transferred to nonhuman animals at similar levels of self-consciousness and with similar capacities for suffering.

At least one philosopher has adopted the biconditional version by accepting that the cost of continuing to use animals is that we must reduce the moral significance we attach to marginal humans. Indeed, Frey (1983; 1987; 2002) is prepared to go as far as to say that some human life has no value at all. 'A life wholly and irreversibly in the grip of senile dementia', he writes (1987: 59), for instance, 'is a life not worth living.' Once this is admitted, of course, there is nothing to stop us from concluding that moral agents have greater inherent value than moral patients and therefore should be treated differently. As Frey (1983: 115–16) admits, then, the 'choice before you is either antivivisection or condoning human experiments', and he chooses the latter 'not with great glee and rejoicing, and with great reluctance' but because 'I cannot think of anything at all compelling that cedes all human life of any quality of greater value than animal life of any quality'.

To a certain extent, of course, this distinction between humans with full-personhood and humans who have fewer, if any, personhood characteristics, is already recognized in practice. We do not, as already indicated, treat children as full persons with the autonomy given to those with such a status and expected by them. Likewise, we recognize that there may be a case for allowing severely mentally and physically disabled humans to die naturally rather than be kept alive artificially. Moreover, it is also correct to say that the medical profession, when faced with the allocation of scarce resources, will, at least partly, base their judgement on the respective levels of personhood involved. Finally, the case for euthanasia is also based on the principle that the quality of human life may have become so low that the individual concerned can no longer be regarded as a person in the full sense of the word. In such circumstances, there may be a recognition that life is no longer worth living.

Of course, these examples are not compatible with the application of the biconditional version of the AMC. In order to be so, we would have to be not only prepared to sanction, say, allowing a seriously defective human being to die rather than administering expensive medical treatment, but also to inflict pain on such an individual in the course of a laboratory procedure. As Leahy (1991: 202) remarks: 'That a hospital lets babies with minimal brains and no conscious potential die would occasion less hostility, and many might even approve . . . Yet if it were known that microcephalic babies . . . were regularly sold to research laboratories, then there would undoubtedly be an outcry.' Likewise, if anyone should be partial to the taste of such a human then there is, morally at least, nothing amiss with using marginal humans as a source of food! Most, if not all of us, I assume, regard such possibilities as morally reprehensible. But we are not basing this moral opposition on the fact that we are exploiting persons, since marginal humans, or at least some of them, are not persons in the way we have defined personhood. Furthermore, we have previously argued that it is illegitimate to distinguish between the moral status of humans and animals on species alone. What we are left with then is the apparently unavoidable conclusion that if we refuse to allow the use of marginal humans in the ways we have described above, then the use of animals for such things is equally morally unacceptable.

Responses to the argument from marginal cases

Responses to the AMC have been a mixture of avoidance and attack. One initial critique is to argue that full moral status should be accorded to members of a species whose *normal* members are full-persons. As Leahy (1991: 204) suggests, 'it would seem reasonable to accord something like honorary status to those existing in its image, as it were, but otherwise enfeebled through age or retardation'. The problem with this, however, is that it arguably makes little sense to accord moral status to a species, rather than to individuals. As Pluhar (1995: 161) correctly points out 'Why should one's own moral status depend upon the endowments – or lack of endowments – of anyone else?' Wise (2000: 253) reveals the illogicality of this view when he remarks that: 'You get straight As; I go to Harvard. I jump thirty feet; you go to the Olympics. You look like Elle MacPherson; I get a modeling contract.'

Some philosophers opposed to the AMC focus on appeals to kinship, that our genetic similarities (the fact that we are all humans) are the key to explaining why we should apply the same moral status to all humans. For Midgley (1983), this amounts to saying that we are emotionally attached to members of our own species. Wenz (1988) provides another version of the kinship theory. His 'concentric circle' theory of justice suggests that our moral obligations to others increase according to their degree of closeness to us at the centre of the circle, and since these others are going to be humans, whether marginal or normal, our moral obligations to all humans are greater than they are to animals. More specifically, Wenz argues that we have negative obligations to non-humans – we must not, all things being equal, interfere with them – but there is no obligation for humans to uphold their positive rights

Wenz (1988: 325) claims that this approach 'mandates sweeping changes in the human treatment of nonhuman animals'. This assertion will depend, of course, on an empirical examination of the treatment of animals in any particular society and legal system. However, Wenz's approach does not seem to amount to much more than the moral orthodoxy. This is because in the event of a conflict between humans and animals, the negative obligations we have towards the latter will have to be sacrificed. So, Wenz starts by proclaiming that it is wrong to trap animals, to experiment on them or even kill them (which is indeed a radical agenda), but then proceeds to remove these prohibitions when human necessity demands it, whether for food, to retain a particular human culture (such as the Inuit) or when scientific research involving animals can be shown to save human life (1988: 325–7).

In response to the kinship approach in general we can argue, first, that it begs the question of why we should base moral judgements on genetics or on kinship. It might be correct empirically that, at some level, we accord greater moral weight to those closest to us. Intuitively, however, we recognize that our obligations to other humans should not necessarily be dependent on our particular relationship to them, so that, for instance, we can sacrifice the interests of other humans in order to benefit our relatives. We recognize, to be more specific, that the kinship approach, because it means the application of differential obligations towards different groups of humans, can be used to justify differential treatment on the grounds of race or gender and so forth (Pluhar, 1995: 162–9).

The second response to the kinship argument is that, even if it is a morally valid claim, it by no means produces the anthropocentric conclusions designed for it. This is because it does not rule out the possibility that a non-human animal may occupy a place near the centre of any particular concentric circle or, in Midgley's terms, may occupy a central place in the emotional life of an individual human. Wenz (1988: 328–9) recognizes this by suggesting that, while in general animals ' "inhabit" more remote concentric circles', and are therefore less important morally, this does not apply to companion animals. In response to this, however, we might argue why should this be restricted to companion animals? After all, animal advocates feel an emotional attachment to all animals, and not just those who are kept as pets. One additional related point here is that it is interesting to note that the moral orthodoxy does not treat companion animals any differently from other animals. Anti-cruelty statutes are designed to protect such animals from unnecessary suffering in the same way as statutes to protect farm or laboratory animals. Of course, if anyone treated a companion animal in the same way as a farm or laboratory animal – kept in a small space, poisoned, burnt, mutilated or whatever – the chances are they would be prosecuted. The infliction of such suffering, however, is deemed to be justified in the one case but not in the other because it is regarded as necessary in the one case and not in the other.

Another response to the AMC is that it underestimates the capabilities of marginal humans, that those of even a severely damaged human are still greater than the most mentally developed non-human. Cohen (1986: 866) provides a representative version of this approach. As he writes, 'what humans retain when disabled, animals never had'. Such an assertion must be subject to empirical examination, however, and it surely exaggerates the degree to which humans and animals differ (Cavalieri, 2001: 77–9). At the very least, it is conceivable to envisage instances where the capabilities of animals might be superior to those of marginal humans. At the very extreme, for instance, a comatose human is surely, according to the full-personhood criteria for moral considerability, less valuable morally than a normal adult non-human mammal. Nevertheless, it is true that the word 'subnormal' when applied to humans covers a large variety of conditions, and that some of these, such as mongoloids, involve considerable intellectual capacities.

One oft-made critique of the inclusion of small children among those classified as 'marginal' is that they will be normal adult humans in the future. They are, therefore, potential persons. Indeed, another way of looking at this is to describe a baby or a child not as a potential person but as a person by virtue of her potential. Indeed, our moral intuition suggests that children matter more to us than adults.[4] This is reflected in the apparently widely accepted principle that in a rescue-type situation, children should be chosen before adults, itself a reflection of the belief that the death of a child is somehow worse than a person dying of a great age. The reason for this, of course, is that death at a young age robs that person of the opportunity to fulfil her hopes and aspirations. It therefore denies the achievement of potential.

However, the above argument that, far from being marginal, babies and small children should be regarded as full-persons because of their potential, is problematic. It is true, of course, that the bulk of children will be normal adult persons in the future. However, it should be noted – as we will explore in more detail in chapter 5 – that the purpose of identifying full-personhood as a key determinant of differential treatment is that, at any one point in time, those with the constituent characteristics can be harmed in much more damaging ways than those without, and there is no dispute that small children do not possess these characteristics to the same degree as normal adult humans. Therefore, potentiality is logically different from actuality. Without an argument explaining why potential persons are the same as actual persons, it does not seem possible to include the former as full-persons. Therefore, it does not explain why, if we are prepared to exploit animals, we should not be morally entitled to exploit infants with a similar degree of personhood (Pluhar, 1995: 107–110). Singer (1993: 153), not for the first time, is worth quoting at length here. He writes:

> It is of course true that the potential rationality, self-consciousness and so on of a fetal Homo sapien surpasses that of a cow or a pig; but it does not follow that the fetus has a stronger claim to life. There is no rule that says that a potential X has the same value as an X, or has all the rights of an X. There are many examples that show just the contrary. To pull out a sprouting acorn is not the same as cutting down a venerable oak. To drop a live chicken into a pot of boiling water would be much worse than doing the same to an egg. Prince Charles is a potential King of England, but he does not now have the rights of a king.

The logic of this position then is that not only is the foetus a potential person but each sperm is too. Are we then to declare that each sperm has moral status on the grounds that one day it might evolve into the President of the United States? (Leahy, 1991: 206). Clearly not, although it should be said that it might be possible to distinguish between the loss of a foetus and the loss of a sperm on the grounds that in the latter case 'there is no . . . identifiable subject of the loss', whereas a foetus is a potential identifiable person (Marquis, 1989: 201–2). Such a position would enable us to dispense with a moral objection to contraception while still maintaining, as Marquis wants to do, that abortion is wrong.

A corollary of the 'potential' adult argument is the view that we should accord full moral status to marginal humans who were formerly normal. One possible justification for this is that to do otherwise is to infringe what such a person would have wanted when a full-person. As with the case of young children, however, such an argument falls foul of the criticism that a moral judgement is being made on the basis of past, rather than current, potentialities, which defeats the object of the personhood criteria. Of course, finally, any success in the granting of maximum moral status to young children and those marginal humans who were formerly full-persons represents only a partial critique of the AMC, in that it does not affect those marginal humans who have always been, and will remain, lacking in full-personhood.

Another common critique of the AMC is that focusing on the devaluation of marginal humans has negative consequences. For some, denying a high moral status to marginal humans, and exploiting them in the same way as animals, might lead to such a confusion of moral responsibility that it could lead to threats against 'normal' humans. This is the slippery slope argument. Singer (1993: 77) explains it as follows:

> Once we allow that an intellectually disabled human being has no higher moral status than an animal, the argument goes, we have begun our descent down a slope, the next level of which is denying rights to social misfits, and the bottom of which is a totalitarian government disposing of any groups it does not like by classifying them as subhuman.

This is part of Singer's critique of the slippery slope argument, and it has an element of sarcasm to it. But it is not too different from the genuine article. Thus, Carruthers (1992: 116) suggests that: 'to think and speak in terms that withhold moral rights from some human beings is to invite people to try to draw yet further distinctions – for example, withholding rights from those who are sexually or intellectually "deviant", or from those whose intelligence is low.' As we saw in chapter 3, Carruthers adopts a contractarian approach to animal ethics, whereby membership in the moral community is restricted to moral agents, those who are capable of claiming their moral entitlements and understanding when others are due theirs. Carruthers recognizes, of course, that such an approach not only excludes non-human animals from moral considerability but excludes marginal humans too. As a result, he needs a device – mainly the slippery slope argument – that enables him to deny access to animals but allow it for marginal humans.

The first point to be made against this argument is that it rests on an empirically verifiable statement that is far from established. As Cavalieri (2001: 82) accurately remarks, the 'serious structural weakness' of the slippery slope argument is the fact that 'certain steps might imply others has not the cogency of a logical derivation but must be experimentally proven each time it is used'. Thus, Carruthers (1992: 116) claims that people would be unable to understand the principle of attaching different types of moral status to different humans. But nowhere does he provide any evidence that this is likely to be the case. Conversely, there are historical examples of stable, compassionate and prosperous societies where differential moral status has been applied. Many societies, for instance, have practised infanticide (Kuhse and Singer, 1985).

Moreover, the perceived threats to normal humans only apply if we accept the bioconditional version of the AMC, that marginal humans and animals should be treated as morally inferior to normal humans. The categorical version, on the other hand, wants to accord a moral equality that would benefit not just animals but marginal humans too. Finally, the slippery slope argument misses the whole point of the moral orthodoxy, which is that normal adult humans *should* be treated in a different way precisely because they have a level of personhood not possessed by animals. It is logically consistent, then, to lump marginal humans together with animals, and there can be no confusion about the existence of normal adult humans in a separate category.

Holland (1984) agrees that the AMC makes marginal humans potentially vulnerable, but rather than using this assertion as a critique of the attempt to challenge the moral orthodoxy, he advocates renewed attempts to show why marginal humans and animals should both have a high moral status. The problem with this criticism is that it ignores the fact that the AMC is intended precisely to deal with the difficulty of developing an ethical framework which can incorporate animals and all humans as moral equals. If Holland is successful, in other words, he automatically makes the AMC redundant. Another pro-animal philosopher, Steve Sapontzis (1987), argues that the AMC *should* be made redundant in that it underestimates the capabilities of animals. Giving some credence, perhaps, to the concerns of those, such as Townsend and Carruthers, who worry about the moral vulnerability of marginal humans, Sapontzis argues that it is degrading, as well as unnecessary, for animals to be linked with severely mentally disabled humans. In response, though, while we should not underestimate the capabilities of animals, no one is seriously suggesting that either animals or marginal humans have full-personhood in the way that normal adult humans have.

Human self-interest in protecting marginal humans provides another critique of the AMC (Narveson, 1977). The arguments employed here are, first, that any one of us normal adult humans might become marginal in the future and we would expect to be treated with respect. Second, marginal humans are likely to have relatives who would want them to be treated with respect. Third, there is nothing to be gained by humans in exploiting marginal members of their species.

The latter two arguments can be dispensed with pretty rapidly. The second point above does not enable us to distinguish between marginal humans and animals. One might say that what happens to animals matters to other animals that are related to them in some way. Similarly, human owners of animals may well think about their animal companions in exactly the same ways that other humans think about the human defectives to who they are related. As an argument, then, for justifying differential (and better) treatment for marginal humans than animals, it palpably fails. Indeed, one can envisage a situation where this approach would justify better treatment for an animal loved by its human companion than for a marginal human who is, maybe, without any close relatives and friends. The third argument above is equally flawed. While it might not be in the best of taste to envisage exploiting marginal humans for the benefit of other humans (and potentially animals) it is not true that no benefit is possible. One constant criticism of the use of animals in laboratory procedures, for instance, is that animal models are not always appropriate for application to humans. The use of marginal humans would clearly alleviate this problem.

The first argument above, that we should respect marginal humans since we would expect to be treated with respect should we become one in the future, would seem to be the strongest. The prospect of becoming a marginal human is a powerful reason for avoiding treating present marginal humans in anything but a dignified fashion. One retort that might be offered here is the view that self-interest does not account for all our moral intuitions, and that the latter should take precedence if we are to avoid charges of either selfishness or speciesism (Pluhar, 1995: 97–101). A more effective response is to make the oft-repeated point that the categorical version of the AMC does allow us to avoid the exploitation of, and therefore show respect to, *both* marginal humans and animals.

Conclusion

This chapter began the attempt to determine what it is that animals are owed morally, after we concluded in chapter 3 that they are worth something. The claim that humans are morally superior to animals is usually based upon the identification of what are suggested to be morally important differences between humans and animals. The suggestion is that humans have characteristics that enable them to be labelled as persons, whereas animals, despite having more capabilities than the ability to experience pain and pleasure, are not full-persons. In this chapter, we offered two possible ways to deny that animals and humans can be distinguished through the use of the personhood criteria. One focuses on the denial that not all animals are non-persons and the other on the denial that all humans are persons. While it is possible to underestimate the intellectual capacities of animals, and particularly the higher mammals, the latter case, enshrined in the argument from marginal cases, is by far the stronger of the two. It has yet to be successfully answered. What we have yet to do is to ascertain why it is that full personhood is morally significant and what it means for the treatment of those with and without it. This is the subject matter of chapter 5.

5

Questions of Life and Death

In the last chapter we explored two major ways of challenging the personhood argument – that is, the view that humans are morally superior to animals because humans are persons and animals are not. These challenges did not dispute that personhood is morally significant, but rather they denied that personhood is an adequate means of distinguishing between humans and animals. This was, first, on the grounds that not all animals lack the characteristics necessary for personhood and, second, that not all humans are persons. This chapter asks what are the implications for the moral status of animals of assuming that the personhood argument does provide the best way of distinguishing between humans and animals? In other words, what follows morally from accepting that the two challenges examined in the previous chapter fail?

At the very least, we have to accept that the vast majority of humans are persons and, even if we dilute the characteristics necessary for personhood to enable us to include some animals, the intellectual capabilities of the vast majority of humans are greater than those of even the most capable animals. The question to pose in this chapter is what follows from acceptance of this undoubted difference between humans and animals. Some moral philosophers have argued that what follows from this is human moral superiority, and an endorsement of the moral orthodoxy which allows for animal exploitation if significant human benefit accrues from it. An alternative approach – what we might call the 'sentiency view' – claims that even if we accept that the vast majority of humans are persons whereas animals are merely sentient, the latter still have a considerable moral status. Thus, although the 'sentiency view' accepts that differences between humans and animals do produce moral differences – particularly in the value of human and animal lives – it argues that they do not produce the degree of moral inferiority the moral orthodoxy requires for animals.

The personhood view stated

Even if it is accepted that humans are persons and animals are not, it might be the case that this distinction is morally irrelevant. We should not necessarily draw inferences about values from facts. There may be a gap, as Holland (2003: 17) explains, 'between the fact of having certain psychological characteristics and the value judgment that creatures that have them enjoy moral status'. This is pertinent, of course, in many moral issues. As Marquis (1989: 186–7) argues in response to the pro-choice argument in the abortion debate that the foetus is not a person and therefore is morally dispensable:

> the pro-choicer is left with the problem of explaining why *psychological* characteristics should make a *moral* difference . . . it is legitimate for the anti-abortionist to demand that the pro-choicer provide an explanation of the connection between psychological criteria for being a person and the wrongness of being killed.

Bearing in mind the dangers of what McGinn (1992: 24–5) has described as 'intelligenceism' – the replacing of one form of illegitimate discrimination, based on species, with another based on intelligence or mental capacities – we should at least investigate the possibility that this factual difference, leaving the arguments of the last chapter to one side for a moment, does enable us to distinguish morally between humans and animals, not least because the view that it does so is widely held.[1] Indeed, it provides the basis for the moral orthodoxy. Singer (1993: 73) sets out the claim with his usual eloquence:

> It has been suggested that autonomous, self-conscious beings are in some way much more valuable, more morally significant, than beings who live from moment to moment, without the capacity to see themselves as distinct beings with a past and a future. Accordingly . . . the interests of autonomous, self-conscious beings ought normally to take priority over the interests of other beings.

Townsend (1979) states this view clearly when he argues that because animals are sentient we are required to act so as to do what is conducive to the living of a pain-free happy life. Because humans are persons, on the other hand, we should respect their autonomy and, as far as possible, allow them to pursue their lives with as little interference as possible. This distinction is justified, Townsend argues, since only beings with beliefs, thoughts and intentions can be harmed by interference which does not involve the infliction of pain. The most destructive interference for a person is death, whereas killing animals would raise no direct moral issues at all, providing it was done humanely. For the advocates of the moral orthodoxy, then, there is 'nothing arbitrary' about the links between personhood and moral status (Feinberg, 1986: 270).

The moral significance of agency

A familiar claim made in defence of the personhood view is that human moral superiority is justified by the fact that, unlike animals, normal adult humans are moral agents, capable of assessing whether a particular action is right or wrong and capable of behaving morally towards others. Rawls (1972: 504–5), as we have seen, for instance, wants to exclude animals from a theory of justice on the grounds that they are not 'moral persons'. A moral person is distinguished by her ability to have a conception of her own good and the ability to apply principles of justice to others. It should be asked whether this moral agency, by itself, really does have any moral significance. As already suggested in the previous chapter, we might reject its significance on the grounds that some humans are not moral agents either. Leaving this aside for now, though, what follows from granting that humans are moral agents and animals are not?

Regan (1984: 151–6) has described those who are not moral agents as moral patients, characterized as individuals who are not able to be held responsible morally for their actions. The first observation here is that the distinction between moral agents and moral patients provides an opportunity for the pro-animal philosophers to circumvent two common criticisms of their position. The first criticism is that it is justified for humans to exploit animals because animals exploit each other. Nature, in other words, is red in tooth and claw, and because humans are part of nature they are entitled to behave in this way too. Singer (1993: 70) describes this as the 'Benjamin Franklin Objection' to vegetarianism, referring to his decision to revert to eating meat after finding the body of a smaller fish in the stomach of a bigger one. The second criticism is that an animal rights position leads logically to the morally problematic – some would say absurd – conclusion that we are morally obliged to intervene to protect animals when they are attacked by other animals. We should, for example, intervene when a wolf attacks a sheep.

The value of classifying animals as moral patients, of course, is that, superficially at least, it enables us to deal with both of the above criticisms. First, because animals are not responsible for their actions they can be forgiven, if that is the right word, for behaving in the way that they do (coupled with the fact that most animals eat other animals to survive whereas the vast majority of humans do not have to). For humans to behave in the same way, eating other animals without a care in the world, would be to deny their ability to make moral judgements, and therefore deny them full moral agency. Second, because predator animals are not morally responsible for their actions we can justify a policy of non-interference when they are attacking their prey.

These responses to the criticisms made against the animal rights/liberation position are not entirely satisfactory. In the first place, one might argue here that pro-animal philosophers want to have their cake and eat it. On the one hand, they want to utilize the fact that animals are not moral agents to absolve them of any responsibility for their actions. This is fair enough. It is difficult to see, irrespective of the evidence that some animal species can behave altruistically, how animals can be expected to behave in any other way. However, they also want to deny the moral relevance of the distinction between humans who are moral agents, and animals who are moral patients, in the sense of allowing us to accord greater moral weight to the interests of humans.

Second, as Pojman (1993: 178) has argued, the policy of non-interference in the way that animals behave towards each other does not follow from the acceptance that they are moral patients. To see that this is so, substitute a human moral patient for an animal in the above argument. If we do so we are committed to the surely morally unacceptable position that we should stand back and do nothing when a morally irresponsible human 'madman' attacks a defenceless human (say a child). The way for pro-animal philosophers to defend their position against this argument is to emphasize that animals usually, although not always, attack and kill other animals for food. Killing in self-defence is much easier to justify than killing for other motives. And where other motives are at play, intervening to prevent an attack by one animal on another does not look so unreasonable. The one obvious example is the devastating impact that domesticated cats sometimes have on bird species. In this case, where cats do not need to kill for food, it is common for humans to try (through, for instance, attaching a bell) to prevent them from 'playing' with and killing birds.

The moral significance of sentiency

We still have to examine in detail the claims made by those who seek to defend the moral orthodoxy on the basis of the different capabilities of humans and animals. In order to assess these claims of complete moral inequality between humans and animals, imagine, first, that humans have the mental characteristics of persons whereas animals are merely sentient, having the capacity to experience pleasure and pain but nothing else. The first point to note here is that if we base moral status on sentiency alone, rather than those characteristics associated with personhood, then it is difficult to maintain a position of moral inequality between humans and animals. This is why the famous passage from the nineteenth-century British utilitarian Jeremy Bentham – that 'the question' of moral status is not 'Can they reason? nor, Can they talk? but, Can they suffer?' (1948: 311) – has such revolutionary implications.

Bentham, and indeed Mill too, although supporting measures designed to improve animal welfare, did not draw revolutionary implications from their utilitarianism. Singer, however, has adopted a version of utilitarianism which claims to justify radical changes in the way that animals are treated, merely as a consequence of their sentiency. In his book *Practical Ethics*, Singer emphasizes that animals have capabilities greater than mere sentiency and these need to be taken into account in our moral deliberations. In his *Animal Liberation*, however, the emphasis is on what derives from the sentiency of animals. For Singer, the answer is an awful lot. Sentiency is not only a necessary condition for having any moral status, but is also a sufficient condition for having a moral status nearly equivalent to that possessed by humans.

Singer, however, makes great use of the argument from marginal cases when he is faced with the different capabilities of normal humans and animals. He is therefore admitting that, without this aid, sentiency cannot do the work that he wants from it. If we reject the argument from marginal cases or, more accurately, ignore it, what exactly are the moral implications of the greater cognitive capabilities of humans? In other words, is the personhood view right after all?

Assuming that humans have the characteristics of personhood and animals are merely sentient would clearly justify differential treatment. It would mean that it is morally unproblematic to do pretty much anything we like to an animal, short of inflicting pain on her. However, what we might call the 'sentiency view' differs from the moral orthodoxy in a crucially important way. The sentiency view case is built on the argument that when it comes to inflicting pain there would seem no reason, all things being equal, to treat an animal's pain as any less important than a human's pain. It might be suggested that the pain felt by an animal is not as great as the pain felt by a human. We have no reason, however, to suppose this to be universally true. Therefore, we are obliged, according to the equal consideration of interests principle, to treat animal and human pain as equivalent.

A crucial additional point here, of course, is that the distinction – between human persons and sentient animals – is too simplistic anyway since, as we suggested in chapter 4, animals can clearly suffer in a wide variety of ways, including, but not exclusively, involving pain. Therefore, where animals can suffer – boredom, exhaustion, frustration and so on – this suffering must be taken into account in our moral deliberations.

Of course, humans suffer in different and, arguably, more intense and varied ways than animals. As Singer (1993: 58) points out, a human dying from cancer, for instance, would suffer more than a nonhuman cancer victim, not least because of the fear that the human has due to greater knowledge of her position. Similarly, it might be argued that the use of normal adult humans in scientific experiments would cause greater suffering, all things being equal, than the use of animals, not least because of the human's fear at the prospect of being used (ibid., 59–60). In this context, imagine a weekly lottery where those having tickets with the numbers drawn would have to submit themselves for painful and possibly fatal scientific experiments! The argument here then is that as Rowlands (2002: 14) points out, 'your greater cognitive and imaginative powers, your ability to think about the future, and so on' mean you are likely to suffer more than an animal does in an equivalent situation.

However, where it can be shown that an animal's suffering is equivalent to a human's, then – according to the equal consideration of interests principle – it must have the same weight in our moral deliberations. And, on occasions, it may be the case that the suffering experienced by an animal – maybe precisely because of more limited understanding – is greater than the suffering of a human in the same situation. Rowlands (2002: 14–15) provides an example to illustrate this point. Imagine that:

you and your dog are taken into a room where you are both given a very painful injection. However, the situation is explained to you (the injection is necessary to save your life, the pain will be relatively short lived, there will be no complications, and then you will be allowed to go) . . . Your dog, however, knows none of these things, and so in addition to the pain of the injection, it has the anxiety associated with unfamiliar surroundings, strange people restraining it, and so on. In this case, your dog seems to suffer more than you do.

It is of crucial importance to note that the principles elaborated above – that animal pain is equivalent to human pain and that humans may, but not always, suffer more than animals – is clearly at odds with what we described as the moral orthodoxy in chapter 2. Let us remind ourselves of that position. One of the best attempts to clarify the moral orthodoxy is provided by Robert Nozick (1974: 35–42). He describes it as 'utilitarianism for animals, Kantianism for people'. So, we are entitled to sacrifice the interests of animals but, since they can suffer, it is necessary to establish that this suffering furthers some human and/or animal benefit, that this benefit cannot be achieved in any other way and the suffering will be minimized as far as possible. However, we are not entitled to treat humans in the same way, to sacrifice their fundamental interests in order to achieve a greater aggregate good for animals or other humans. The kind of human benefit necessary to justify animal suffering is by no means clear-cut, and this explains why there is a political debate surrounding animal welfare. As chapters 7–9 will reveal, the line beyond which animals are deemed to suffer unnecessarily has changed over the years, making improvements to the welfare of animals possible.

According to the moral orthodoxy – more commonly known as the animal welfare position – humans are entitled to inflict suffering on animals (including but not exclusively pain) if a substantial human benefit accrues. But, surely, adherents of the moral orthodoxy are not able to infer this conclusion from the fact that animals are sentient and humans are persons. The logical flaw here is the argument that because there are some characteristics humans possess but animals do not then *all* human interests become more morally important than *all* animal interests. But this position clearly does not treat like interests equally because, for instance, the pain suffered by animals (and I repeat we have no reason to think that the capacity of a human to experience pain is any greater than that of an animal) is disregarded if humans can benefit from it, and yet the idea of inflicting pain on humans for the benefit of animals is never entertained. It may be the case that humans can be shown to suffer more than animals in certain circumstances, as indicated above. But this does not justify a blanket principle stating that on all occasions human interests should come first and animal interests second.

Three principles derive from the sentiency view. First, the only area where the interests of normal adult humans ought to take precedence over those of animals is in their respective interests in living. If it can be established – as I think it can – that human lives are worth more than animal lives, then, all things being equal, the practice of sacrificing animal lives in order to protect human lives would seem to be justified. Second, it is much more problematic, although not impossible, to justify inflicting suffering on animals in order to protect human lives. On the grounds that animals are sentient, Bentham (1948: 310–11) clearly thought this was illegitimate. As he wrote:

> If the being killed were all, there is very good reason why we should be suffered to kill such as molest us: we should be the worse for their living, and they are never the worse for being dead. But is there any reason why we should be suffered to torment them? Not any that I can see.

Third, what is clearly ruled out by the sentiency view, though, is the infliction of suffering on animals for human benefits that fall short of the protection of human lives. Chapters 7–9 reveal that this would rule out many of our current practices involving animals.

Human and animal lives

We have been assuming, in this chapter, that human lives are more valuable than animal lives. Is this, in fact, true? In practice, in developed societies at least, human life is regarded as special in some way, and its perceived unique value is seen in the agonized debates in such societies about euthanasia and abortion. By contrast, animal life is regarded as shockingly expendable. I use the adjective 'shockingly' here because, when the reality of the casual way in which animal lives are treated is made starkly apparent, many (who would not, by any means, want to be described as advocates of animal rights) feel uncomfortable about it. The sheer scale of the killing here beggars belief. In the United States alone, no less than 8 billion animals are killed each year for food, or 23 million a day or a staggering 260 every second. And this is the situation only for food animals. Over 200 million animals a year are killed by hunters in the United States, while millions of animals are killed after being used in scientific procedures (Francione, 2000: xx).

The expendable nature of animal lives became all too apparent during the foot-and-mouth outbreak in Britain in 2001. As was pointed out in the introduction to this book, in many ways the killing of thousands of animals did not raise additional ethical problems to the 'normal' practices of agribusiness. Indeed, in some ways it resulted in better welfare for the animals. What shocked people was the low worth put on animal life. Foot-and-mouth in most cases is not a fatal disease and, while uncomfortable, is not horribly painful for the animals. Moreover, many of the animals killed were not infected anyway, but were simply slaughtered in order to prevent the infection from spreading. The key to it all was economics. Affected animals are worth less because they weigh less and because under present rules they cannot be exported.

The sanctity of human life and the disregard for animal life is, as Singer (1993: 88–9) explains, a product of the influence of Christianity. Despite the attempts by theologians such as Andrew Linzey (1987) to reinterpret Christian mores towards animals, the view that they were placed by God under man's dominion – and therefore could be treated as humans saw fit, providing that human property laws were not flouted in the process – has held sway. But what value should a secular ethical theory place on animal (and human) life? It is worth bearing in mind two distinctions at this point. First, there is a significant difference, of course, between saying that human lives are worth more than animal lives and saying that the death of an animal does not matter at all. Second, there is an equally significant difference between on the one hand, in a so-called lifeboat scenario, choosing the life of a human over an animal and, on the other, saying that animal lives can be sacrificed even if a human life is not at stake. In each case, the second options obviously grant much less protection for animals. When pro-animal philosophers talk about human lives being more morally significant than animal lives they are usually referring to the stronger first options in each case.

If we accept that animals are merely sentient, then the killing of an animal enjoying a pleasant life should, one thinks, be avoided, although it would be justified if by so doing the lives of self-conscious beings were preserved (for reasons explored below). Contrary to this, some argue that a painless death is morally unproblematic for a being without a sense of itself as a distinct identity with a past and a future. This conclusion is particularly associated with Singer (1993: chapter 4), who adopts a version of preference utilitarianism, whereby right and wrong actions are judged by their capacity to produce an aggregate of preference satisfactions (see chapter 6). Clearly, if it can be shown that animals do not have a strong preference to continue living, then they 'cannot have a preference for their own future existence, as against non-existence' (Carruthers, 1992: 82). As Singer (1993: 89–90) himself remarks, it might be 'intrinsically wrong to kill' those animals, such as pigs and dogs, who 'are self-aware to some degree, and do have thoughts about things in the future', but 'there are other animals – chickens maybe, or fish – who can feel pain but don't have any self-awareness or capacity for thinking about the future' where painless killing may not raise any ethical issues at all.

Clearly, having an interest in avoiding pain is not enough to have an interest in living. Indeed, dying may be a preferable option to someone whose life is dominated by unbearable pain. Even here, though, at the very least, a consequence of the painless death of a sentient being enjoying a pleasant life would be a reduction in the amount of pleasure in the world, and so, on utilitarian grounds – that an act should be judged according to the extent to which it produces a total balance of pleasure over pain – we would need to replace an animal killed with another equivalent one (Singer, 1993: 120–1; 132–3). It also seems to follow that we are justified, in the case of a conscious but not self-conscious being, in cutting short an unpleasant life. Indeed, this is probably the one area in practice where the treatment of animals is morally preferable to the treatment of humans. While humans are kept alive in all kinds of circumstances where the kinder option would probably be to put them out of their misery, animals in pain and with no chance of making a recovery are often painlessly killed.

We saw, though, that at least some animals are much more than merely sentient, and also have considerable cognitive abilities. Equally, the average normal human has greater mental capacities than any normal animal. What then? How do we judge the harm caused by death? Here, there is a consensus among pro-animal philosophers that human life is more valuable than animal life. Even Regan (1984: 324–5), who does attach a right-to-life to mammals over the age of one, claims that in the event of a choice between saving the life of a human and the life of an animal, the human would normally win out. To illustrate this he asks us to imagine an overcrowded lifeboat containing four humans and a dog, where there was no hope of survival for any of them unless one was thrown overboard. Regan argues it should be the dog that goes on the grounds that the death of the dog 'though a harm, is not comparable to the harm that death would be for any of the humans'. Indeed, he wants to go further than that by saying that one human life is worth any number of animal lives in a lifeboat situation. This follows from the application of his 'worse-off' principle, whereby, since a human loses more from death than an animal, in the event of a choice we ought to choose the life of a human over any number of animals.

This latter assertion is disputed by other pro-animal philosophers.[2] But in general terms they would agree that a normal human life is worth more than any animal life. The reason for the greater value placed on human life relates to the harm caused by death. There are two distinct ways in which harm might be caused by death. The first, what DeGrazia (2002: 59–61) calls the 'desire-based account', postulates that death causes harm because it denies a desire to stay alive. DeGrazia is probably right to assert here that no animals, except perhaps the higher mammals, even understand the concept of staying alive, let alone the desire to do so. As a result, death is not a harm for animals according to this account of the harm caused by death. Normal adult humans, on the other hand, clearly do possess the concept of death and most do have a desire to stay alive. 'To take the lives' of such self-conscious beings, as Singer (1993: 90) points out: 'is to thwart their desires for the future. Killing a snail or a day-old infant does not thwart any desires of this kind, because snails and newborn infants are incapable of having such desires.' DeGrazia (2002: 61) also identifies an 'opportunities-based' account of the harm caused by death. Unlike the desire-based account, this view does not depend upon an individual's awareness of the opportunities lost by death. Rather, 'death is an instrumental harm in so far as it forecloses the valuable opportunities that continued life would afford'.

The nature of this thwarting of desires, then, is not about individuals feeling frustrated, angry or unfulfilled, since they will not be alive to feel such things. Clearly, though, it is important to recognize that great anxiety is likely to be caused by a fear of death, a feeling that will not be present in a being that has no conception of its own future. But assuming the death was instantaneous and unexpected, it is the lost opportunities that are thwarted. In other words, there are harms of deprivation. So, labouring the point somewhat, it is wrong to claim that painless death causes no harm because we are not aware of it. We can clearly be harmed even though we are unaware of the fact. Carruthers (1992: 76) illustrates this point by asking us to imagine being defrauded, without our knowledge, out of an inheritance we were entitled to by an unscrupulous lawyer. 'Here I may rightly be said to have been harmed by the lawyer's action', Carruthers tells us, 'even though I never feel the lack of the money' because of the 'satisfactions that I would have enjoyed had the lawyer not interfered'.

DeGrazia (1996: 238) is right here to suggest that it is not easy to justify greater human opportunities lost by death on the grounds merely that we have more numerous opportunities than animals do. Even though this may be true, it is problematic not least because animals would lose some opportunities which humans would not. For example, 'death robs the dolphin, but not the human, of the pleasures of echolocation (sonar), and robs canines, but not us, of an immense olfactory world'. Instead of the number of opportunities, we are on stronger ground if we point to the richness of the opportunities available to humans, compared to animals, and therefore the loss of these opportunities upon death.

For a person, then, death means that a future is taken away, consisting of 'a constellation of experiences, beliefs, desires, goals, projects, activities, and various other things' (Rowlands, 2002: 76). If the life is taken of a being that does not have this 'constellation of experiences', or has them to a lesser degree, it is difficult to see that being can be harmed to the same extent, providing the death is painless. As Sapontzis (1987: 218) remarks, 'thanks to our superior intellect, we are capable of appreciating fine art, conceptual matters, moral fulfilment, flights of imagination, remembrance and anticipation, and so on in addition to what animals can experience'. Singer (1993: 107) likewise observes that:

> In general it does seem that the more highly developed the conscious life of the being, the greater the degree of self-awareness and rationality and the broader the range of possible experiences, the more one would prefer that kind of life, if one were choosing between it and a being at a lower level of awareness.

A useful way of clarifying the distinction between the value of the life of a person and the life of a being with little or no conception of, or opportunities presented by, a future is provided by Rachels (1983: 280–2). He distinguishes between an individual being alive and having a life. The former refers to a 'functioning biological organism', while the latter is about a notion of biography rather than biology – about, that is, an individual's attitudes, beliefs, actions and relationships. Clearly, in the sense defined, only persons can have a life in the biographical sense, whereas non-persons have a life in the biological sense. The former life, too, would seem to be more worthwhile. This is what makes it possible to talk quite sensibly of a life (in the biological sense) not worth living (in the biographical sense) in the case, say, of a seriously retarded human.

In the same vein, Tooley (1983: 117–18) considers the difference between killing someone and, while not biologically killing them,

destroying their upper-brain, the site of 'the neuro-physiological basis
... of higher mental functions such as self-consciousness, delibera-
tion, thought and memory'. For most people, Tooley surely rightly
suggests, the latter would be regarded as morally on a par with the
former on the grounds that it involves the destruction of a person.
Therefore, 'the wrongness of killing normal adult human beings
derives from the fact that killing in such cases involves the destruction of a person'.

The distinction Rachels makes is similar to the one made by Frey
(1987), which we encountered in chapter 4, between control and
preference autonomy. Autonomy matters, he argues, because of what
it enables us to make of our lives. Normal humans can exercise the
control version of the concept. This involves individuals themselves
choosing what they want to achieve and organizing their lives in
pursuit of this goal. We will not be autonomous to the extent that
we allow ourselves to be coerced by others and to the extent that we
allow our life plan to become subservient to our 'first-order' desires
– eating, drinking, drugs and so on. Animals, Frey argues, can only
exercise what he calls preference autonomy which requires merely
that beings be able to have desires, or preferences, and have the ability
to initiate actions with a view to satisfying them. As a result, animal
lives are less valuable than human lives or, to use what is perhaps a
more appropriate phrase, human lives are richer than animal lives
and therefore the loss of such a richer life is much greater. In Singer's
(1990: 21) words:

> to take the life of a being who has been hoping, planning and working
> for some future goal is to deprive that being of the fulfilment of all
> those efforts; to take the life of a being with a mental capacity below
> the level needed to grasp that one is a being with a future – much
> less make plans for the future – cannot involve this particular kind of
> loss.

There are at least three major responses we can make to an argument which focuses on the greater richness of the opportunities available to humans. The first response is that, although the greater
richness of opportunities argument means that human and animal
moral patients have less to lose from death than do human persons,
this is not nevertheless to say that moral patients, including animals,
lose nothing by death. Indeed, according to the opportunities-based
account, to be harmed by death only requires sentiency since
death prevents the future possibility of pleasurable experiences. As
Rowlands (2002: 94) points out:

Holding on to a future, even in this weak sense, is unarguably a vital interest of the animal, for if this interest is thwarted, then all its other interests are automatically thwarted too. The animal may have less invested in the future, but in losing a future it still loses out on all the opportunities for satisfaction that the future brings with it.

While it is wrong to kill an animal, then, it is not as great a wrong as killing a human. So, if we had to choose between saving the life of an animal and a human we should choose the latter. It is important to recognize too that this conclusion is consistent with the equal consideration of interests principle. We have not sacrificed the principle that we should accord equal weight to the comparable interests of humans and animals because we have decided that humans have a greater interest in staying alive.

The second response, which should be very familiar to the reader by now, is that not all humans have the rich opportunities available to 'normal' humans. The employment of the argument from marginal cases suggests that human and animal moral patients may well have the same opportunities. As a result, the harm caused by the death of an animal will, in some circumstances, be as great as the harm caused by the death of a human. As Singer (1993: 132) remarks, while animals do not have the same level of self-consciousness as the average human, the case against killing them 'is as strong as the case against killing permanently intellectually disabled human beings at a similar mental level'. In other words, the success of the pro-animal philosopher's project – to make the death of animals as morally important as the death of humans – depends upon the success of the argument from marginal cases. If we don't accept it then, as we have suggested, the case for regarding human lives as more important than animal lives would seem to be unanswerable.

However, the third response to the richness of human opportunities argument is to deny its force. This response, particularly associated with Sapontzis (1987), is, in part, based on the view that it underestimates the capabilities of animals. This is a debate we covered in chapter 4. There it was suggested that there are severe problems with trying to deny major differences in the intellectual capacities of humans and animals. There is no doubt that, in the words of DeGrazia (1996: 245), 'different animals have different potentials or capacities, and the exercise of some – those of greater complexity – is more valuable than that of others'. But while some animals – most notably non-human primates – may have considerably rich life opportunities that are harmed by death, these opportunities are not shared with most animal species. Moreover, the life opportunities of non-human primates are still probably not as rich as those of 'normal' humans.

The case against the force of the richer human opportunities argument is also based on two other factors. First, even if we accept that animal experiences are less sophisticated than those of humans, there is still the possibility that they may be more intense than ours. Humans 'are notorious', Sapontzis (1987: 220) writes:

> for not getting full enjoyment from present pleasures because they have fixated on past sorrows or are fretting about future difficulties, while animals, like dogs playing on the beach, do not seem to have their present enjoyment thus diluted. Now, if animal feelings are more intense than ours, then this extra intensity could counterbalance the extra feelings our extensive temporal capacity provides us.

The claim by Sapontzis, however, would appear to be a contingent one. As we saw earlier, human capacity for suffering may be greater than that of animals in any particular situation. The greater richness of opportunities available to human moral agents, however, would seem to be universal and permanent.

Second is the claim that, as we saw above, animals have experiences humans do not and these may be extremely enriching. As Sapontzis (1987: 219) remarks, 'we cannot enjoy the life of a dog, a bird, a bat, or a dolphin. Consequently, we cannot appreciate the subtleties of smell, sight, sound, and touch that these animals can apparently appreciate.' At the very least, therefore, we should exercise caution before claiming that the subjective experiences of animals are somehow inferior to human experiences.

This reminds one of Mill's (1972) famous, and ultimately flawed, attempt to justify a preference for what he regarded as the 'higher' pleasures over the 'lower' ones. 'It is better to be a human being dissatisfied than a pig satisfied, better to be Socrates dissatisfied than a fool satisfied,' Mill wrote, arguing, in support of the statement, that those who had experience of both forms of pleasure would always prefer the higher ones. From an objective viewpoint we might throw caution to the wind and state that non-human experiences are not as sophisticated and enriching as human ones. But then does this make human lives better? Despite Singer's best efforts to make comparisons between being a human and a horse (1993: 89), it is tempting to agree with Carruthers (1992: 89) when he writes: 'How are we, fairly and realistically, to compare the life of a horse with the life of a human being, given the vast changes in cognitive powers and dispositions that would be necessary to move from the one to the other?' Nevertheless, as DeGrazia (1996: 248) remarks, there is a 'stubborn conviction' among many philosophers 'that the lives of normal humans *must* be of greater value than the lives of many, if not all, nonhuman animals'. Whether this is the case will have to remain a somewhat open question for now at least.

Conclusion

What this chapter has revealed is that, even if we ignore the implications of the claims that animals, like humans, can be persons and that not all humans are persons, the moral orthodoxy relating to the relationship between humans and animals would appear not to be wholly justified if we invoke the equal consideration of interests principle. In other words, it is possible to challenge the moral orthodoxy in fundamental ways without having to prove anything more than that animals are sentient and can suffer in ways that do not always involve pain. If we accept that humans are persons and animals are not, then differential treatment is morally justified, and, in particular – all things being equal – it is a greater wrong to kill a human than it is to kill an animal. However, the moral orthodoxy, by sanctioning the infliction of suffering on animals for a wide range of human benefits, goes much further than the like treatment of like interests permits. The only justification for the infliction of pain and suffering on animals from the perspective of the equal consideration of interests principle is, first, when it can be shown that human suffering is greater than animal suffering and, second, when human life is at stake, since humans have a greater interest in living than animals do. It is not easy to demonstrate that, even in the majority of cases, humans suffer more than animals. As Rowlands (2002: 15) rightly points out: 'When people claim that animals don't suffer "in the same way we do", what they are saying is probably right. But, unfortunately, they then tend to slide from this to the claim that animals "suffer less than we do". And this is almost certainly wrong.' If all of the foregoing analysis is right then the key question, to which we will return in chapters 7–9, becomes how far animal exploitation in practice can be justified on the grounds that human lives are protected.

6

Rights, Utility, Contractarianism and Animals

Let us assume we have established that animals have a much higher status than the moral orthodoxy allows and are approaching moral equality with humans. What then? How does that translate into prescriptions about how we treat animals and, indeed, humans too? Traditionally, in moral philosophy, the answer to this question has revolved around a discussion of the competing merits of utilitarianism on the one hand and rights on the other. Animal ethics is no exception. There has been sometimes ferocious debate between advocates of a utilitarian approach to animal liberation (associated with Singer) and advocates of a rights approach (associated principally with Regan). This debate will be summarized in the pages that follow.

Before we engage in a consideration of the debate between advocates of either rights or utilitarianism, two caveats need to be made. In the first place, more recent animal ethics has shown signs of moving beyond this debate. Second-generation animal ethicists tend to take a much less homogeneous line than many of the first-generation scholars. For example, Midgley (1983) focuses on social bonds as important ethical parameters, and Sapontzis (1987) combines an interest in utility, rights and virtue. DeGrazia (1996, chapter 2) adopts what he calls the 'coherence model' of ethics whereby 'no set of ethical norms is granted epistemic privilege' or is set in stone. Rather, a process similar to Rawls's 'reflective equilibrium' is adopted, whereby ethical judgements are regularly checked against 'common-sense' moral principles. Finally, Warren (1997) adopts a 'multi-criterial concept' of moral status, incorporating elements from different moral traditions.

The second caveat is that mention should also be made of a major alternative to rights and utilitarian approaches. The last three chapters have revealed how difficult it is to determine what the moral status of animals is. Arguments employed are vulnerable to the claim that moral questions are inherently subjective and impossible to resolve. For example, moral equivalence between humans and animals, as we have seen, is dependent largely on the success of the argument from marginal cases but this has been the subject of numerous critiques. Wouldn't it be better then if we could find an objective means of deciding upon the moral status of animals which most could accept? Such a possibility has been suggested by advocates of a so-called 'contractarian' approach to animal ethics, and it is to this we turn first.

Contractarianism and animals

A contractarian, or contractual, approach to ethics is, following Carruthers (1992: 35), 'an attempt to justify a system of moral principles by showing that they *would* be agreed upon by rational agents in certain ideal circumstances'. The attempt to use a social contract approach to justify according a high moral status to animals is predominantly associated with an attempt to revise John Rawls's theory of justice (1972). Rawls, in what has been described as the most important work of political philosophy in the post-1945 period, revived the social contract tradition – associated with British political theorists such as Locke and Hobbes – to develop a contemporary liberal theory of justice. His principles of justice were derived from an imaginary 'original position' in which it was asked what principles of justice would individuals decide upon if they were shorn of any knowledge of what their own circumstances would be. Under this so-called 'veil of ignorance', Rawls assumes that individuals would adopt a no-risk strategy whereby they would adopt principles which would ensure that if they turned out to be disadvantaged members of society they would be protected.

Now, Rawls's theory has been subject to enormous scrutiny from all kinds of perspectives. From our perspective, what is significant is that Rawls excludes animals entirely from his theory of justice. This is justified, as we saw, on the grounds that animals are not moral persons. There are, for Rawls (1972: 505), two characteristics of moral personhood. First, moral persons, 'are capable of having . . . a conception of their good (as expressed by a rational plan of life); and second they are capable of having . . . a sense of justice, at least to a certain minimum degree'. This is equivalent to the moral agency justification for according to humans a higher moral status than animals, referred to in chapter 5. Only those who can understand what it means to be just, claim it for themselves and respect the justice claims of others, then, are accorded moral personhood and therefore entitled to be recipients of a theory of justice.

It is important to note at this point that Rawls does not intend to exclude animals from any moral consideration. Despite his Kantian roots, his is not a theory emphasizing that we owe only indirect duties to animals. And, given the importance Rawls attaches to moral intuition, it would be strange if he were to offer a theory which was at odds with the consensus, in the West at least, that animals do have some moral standing. What Rawls does suggest is that a theory of justice can be distinguished from a wider theory of morality and it is within the latter we can include moral precepts concerning animals. He does not provide any details about how he thinks animals ought to be treated, limiting himself to general statements such as:

> It does not follow from a person's not being owed the duty of justice that he may be treated in any way that one pleases. We do not normally think of ourselves as owing the duty of justice to animals, but it is certainly wrong to be cruel to them. (Rawls, 1963: 302)

and:

> it is wrong to be cruel to animals . . . The capacity for feelings of pleasure and pain and for the forms of life of which animals are capable clearly impose duties of compassion and humanity in their care. (1972: 512)

Rawls does not therefore reject the case for some animal protection. Rather, he claims that justice is a much narrower area of inquiry than ethics, and the treatment of animals is an issue that is incorporated within the latter and not the former. This distinction is explored in greater detail in his *Political Liberalism*. A conception of justice, he argues, only concerns the basic political structure. As a result, 'the status of the natural world and our proper relation to it is not a constitutional essential or a basic question of justice' (1993: 246).

From all of this, two main issues arise. First, was Rawls right to exclude animals from his theory of justice? My answer to this question is no. Second, if Rawls was wrong, have we found a way of demonstrating objectively that animals are deserving of considerable moral status? My answer to this question is also no.

In answer to the first question, an initial criticism of Rawls's position is that by excluding animals from a theory of justice he may, albeit inadvertently, be condemning them to moral irrelevance. This relates to the liberal emphasis on moral pluralism and will be explored in chapter 10. For now, it should be noted that animal protection is likely to be enhanced by extending membership of the justice 'club' to animals. Justice, it is commonly believed, is our most politically powerful ethical language and carries greater moral weight than notions of kindness, mercy and charity.

Demonstrating that animals would benefit from being incorporated into a theory of justice is very different from an argument justifying this outcome. As far as an adaptation of Rawls's theory is concerned, the route towards this goal is through showing that animals can be beneficiaries of his original position. Since the publication of *A Theory of Justice* in 1972 there have been a number of such attempts.[1] The attempts to revise Rawls in a way which benefits animals have been very similar. All, in Dombrowski's words (1997), 'think that he, like Columbus, has made a great discovery, but he is mistaken about the precise character of that discovery'. The central pillar of the critique of Rawls is the argument from marginal cases that we discussed in detail in chapter 4. Here the problem for Rawls is that by insisting on moral personhood as the major ground for inclusion in a theory of justice he also excludes human moral patients who, like animals, do not have the necessary characteristics. Rawls recognizes this problem at various points but tends to gloss over it. Consistency demands, however, that if marginal humans are to be beneficiaries of his theory of justice then animals ought to be too. As Dombrowski (1997: 63) rightly concludes here: 'To choose in favour of marginal cases but not animals solely on the basis of species membership is . . . to be speciesist.'

Neither human nor animal moral patients are able to make decisions in the original position but it is not clear why they cannot be beneficiaries of the decisions made, maybe through having rational agents to speak on their behalf. All that is required for this to be possible is a 'thickening' of the veil of ignorance so that the participants do not know whether they are going to be marginal humans or even whether they are going to be members of the human species at all. As a result, if we take Rawls's risk minimization strategy as given, the participants in the original position would adopt principles which would protect them if they turned out to be animals. More specifically, Rawls's 'difference principle', that social and economic inequalities are to be arranged so that they are to the greatest benefit of the least advantaged, would be extended to incorporate not only vulnerable humans but animals too.

At this point the criticism emerges that if we expand the beneficiaries to include non-rational agents then this could result in principles of justice applying to inanimate objects such as stones or mountains. In response to this we could argue the case for extending moral standing beyond those who are sentient, a position defended by some environmental ethicists (Singer, 1988). Alternatively, in order to avoid the counter-intuitive conclusion that we should grant moral standing to stones, mountains and so on, we could add the restriction that beneficiaries of decisions taken in the original position need to be able to appreciate the benefits they receive, thereby restricting it to those entities that are sentient. The problem with this is that we are then throwing an arbitrary moral principle into the works – the principle that only sentient beings are morally worthy – when the whole point of the contractual exercise is to develop moral principles from scratch. In the end, we come back to the marginal humans argument, that if we exclude animals as beneficiaries on the grounds that they are not rational agents, then we are bound to exclude marginal humans too.

In response to the second question above, asking whether we have found an objective process whereby the high moral status of animals can be justified, Rowlands (1998: 3) wants to claim that a contractarian account 'provides the most satisfactory theoretical basis for the attribution of moral rights to nonhumans' and is therefore the 'greatest ally' of animal rights. However, Rowlands and others have failed in their attempt to provide an objective account justifying a high moral status for animals independently of the normative arguments employed in the preceding chapters of this book because the contract by itself cannot do the work that pro-animal exponents want it to do (Garner, 2003).

It can be conceded that a large number of the normative arguments employed by pro-animal philosophers, many of which have been encountered in this book, are inherently subjective and as such difficult to establish conclusively. The problem with a reliance on the contractarian approach, however, is precisely that it is dependent upon many of the same set of normative arguments. Rawls admits that he is not totally reliant on the heuristic device of the contract to derive his principles of justice. Rather, he adopts a procedure described as 'reflective equilibrium', whereby the principles derived from the original position are checked for consistency with our moral intuitions (Rawls, 1972: 20).

Inevitably, then, the principles of justice arrived at will be, at the very least, influenced by already existing moral conventions. Indeed, his notion that only moral persons can be beneficiaries of a theory of justice is itself a product of the pre-existing value he places on humans and animals. Likewise, the contention of those who insist that animals can be included is equally a product of the belief that moral personhood should not be the main criterion for according moral status. As Jones (1994: 106) correctly remarks, then, 'most of the moral work will be done by the background moral assumptions that provide the context for the hypothetical contract rather than from the contracting process itself'. It is with some relief, then, that we can conclude that the preceding chapters, seeking to establish normative principles about the moral worth of animals, have not been a complete waste of time!

Varieties of utilitarianism

It is somewhat ironic that animal rights is the label most often attached to the position that humans and animals are morally equivalent. This is because one of the earliest, best-known, and most successful attempts to accord moral considerability to animals is provided by Peter Singer, who eschews rights in favour of utilitarianism. Utilitarianism dates back at least as far as the work of the nineteenth-century British political theorist and social reformer Jeremy Bentham. Utilitarianism has been an extremely influential doctrine, particularly in Britain. Indeed, for much of its existence, it held sway over rights in theory and practice and only relatively recently has it been subordinated to the emphasis on rights.

Utilitarianism is the best-known example of a goal-based consequentialist ethical theory – often called a teleological theory – which asks us to 'maximise the occurrence of intrinsically valuable, and to minimize the occurrence of intrinsically disvaluable, states of affairs' (Thomas, 1993: 74). Bentham adopted an approach which has been described as hedonistic or classical utilitarianism, in the sense that he based his theory of morality on the simple premise that what we ought to do is to maximize happiness (which he defined in terms of pleasure) and minimize unhappiness (which he defined in terms of pain). An alternative version, associated with Singer, is so-called 'preference utilitarianism' whereby we should act so as to maximize the satisfaction of wants as told to us or gauged by us.

A theory that bases moral judgements on sentiency, and not rationality, is peculiarly suited to incorporate the interests of animals. Bentham and J. S. Mill, a later utilitarian, were not slow to recognize this. In a much-quoted passage, Bentham (1948) wrote in his *Introduction to the Principles of Morals and Legislation*, originally published in 1789, that:

The French have already discovered that the blackness of the skin is no reason why a human being should be abandoned without redress to the caprice of a tormentor. It may come one day to be recognized, that the number of the legs, the villosity of the skin, or the termination of the *os sacrum*, are reasons equally insufficient for abandoning a sensitive being to the same fate. What else is it that should trace the insuperable line? Is it the faculty of reason, or, perhaps, the faculty of discourse? But a full-grown horse or dog, is beyond comparison a more rational, as well as a more conversable animal, than an infant of a day, or a week, or even a month old. But suppose the case were otherwise, what would it avail? The question is not, Can they reason? Nor, Can they talk? But, Can they suffer?

Similarly, Mill (1969: 184) wrote, in 1874, that:

Granted that any practice causes more pain to animals than it gives pleasure to man; is that practice moral or immoral? And if, exactly in proportion as human beings raise their heads out of the slough of self-ishness, they do not with one voice answer 'immoral', let the morality of the principle of utility be for ever condemned.

Another nineteenth-century utilitarian, Henry Sidgwick, also saw the implications of a sentiency-based ethic. 'It seems arbitrary and unreasonable', he wrote in a book originally published in 1874, 'to exclude . . . any pleasure of any sentient being' (Sidgwick, 1966: 414).

The logic of Bentham's position (although not Mill's since he, as we saw in chapter 5, seeks to revise Bentham's utilitarianism by arguing that the so-called 'higher' pleasures – those associated with the faculties of personhood – are preferable to lower ones) is that an animal's interest in experiencing pleasure and avoiding pain should be equivalent to a human's. For whatever reason – maybe social conventions, or logical inconsistency – Bentham fails to do this and, instead, adopts a conventional animal welfare position. As he wrote in a letter to the *Morning Chronicle* in 1825:

I never have seen, nor ever can see, any objection to the putting of dogs and other inferior animals to pain, in the way of medical experiment, when the experiment has a determinate object, beneficial to mankind, accompanied with a fair prospect of the accomplishment of it. But I have a decided and insuperable objection to the putting of them to pain without any such view. (Quoted in Clarke and Linzey, 1990: 136)

About a century and a half later, another utilitarian, Peter Singer, did draw the logical conclusion from a utilitarian ethic and came up with a formidable challenge to the moral orthodoxy. For Singer, equivalent human and animal interests ought to be considered equally so that – all things being equal – an animal's preference to avoid pain should be treated equally with a human's. This is not equivalent to saying that humans and animals have rights since, as a utilitarian, Singer is committed to the proposition that we ought to aggregate preferences so as to arrive at the situation where their satisfaction is maximized. Nevertheless, Singer still thinks that his version of utilitarianism does rule out most of the major ways in which animals are exploited and, in particular, necessitates ending modern systems of animal agriculture and the use of animals in scientific procedures.

A critique of utilitarianism

Utilitarianism rarely produces a non-committal response, its defenders being as impassioned as its attackers. It is applauded by some for its secular character so that the goal it seeks to promote 'does not depend on the existence of God, or a soul, or any other dubious metaphysical entity'. In addition, by focusing on the consequences of an action, and not the motives of those responsible, it asks us to consider those who are affected by it, a laudable goal (Kymlicka, 2002: 11). Third, utilitarianism 'provides a clear and definite procedure for determining which acts are right or wrong' (Brandt: 1992: 113). Finally, as will be discussed in detail below, utilitarianism is flexible enough to justify the attainment of what most would regard as important social goals. Indeed, armed with utilitarian ideas, the nineteenth-century 'Philosophical Radicals' were the popular driving force behind a thoroughgoing critique of English society, culminating in significant social and legal reforms.

Utilitarianism has also been much criticized. In the first place, it is arguably a doctrine that has had its day. As Kymlicka (2002: 45) astutely recognizes, in the nineteenth century utilitarianism was on the side of the majority against the ruling minority and was therefore a force for change in an increasingly democratic climate. Now, in a society where basic civic and political rights have been achieved, it no longer has this role. Indeed, 'many of the burning political questions have centred on the rights of historically oppressed *minorities*', and utilitarianism, as we shall see, has great difficulty in justifying the protection of minority rights.

There are many other more technical difficulties with utilitarianism. It has been criticized first for its failure, in the classical version at least, to provide content to pleasure and pain. To say that humans want pleasure and seek to avoid pain may, at least for the vast majority, be a truism, but it remains inadequate as a guide for action if we cannot define more accurately what pleasure and pain is in practice. It is partly for this reason that J. S. Mill, as we saw in the previous chapter, sought to distinguish between what he called higher and lower pleasures, arguing that the higher pleasures are infinitely more preferable.

However, once we start to provide content to pleasure and pain then doubts are raised about its accuracy as a guide to what humans want. Many, for instance, would no doubt disagree with Mill and say they prefer the lower pleasures. Others may value things that cannot, without distorting the language, be described as pleasure. We can get round this problem to some degree by converting the original hedonistic version of utilitarianism, centring on measuring pleasure and pain, into preference utilitarianism. In this version, promoted by Singer, we add the assumption that each person is the best judge of their own happiness. A moral act, then, becomes one that maximizes preferences, as stated by individuals. This appears to be a more valid position, although it is not without its problems. In the first place, it assumes, sometimes erroneously, that each person actually is the best judge of his own happiness or well-being. In this sense, as Kymlicka (2002: 15) remarks, 'our preferences are predictions about our good' rather than certainties to achieve it. We may be mistaken. Moreover, preference utilitarianism assumes that individual preferences are not themselves being influenced by other, powerful, forces in society (Lukes, 1974).

Utilitarianism has also been criticized for what is alleged to be the inoperable system of calculations involved. That is, isn't the process of calculating the amount of pleasure or pain or preferences involved in any particular act really beyond us? We can never be totally sure of the total consequences of any act. The problems here might not be insurmountable in some more local and small-scale actions, but the larger and more complex the act the greater the difficulties of measurement become. To illustrate this, imagine the problems of determining on utilitarian grounds whether the dropping of atomic bombs on Japanese cities was justified at the end of the Second World War. Not only would we have to find out how many deaths occurred as a result of the action, both as a result of the immediate impact but also as a result of the later impact of nuclear fallout. In addition, we would have to calculate how much suffering would have occurred had the war continued as a result of the nuclear devices not being used. But we can't possibly know how long the war would have lasted had the bombs not been dropped, nor for sure whether the bombs were the decisive factor in bringing it to an end.

The most commented upon criticism of utilitarianism, which has purchase both as a general critique of the doctrine as well as a weakness from an animal protection perspective, is its aggregative character. Utilitarianism, or at least the version known as act utilitarianism, holds that determining the rightness or wrongness of an act can be determined by measuring the overall balance of pleasure (or preferences) over pain (or the denial of preferences). Bentham sometimes defined this principle as the greatest happiness of the greatest number, although more often merely the greatest happiness, a significant difference that will be discussed below.

The problem with the aggregative principle central to utilitarianism, as has been exhaustively noted, is that it would appear to justifiy sacrificing the interests of individuals if by so doing an aggregative amount of the desirable objective is obtained. As a result, it 'entails very counter-intuitive solutions to questions of distributive justice' (Carruthers, 1992: 27). In Jones's words (1994: 62): 'There is no end to the horror stories that can be concocted to illustrate the awful possibilities that utilitarianism might endorse.' The persecution of a racial minority in the interests of a racist majority, the execution of an innocent person in the interests of social stability and calm, and the killing of a healthy individual so that his organs can be transplanted into a number of sick individuals, have all been cited as possible outcomes justified by a utilitarian calculation.

Imagine then, as Singer claims, that utilitarianism enables the equal consideration of animal and human interests. In this situation, with the aggregative procedure still in operation, it would justify sacrificing human and animal interests if by so doing happiness, pleasure or preferences were maximized. For example, if there was a possibility of finding a cure for a disease such as cancer by using humans or animals in scientific research, a utilitarian, or at least an act utilitarian, would surely have to sanction it. The fact that most people would regard such a use, of humans at least, as morally repugnant, suggests that intuitively we regard it as immoral to sacrifice the fundamental interests of humans even if the greater good is served in the process.

There are a number of ways in which utilitarian sympathizers could respond to this critique. It might be suggested, first, that in cases where fundamental interests are not at stake, the utilitarian aggregation principle may appear justifiable. Indeed, the sacrifice of some interests for what are perceived to be greater social and economic goods is a common occurrence. This is why, for instance, utilitarianism provides such strong intellectual support for the collective public provision required by the welfare state. Even here, though, there is a strong attack on such principles from the libertarian right who regard redistributive taxation as an illegitimate interference in the lives of individuals.

The defence noted above doesn't hold, of course, for the sacrifice of more fundamental interests. At least three responses in defence of utilitarianism might be made here. In the first place, a utilitarian calculus need not merely be a head count of those affected by an act. Rather, we are entitled to take into account the intensity of the feelings generated. Consider an example, provided by Carruthers (1992: 28), of a doctor who has a limited supply of a drug that can, in large quantities, be used to save the life of a human with a particular disease and in small quantities be used to treat acne. Imagine, then, that our doctor is faced with choosing between saving one human life and providing acne treatment for 100. Now, adopting Bentham's greatest happiness of the greatest number principle would result in us accepting that providing treatment to the 100 acne sufferers is the moral thing to do.

Utilitarians are not condemned to accept this counter-intuitive outcome however. We can avoid it by allocating a weighting to the pleasures and pains involved so that, say, we arrive at 1,000 units of pain for the individual deprived of the life-saving drug and 1 unit of pain for the 100 individuals deprived of the acne treatment. As a result, a utilitarian would now regard giving the drug to the individual as the most moral outcome since he will suffer 1,000 units of pain if deprived while the 100 deprived of the acne treatment will receive 100 units of pain if they are deprived. Of course, this solution is no guarantee against what most would regard as counter-intuitive outcomes. For imagine that there are 2,000 individuals who could benefit from the acne drug. In this scenario, it would be moral, according to utilitarianism, to sacrifice the fundamental interests of the individual who needs the drug to live and give it to the 2,000 who require it for acne treatment, since their total amount of pain is greater (at 2,000 units) than that experienced by the individual (1,000 units).

The second response we might make to the potential for counter-intuitive outcomes due to the aggregative principle of utilitarianism is to challenge intuition. Why should moral intuition always be right? Indeed, one of the main aims of Singer's utilitarian philosophy is to challenge widely held views about such issues as euthanasia as well as the treatment of animals. As we shall note below, one of the criticisms of rights theory is that it is too inflexible, preventing us from sacrificing the rights of the few in order to promote the common good when it is overwhelmingly in the interests of the vast majority to be able to pursue it.

Third, the problem of the aggregative nature of act utilitarianism has led some to dispense with it in favour of an alternative rule utilitarianism. Act utilitarianism, as we have seen, seeks to judge the utility of the consequence of every act. Rule utilitarianism, on the other hand, judges actions in terms of their conformity with a set of rules. So, even if in a particular instance the consequences of an act may be undesirable in terms of a surplus of pain over pleasure, providing it follows a rule that has been designated as one which if generally accepted maximizes utility the act should still be followed. The paradigm case here is a rule that says we should not lie. In particular circumstances, it may be justifiable in terms of a utilitarian calculus that lying is the right and moral thing to do. However, we may decide that a general rule imploring us to tell the truth will, on balance, maximize pleasures or preferences.

The application of rule utilitarianism, it might be argued then, resolves the aggregation problem inherent in act utilitarianism, because we can introduce a rule whereby, for instance, utility will be maximized in the long term if we do not infringe the fundamental interests of individuals in order to promote the common good. In this way, utilitarianism can be reconciled with the rights view (Brandt, 1992: 196–212). Moreover, not only does rule utilitarianism claim to remove the counter-intuitive outcomes produced by act utilitarianism, it also helps to resolve some of the calculation problems we discussed above. This is because by utilizing rule utilitarianism we do not have to calculate the likely consequences of any particular act but can instead follow a particular rule we have decided will maximize utility in the long term.

Rule utilitarianism is not a satisfactory solution to the counter-intuitive outcomes that can emerge from act utilitarianism. It has been widely noted that unless the rules are drawn so broadly as to take into account every possible eventuality, then a particular rule does not maximize utility and therefore to continue accepting it becomes a form of rule-worship, so that even when breaking the rule in particular circumstances will clearly maximize utility, and where the future use of the general rule is not threatened by breaking it in an individual instance, rule utilitarianism still insists that the rule be obeyed (Smart, 1973: 10). The option of drawing rules so broadly is an equally ineffective solution because so many caveats and sub-clauses to rules will be necessary that it quickly collapses into act utilitarianism (Lyons, 1965). Indeed, for Smart (1973: 11–12), such are the number of modifications that would be necessary that 'an adequate rule-utilitarianism would not only be extensionally equivalent to the act utilitarian principle . . . but would in fact consist of one rule only, the act utilitarian one: "maximise probable benefit"'.

Utilitarianism and animals

But what of animals, you might be asking by now? Well, Singer's version of utilitarianism has faced its biggest criticism from advocates of animal rights who claim that it cannot provide the philosophical basis for the abolitionist objectives Singer argues are justified (see Regan, 1984: chapter 7). There are two aspects to this. The first relates to what utilitarianism has to say about the killing and death of animals. Classical utilitarianism, as was indicated in chapter 5, finds it difficult to find anything wrong with painless killing, since it bases the rightness or wrongness of an act on the amount of happiness produced. There might be indirect reasons for regarding killing animals as wrong (such as the effect it will have on others or because it involves the infliction of pain), and it may be necessary to replace those animals we kill with others in order to maintain the same balance of happiness in the world. Killing animals painlessly is not, by itself however, a wrong.

Other versions of utilitarianism face similar problems in justifying the wrongness of killing animals. One could consider adapting rule utilitarianism to include a provision that it is wrong to kill animals. But rule utilitarianism, as we saw, is difficult to sustain, and, in this case, would find it difficult to justify prohibiting the killing of animals, or humans, if significant benefits are likely to accrue. Moreover, a rule that it is legitimate to kill animals providing that humans benefit significantly from it is as likely, if present practice is followed, as one prohibiting killing irrespective of the consequences. Preference utilitarianism can, all things being equal, provide a justification for not killing animals on the grounds that animals have a preference not to be killed. However, as we saw, Singer has admitted that human lives are more important than animal lives and the latter can be sacrificed for the former.

The second aspect of utilitarianism's weakness when it comes to the protection of animals is that, as we indicated above, *even if* we do not hold the principle that animal lives are worth less than human lives, animal killing is still justified if, on balance, more preferences are satisfied by so doing. As Singer (1993: 95) himself says: 'the wrong done to the person killed is merely one factor to be taken into account, and the preference of the victim could sometimes be outweighed by the preferences of others.' So we are back to the aggregation problem again. In short, because it is a consequentialist theory, no utilitarian could rule out the sacrifice of animal interests prior to the consequences of an act being known. As a result, utilitarianism cannot rule out a priori using animals for food production or as scientific research tools in the laboratory. A moral judgement will depend upon weighing up all the costs and benefits which, of course, will vary from case to case. Regan (1984: 218–24), for one, argues that it is distinctly possible that a utilitarian analysis would justify almost any use of animals, including, under certain circumstances, their use for food and experimental purposes Whether this is so will be examined further in chapters 7–9.

It should be noted here that much of the criticism of Singer from the animal rights camp is misplaced. He is placed by some in the animal welfare camp but this is to misunderstand his position. We can see that this is so by distinguishing between speciesist and non-speciesist versions of utilitarianism. The former allows for the interests of animals to be sacrificed if by so doing a significant human benefit accrues. As we saw, this position has been equated with according rights to humans and utilitarianism to animals and is therefore, strictly speaking, not a version of utilitarianism at all. What Singer would describe as a speciesist version of utilitarianism would be one prepared to aggregate interests, but in such a way that human interests count for much more than animal ones. By contrast, Singer himself adopts a non-speciesist version in which the interests of humans and animals must be considered equally. As a consequence, if we are to consider allowing experimentation on individuals for the pursuit of scientific knowledge, we should consider using humans for such work as much as we consider using animals. Singer, of course, thinks that in most circumstances we should use neither.

Rights

Such are the criticisms of utilitarianism that rights theory seems attractive as an alternative ethical theory in general and in terms of its capacity to protect the interests of animals. In contrast to utilitarianism, rights are a major part of the deontological tradition of moral thought. As Benton (1993: 82) points out: 'A deontological moral view is one according to which the difference between morally right and wrong action is not, or at least is not *solely*, a matter of consequences.' In other words, the attractiveness of rights theory is that it builds protective fences around individuals whose fundamental interests cannot, under normal circumstances, be sacrificed in order to promote the general welfare.

It is customary to make two important distinctions when talking about rights. In the first place, we can distinguish between legal rights and moral, or natural, rights. The former refers to the rights existing as a result of statutes protecting and promoting certain forms of behaviour, whereas the latter refers to rights existing as a moral entitlement whatever the prevailing legal system permits and prohibits. The so-called 'legal positivists', including Bentham, argued that the only sense in which rights can be said to exist is in their legal form. Moral rights are, in Bentham's famous phrase, 'nonsense upon stilts' (Bentham, 1948: 501).

Those who hold that we can talk sensibly about moral rights tend to sub-divide them into acquired and unacquired types. The former – often described as special rights – are those rights that derive from a particular agreement between individuals, the making of a promise being the paradigm example, or are those attached to a particular office or position. These type of rights are therefore not universal, but only involve those who have made the agreement or compact or who occupy office or position. The latter type, on the other hand, are possessed independently of any particular agreement and are held by whole groups of beings, usually as a result of some general characteristic possessed by all of them. When one refers to human rights and, indeed, animal rights too, it is the unacquired moral version to which we are referring.

A critique of rights

After a long period in the shadows of utilitarianism, rights made something of a comeback in academic political philosophy in the post-Second World War world, not surprisingly in the context of the atrocities committed by totalitarian regimes in the name of state goals (Waldron, 1987: 154). The return of rights theorizing in academic political philosophy was accompanied by attempts – enshrined in the 1948 United Nations Declaration of Human Rights – to establish a set of rights that ought to be protected in practice.[2] Writing in the 1980s, Waldron (1987: 156) could remark that: 'From a position of relative disrepute at the beginning of the century, rights seem to have become the new fashion in modern political philosophy.'

Despite this, the concept of rights is not without its difficulties. As Midgley (1983: 61) points out: 'As any bibliography of political theory will show', the concept of rights 'was in deep trouble long before animals were added to its worries'. Liberal rights theory is criticized not only by utilitarians, Burkean conservatives and Marxists (on which see Waldron, 1987), but also these days by the disparate set of thinkers who have been labelled communitarians (see Kymlicka, 2002: chapter 6). A full examination of the communitarian critique of rights is beyond the scope of this book, although elsewhere (Garner, 2005: chapter 4) I have examined the case for recommending communitarianism as a body of thought particularly amenable to the protection of animal interests. The major criticisms of rights, which we shall look at in turn, are that they lack a viable foundation, are too abstract, inflexible and individualistic.

One of the major problems of rights is their foundation. In other words, on what grounds are they to be accorded to individuals? Initially, it was argued, most notably by Locke, that rights were given by God, as part of His natural law. In a more secular age, however, a theocentric view of the world has much less force. It is by no means clear how rights are to be justified in the absence of widespread acceptance of divine power and wisdom.

Contemporary rights theorists tend to rely on the argument that rights are necessary in order to ensure that humans, possessed of certain characteristics, flourish. Exponents of animal rights then simply extend the concept to animals on the grounds that they too are the kind of beings who require rights in order to flourish. For Regan, as we have seen, rights ought to be given to beings who have the characteristics of subjects-of-a-life who, in turn, have inherent value and therefore cannot be treated as a means to an end. But, as Rowlands (1998: 49) argues, these judgements about what a flourishing human life ought to be like are subjective ones, and need to be justified more coherently than they have been. For example, Regan seems to place a great deal of store on the concept of inherent value as the key criteria, possession of which automatically translates into rights. Yet, as Rowlands (1998: 110–18) observes, it remains 'mysterious,' because its status, content and origins is never fully explained, 'ad hoc', in the sense that it is only introduced in order to make his theory conform with already existing moral beliefs, and 'unnecessary', because it can easily be replaced by the much less mysterious notion of an entity being subjectively inherently valued (see also Warren, 1997: 91–2).

Second, rights have been criticized for being too abstract. That is, they have been accused of neglecting local variations and the importance of tradition. As Waldron (1987: 167) points out:

They push aside all the detail of local custom, complex practice and ways of doing things that have evolved to suit particular environments, and replace them with norms of right that are supposed to apply uniformly and without exception across all the circumstances of human life.

Benton (1993: 90–2) has applied this abstraction criticism to the ability of rights to adequately reflect the moral status of animals. Commenting upon Regan's account of animal rights, Benton confirms that he provides a conventional emphasis of their universal character (except that they apply to some animals as well as humans). Rights are to be held equally by those beings deemed to be subjects-of-a-life and therefore no moral account is taken of either individual characteristics or circumstances. For Benton – in a similar vein to the more heterogeneous accounts of animal ethics provided by philosophers such as DeGrazia and Warren noted earlier – universal rights account prevents us from recognizing and acting upon the very different needs of animals experiencing very different circumstances. As he writes (Benton, 1993: 92), 'given the diversity of moral dilemmas posed by our relations to animals, it seems on the face of it unlikely that the single philosophical strategy of assigning universal rights of a very abstract kind to them would be a sufficient response'.

This is because protecting the interests of, for example, farm animals, experimental animals, wild animals and companion animals raises very different moral issues. For one thing, the institutionalized exploitation now the norm in the first two uses of animals has no real resonance in the latter two. Moreover, the relationship between a domestic pet and his/her 'owner' is very different from the other three in the sense that individual responsibility can be more easily assigned and enforced. Might it not be appropriate, then, to talk about acquired or special rights in the context of domestic pets rather than universally recorded natural rights? Might it not also be appropriate (as discussed on p. 102) to jettison rights in the case of animals subject to institutional exploitation in favour of an emphasis on tackling the economic and social factors responsible for this exploitation?

The third problem with rights relates to the degree to which they are absolute in the sense that they should never be overridden. It is tempting to argue that rights ought, as far as possible, to be absolute as an expression of the protection they provide for individuals. The problem is that in virtually all cases it is possible to think of circumstances in which there would seem to be a strong moral case for saying that a right should be overridden. Take the example of what

most would regard as a right that should be protected at all costs –
the right not to be tortured. It might be thought that this right should
be absolute. But one can think of circumstances in which most would
feel compelled to abandon it. Imagine we have captured a terrorist
who has planted a bomb that will kill hundreds, maybe thousands,
of people should it detonate. Wouldn't we be under the most enormous moral pressure to torture the terrorist to find out the location
of the bomb?

We would seem to be faced with a difficult choice here. We can
either insist that rights are absolute even when there is a clear moral
case for overriding them, or we admit that rights can be overridden,
thereby threatening 'so to muddy the water that it will cease to be
clear what, morally, having a right amounts to' (Jones, 1994: 193).
Having said this, it is not being argued here that there is a danger
that if we accept that rights are not absolute then rights theory
quickly collapses into utilitarianism. As a matter of course, utilitarians will seek to adopt the act that maximizes aggregative utility
without considering the potential rights infringements that might
occur as a result.

By contrast, rights theorists agonize over the circumstances in
which a particular right might be overridden. Ordinarily, rights act,
in Dworkin's words (1978: 90–4), so as to trump utilitarian considerations, or, in Nozick's words (1974) 28–33), to act as side-
constraints against them. Where rights are not regarded as absolute
they are widely known as 'prima facie' rights to denote the fact that
under normal circumstances I should expect to have a particular
right, but under extraordinary circumstances it may be overridden.
As Jones (1994: 195) remarks: 'If rights yield too easily and too
perfunctorily in the face of competing concerns, they will cease to
warrant description as "rights"', and are likely to collapse into a
utilitarian calculus.

Much of the discussion about the extent to which rights are
absolute is not undertaken in the context of a conflict between individual protection and societal welfare in any case. Rather, rights theorists have spent a great deal of effort contemplating what happens
when rights conflict. What do we do, for instance, in the event of a
right to property conflicting with a right to free movement? Similarly,
does the right to free speech extend to making racist comments that
threaten the rights of those against whom the comments are directed?
In other words, how do we go about prioritizing rights? Which are
more important than others?

Some argue that it is possible to exaggerate the necessity of con-
flictual rights. Rights tend to conflict, it is suggested, when care has

not been taken in defining their boundaries. In the above example, for instance, the right to free speech can easily be qualified so that it excludes a right to engage in racist talk (Jones, 1994: 199). Not all conflicts can be avoided, however, and increasingly debates about prioritizing rights have to be held within the context of competing general political ideologies. For example, conflict between rights is particularly acute in the context of the debate between traditional negative rights – such as rights to life, liberty and property – promoted by classical liberals, and the newer social and economic rights promoted by radical liberals and socialists. Finally, in addition to conflicts between different rights, we should not forget that there may also be conflicts between different rights holders. In the familiar lifeboat scenarios, who would we save if we had to make a choice?

One of the most sustained attempts to provide principles justifying the overriding of rights has been provided by Tom Regan (1984: chapter 8). He develops three principles relating to the circumstances in which rights may be overridden. The first is the so-called 'miniride' principle. Here, it is justifiable to harm innocent individuals if by so doing a larger number can be saved from a comparable harm. The second is the 'liberty' principle whereby individuals have the right to harm others in order to protect themselves from comparable harms. The third is the 'worse-off' principle, which we encountered in chapter 5, whereby it is morally impermissible to inflict a major harm on an individual or individuals in order to save any number of other individuals from a lesser harm.

The worse-off principle allows Regan to argue that the death of a human is worth more than the deaths of any number of moral patients because the harms are not comparable. We argued in chapter 5 that there are weaknesses with Regan's argument here. On the positive side, Regan is able to show through the worse-off principle why it would be always morally wrong, referring back to our illustration earlier, to give the drug for the treatment of acne to the many rather than the individual who needs it to counter the effects of a fatal disease. This would seem to be one area where rights theory is closer to our moral intuition than utilitarianism.

We have seen that if rights theory is to differ from utilitarianism then it must be prepared to protect individuals against measures to promote the general welfare. Benton (1993: 87) sums up nicely Regan's insistence on this when he writes that animals must never 'be treated as individual bearers of "inherent value", never as replaceable "receptacles" of value, or as mere means to human ends'. The question that then arises is whether the general welfare is never sufficiently important to justify sacrificing the interests of some individuals? This question is equally applicable if we attach rights to humans only or if we extend rights to animals. For instance, can it be right to, say, pass up the opportunity to sacrifice the interests of animals and/or humans in some scientific experiment even if we strongly suspect it will lead to a major medical advance? At present we are not forced to make such a decision precisely because animals are not regarded as sufficiently important morally to be granted rights. We therefore sacrifice their interests in a utilitarian fashion, whereas humans as rights holders are not permitted to be treated in this way.

In practice, a utilitarian would no doubt claim, individual interests are infringed on a regular basis in order to pursue goals which are regarded as socially beneficial. The most notable examples are interventions in property rights and, in particular, the levying of taxes. Calls by libertarian philosophers, such as Nozick (1974), to regard these interventions as unjust have largely fallen on deaf ears. From time to time, too, the sacrifice of fundamental human interests is justified by invoking utilitarian-type arguments. The best recent example has been the arguments employed by Tony Blair to justify military action against Iraq, which have been along the lines that the resulting loss of life is worthwhile, given the lives saved and general happiness increased as a result of the toppling of Saddam Hussein.

In addition to the charge of inflexibility, rights have also been criticized for their overly individualistic nature. They have been regarded as antisocial, always emphasizing the limitations on societal and state intervention in the lives of individuals rather than the responsibilities individuals might have to society. More pertinent, in a book about animal rights, is the difficulty of assigning responsibility for infringing a particular right. This criticism is particularly associated with the Marxist social theorist Ted Benton. For Benton (1993: 89), 'possession of a right depends on having a valid claim against some assignable individual', and yet the institutionalized exploitation of animals, in factory farms and laboratories, is peculiarly unsuitable to this kind of individualistic expectation. Take modern intensive animal agriculture, for instance, where the animals and the equipment which is used to raise and slaughter them is owned by large and complex agribusiness corporations. To whom should we attach responsibility for the infringement of animal rights in this instance?:

Should we assign responsibility to the operatives who administer and maintain the animals and the physical plant, to their managers, or to the business executives who run the enterprise, or to the investors in the pension schemes who supply its capital, or to the food processors and retailers who demand standardized and predictable supplies of meat at set prices, or to consumers who demand cheap food and ask no questions, or to legislators who fail to outlaw these practices, to a civil service which fails to enforce what legislation there is, or to a citizenry that fails to act against abuse? (Benton, 1993: 89–90)

Finally, the criticism arises, again from the left of the political spectrum, that there is a crucial difference between the formal granting of rights and the protection of individual interests in practice. The argument here is that rights are only necessary in a society where individuals are likely to have their interests infringed, and the formal granting of rights does nothing, by itself, to mitigate the social and economic factors that cause the exploitation of individuals. As Benton (1993: 95) remarks: 'As both women's rights and black liberation campaigns have experienced, prevailing structures of economic, cultural and political power may continue to obstruct the realization of juridically acknowledged rights.'

There is a clear parallel here with the treatment of animals. The protection afforded to animals by rights will only be effective if there is a broad societal consensus that their moral status is sufficiently high to justify protection against exploitation. And, of course, by the time this position has been reached, according formal rights to animals will be unnecessary, or at least much less important. Rights theory, then, rather side-steps the key issues. The crucial question now becomes: how do we get to a position where there is a sufficiently large and/or influential group of people who accept the moral considerability of animals to make the protection of animals a genuine possibility? We will return to this question of agency in chapter 10.

Conclusion

In preceding chapters of this book we have examined various approaches to the moral status of animals. These range from the view explored in chapter 3, that we owe no direct moral duties to animals, to the view covered in chapter 5, that animals have a moral status which is close, if not equivalent, to that of humans. Add in the argument from marginal cases successfully and actual equivalence is achieved. Between these two positions is the moral orthodoxy that grants some moral status to animals, but insists that humans are morally superior and our interests should take precedence over those of animals. In this chapter, we have examined three major moral theories – rights, utilitarianism and contractarianism – that seek to tell us how to distribute the moral status that is attached to humans and animals by each of the approaches discussed above. Two major issues are left to be discussed. The first, covered in chapters 7–9, is concerned with applying the approaches identified to the various ways in which animals are used by humans. The second, covered in chapter 10, is concerned with the question of political agency. In a nutshell, if it is accepted that there is a need for animals to be accorded greater moral status than the currently dominant moral orthodoxy allows, how is this change to be effected?

7

Should We Eat Animals?

It is appropriate to begin an examination of the relationship between the ethical theories discussed in this book so far and the way animals are, and ought to be, treated in practice, by looking at the raising and killing of animals for food. For one thing, the sheer scale of the practice beggars belief. For another, the relatively recent use of increasingly intensive forms of animal agriculture raises acute welfare problems, which may make them morally illegitimate from even the standpoint of the moral orthodoxy. Eating animals, as Singer (1993: 62) points out, is 'the oldest and the most widespread form of animal use . . . the foundation stone on which rests the belief that animals exist for our pleasure and convenience'. This leads to the key question: is vegetarianism, or even veganism (the latter distinguished by the prohibition on the consumption of all animal-derived products) mandatory?

Factory farming

The number of animals raised and killed for food is phenomenal. In the United States alone it is estimated that some 103 million pigs, 38 million cows and calves and a staggering 9 billion broiler chickens are slaughtered each year. This amounts to about 27 million animals slaughtered per day and more than a million every hour (Regan, 2004: 96). Such big numbers translate into big profits. In the United States the meat and poultry industries produce an income of $90 billion a year (Mason, 2002: 201). The primary reason why the number of animals killed for food has soared is that humans have developed increasingly efficient and cost-effective ways of converting animals into meat. This growing intensification – commonly known as 'factory' farming because it is undertaken in buildings reminiscent of industrial plants and involving standardized and mechanized procedures that are capital, but not labour, intensive – has provided the most fertile arena for animal advocates and is at the centre of the political debate (see Harrison, 1964 for an early critique of factory farming).

It should not be thought that the conversion of animals into food was idyllic before the advent of intensification. Nineteenth-century accounts of the treatment of farm animals by writers such as Thomas Hardy should free us from that misapprehension. For one thing, in an age without motor transport, animals were often herded for very long distances without much in the way of food, water or rest. The killing was also very primitive and cruel. The evolution, since 1945, of factory farming does represent, however, a new dimension in man's inhumanity to animals. Nowadays, the vast majority of animals raised for food are raised in the intensive manner described in this chapter.

The dominance of factory farming is particularly evident in the case of poultry. The vast majority of laying hens and broiler chickens – designed for meat – are subject to intensification. Modern poultry units are subject to vertical integration where one corporation – such as Tyson Foods and Perdue Farms in the United States – controls the whole process from birth to death, usually on one site. The use of battery cages – where a number of hens are kept indoors in cages with minimal room for movement – is the most potent symbol of factory farming. Less well known is the intensive rearing of broiler chickens, those reared for their meat. Here, many thousands of birds are kept in windowless broiler sheds fattened by excessive feeding for a short period of time – about seven weeks – before being sent for slaughter. Poultry plants are usually run with military precision, and the label 'factory' farming has never been more apt (Browne, 2002).

It is not just poultry that is subject to intensification. The raising of calves for the veal trade is the best-known example of the confinement of mammals. Calves reared in the classic so-called 'crate' system are not only confined in such a way that they are unable to turn round, but they are also deprived of the necessary nutrients, in order to keep their flesh pale, and of the company of other calves. Not all veal systems currently operate the classical system, some now allowing greater movement, better diets and less isolation.

Pigs are increasingly raised in intensive ways too, particularly in the United States where the vertical integration common in the poultry industry has been increasingly replicated. Smithfield Foods Inc. of Virginia, the world's largest producer of pig meat, owns 700,000 sows (getting on for a quarter of the total national stock), has annual sales of about $6 billion and kills 82,300 pigs every twenty-four hours, almost half in the world's largest slaughterhouse which it owns (Scully, 2002: 250–9). In the most intensive systems, particularly evident in North Carolina, pigs are confined indoors for their entire lives, whether as breeding sows or hogs bred for their meat. A graphic, and alarming, portrait of this system is provided by Scully (2002: 247–86). It is now common practice in the United States and Europe for pigs being fattened for slaughter to spend their lives standing on pens with metal or concrete slats. In addition, sows are subject in many countries (although not now in Britain) to confinement by stalls and tethers during pregnancy, and the farrowing crate during and after the birth of piglets.

Intensive animal agriculture is not characterized entirely by indoor housing and confinement. Beef cattle, for instance, are not usually kept indoors, although in the United States, the so-called 'feedlot' – a densely populated concrete fenced area – which provides a poor environment for cattle, is common. Dairy cows, likewise, are not always confined – although some are – but fare even worse than beef cattle. Demands for increased milk yields, promoted by the use of hormones in the United States, requires a constant cycle of impregnation, birth and lactation. As a consequence, dairy cows suffer more infections and wear out more quickly. The natural lifespan of a cow is more than twenty years but most are slaughtered at about four years old, when they are deemed to be spent.

The costs of animal agriculture – to animals

Is killing animals for food necessary? Does it provide for significant human benefits? If not, animal agriculture is illegitimate even from the perspective of the moral orthodoxy. This is because the fact that animals suffer as a consequence of modern intensive agriculture should be taken as a given. Regan (2004: 89–90) eloquently sums it up with little exaggeration: 'The vast majority of these animals, literally *billions* of them, suffer every waking minute they are alive. Physically, they are sick, plagued by chronic, debilitating diseases. Psychologically, they are ill, weighed down by the cumulative effects of disorientation and depression.' The fact that the general public in many countries would be prosecuted for keeping animals in some of the ways they are commonly kept by farmers illustrates the point that suffering can be taken for granted. In Britain, to give one example, to keep a bird in a cage where it cannot spread its wings is illegal under the 1911 Protection of Animals Act. But this is precisely what is allowed in the battery cage. The difference, then, must be in the degree to which this suffering is necessary in the sense that it serves significant human purposes.

Of course, as with all areas of animal welfare, the level of suffering inflicted on animals in the process of converting them into meat will vary from country to country and from region to region. In Europe, for instance, it is generally recognized that Northern countries have better animal welfare records than Southern countries. Likewise, it is generally recognized that Northern European countries have better records than the United States (see Garner, 1998). In the latter, for instance, there is no federal legislation regulating the husbandry of farm animals and not much regulating their transportation and slaughter. Poultry, for instance, are excluded totally from the provisions of the US Humane Slaughter Act. In addition, state legislation tends to be weak and poorly enforced. In some parts of the world, too, in complete contrast with Northern Europe, animal welfare law is non-existent. Despite these differences, however, the structure of intensive animal agriculture is remarkably uniform, with confinement in cages (laying hens), sheds (broiler chickens) and stalls (pigs) being the norm.

Let us now elaborate on some of the suffering that modern agriculture inflicts on animals. This can involve pain, although, as we have seen, it often goes beyond this. Animals suffer pain from being confined. This can be through injuries to limbs, a common occurrence in poultry. Broiler chickens, provided with little exercise and fed an enormous amount, grow so big that their legs have problems supporting their bodies. This is in addition to the injuries that are likely to be sustained in a crowded and frightening environment. The chances of veterinary attention for sick or injured birds is remote in such an environment, and hardly cost-effective for the producer. Similarly, battery hens, deprived of exercise and sunlight, tend to suffer from brittle bones which regularly break when the spent hens are removed from cages and sent to the abattoir. Beak trimming, too, necessary to prevent broiler chickens from pecking each other in the confined space they find themselves, is undoubtedly a painful procedure (Fraser and Broom, 1990: 271).

Mammals subject to intensive animal agriculture also undoubtedly suffer. Dairy cows, although not confined in the same way as poultry, pay the price of increased productivity particularly in terms of increased susceptibility to infections, most notably an infection of the

udder known as mastitis. Veal calves too 'endure the pain and discomfort of swollen joints, digestive disorders, and chronic diarrhoea'
(Regan, 2004: 92). In factory farmed pigs, foot and leg injuries, the
result of standing on inadequate flooring, is common. Scully, an
American writer, describes the physical problems he encountered in
a hog unit (2002: 267). 'Sores, tumours, ulcers, pus pockets, lesions,
cysts, bruises, torn ears, swollen legs everywhere.'

Factory farming undoubtedly also causes other forms of suffering
to animals. Supporters of factory farming often point to the high productivity rates of animals as evidence that suffering is minimal. Productivity, however, should not be equated with absence of suffering
(Dawkins, 1980: 27–32, 34, 48–9). As we have seen, broiler chickens grow to an unnaturally large size under intensive conditions, but
while they are worth more this is accompanied by serious welfare
problems due to confinement. Intensive systems are generally cost-
effective because they are not labour intensive, but the confinement
that enables this to occur is itself the subject of serious animal welfare
concerns.

The confinement of animals means that they are usually unable to
perform behaviour patterns associated with their species. Hens in
cages, for instance, are unable to stretch their wings, fly, dust bathe
or build nests. By itself, this is not an entirely adequate critique of
confinement. For one thing, it assumes animals bred for captivity
have the same requirements as their free-range ancestors. In addition,
the suffering caused by confinement has to be balanced against the
suffering experienced by animals farmed extensively, who are more
likely to contract diseases and be attacked by predators.

There is additional evidence, however, that confinement causes suffering. Put simply, the level of boredom produced by confinement
must have catastrophic consequences for the psychological health of
factory farmed animals. Physiological evidence reveals that animals
experience high levels of stress as a result of being confined. Even
more importantly, confined animals exhibit clear signs of abnormal
behaviour. This includes self-mutilation, the mutilation of other
animals, misdirected behaviour such as homosexual acts among
animals kept in single-sex groups, apathy and hysteria. Above all,
confined animals (in zoos as well as factory farms) engage in so-called
'stereotypical' behaviour such as rocking backwards and forwards,
rubbing continuously against objects, head shaking, eye rolling, sham
chewing, tongue rolling and bar biting.[1] Scully (2002: 268) described
the 'social defeat' he found in the American hog unit visited: 'every
third or fourth stall some completely broken being you know is alive
only because she blinks and stares up at you . . . creatures beyond the

powers of pity to help or indifference to make more miserable, dead to the world except as heaps of flesh.'

The fact that animals suffer more than just pain as a result of confinement was confirmed by the results of an inquiry set up by the British government in 1965. The Brambell Report (HMSO, 1965) – named after its author, a noted zoologist – proposed that new legislation be created applying specifically to farm animals. This was done in the form of the 1968 Agricultural (Miscellaneous Provisions) Act. More importantly, Brambell also proposed that animal welfare legislation be based on the fulfilling of the 'five freedoms' which should allow an animal to turn around, groom itself, get up, lie down and stretch its limbs. These proposals were largely ignored at the time but the 1968 Act allowed for the creation of regulations which, over the years, have gradually begun to diminish the scale of factory farming (see below).

The transportation and slaughter of animals is not part of factory farming as such, and arguably could be practised in ways that minimized or even eliminated pain and other forms of suffering. The economic needs of modern animal agriculture, however, rarely achieve these goals. The transportation of animals, particularly across national borders, can often result in animals suffering pain – through things such as bruising, broken limbs and so-called 'shipping fever' – even when conducted within the law. The degree of suffering inflicted will obviously vary depending on things such as the distance travelled, the accommodation provided and the seriousness with which the operators take their animal welfare responsibilities. The evidence is that the laws, often inadequate, are regularly deliberately flouted or that things go horribly wrong unintentionally, as with the death of many thousands of animals en route from Australia to the Middle East (Wilkins, 1997: 4).

In most developed countries, the slaughter of animals is meant to minimize pain. To this end, stunning is required so that animals are unconscious before having their throats cut. In addition, various other pre-mortem regulations have been introduced to ensure that animals do not suffer fear or panic before being slaughtered. For various reasons, however, the slaughter of farm animals is not as pain-free as some of the industry's publicity would have it.

First, despite the fact that it is widely believed to cause considerable pain, the ritual slaughter of animals, where animals are denied pre-stunning, is still permitted in many countries. Second, one should not assume that pre-stunning – in most cases the infliction of an electric shock that induces unconsciousness – is painless. Third, and most significantly, evidence suggests that animal welfare regulations are regularly broken, usually because of the profit motive which ensures that animals are moved swiftly through the slaughterhouse process, with no incentive to stop the line if something goes wrong. This includes ineffective use of stunning equipment, with the obvious appalling conclusion that some animals are conscious while having their throats cut or while being submerged in boiling water. Not surprisingly, the turnover of staff in slaughterhouses is often rapid, and staff may be inexperienced and/or have little concern for animal welfare.[2] It is probably the case that these cases of extreme cruelty are rare but as Scully (2002: 282) points out, such is the volume of animals being slaughtered that this can amount to a considerable number. If, for example, only 1 per cent of pigs in the United States are not stunned properly this amounts to over 1 million per year.

The costs of animal agriculture – to humans

Having examined the cost to animals of intensive animal agriculture it is appropriate here to mention that it has been argued that there are other *human* costs of this system of producing food. In the first place, in most societies eating animals is not necessary for good health or longevity. Indeed, the consumption of meat – because of its high fat and cholesterol levels – has been associated with human health problems, whether that be the long-term impact of the consumption of saturated fats or the more specific health scares such as salmonella, mad cow disease and the use of antibiotics on animals. Animal agriculture, and particularly intensive versions of it, also has environmental consequences. It uses vast amounts of water, heating and lighting, it pollutes water, and damages wildlife habitats in general.[3] In one of the most extreme examples, in 1997 the North Carolina legislature was forced to impose a moratorium on the construction of new intensive hog farms because of growing concerns about the water pollution caused by the disposal of huge amounts of pig waste from existing units (Bauston, 2002: 179; Scully, 2002: 249).

In the last two decades or so British animal agriculture has staggered from one crisis to the next. What is interesting is that in most cases these crises – all of which have impacted negatively on human beings – have their source in the use of intensive agricultural methods. The growing incidence of salmonella is one example. It is so much more difficult to control salmonella, and other diseases, in the cramped conditions of an intensive battery unit. BSE, likewise, was caused by the unnatural practice of feeding cattle with the brains and vertebrae of other animals. Finally, foot-and-mouth was caused by unscrupulous and reckless behaviour by one farmer, coupled with the centralization of abattoir provision and the consequent need for animals to be transported greater distances, thereby making it more difficult to contain the outbreak (Fort, 2001).

Modern animal agriculture is also implicated in the impoverishment of the developing world. This is because it is suggested that raising and killing animals for food is an extremely inefficient form of food production, since a disproportionately small amount of animal protein is produced from a large amount of feed protein. The logical conclusion is it would be better to 'cut out the middle man' and grow crops for human consumption (Mason and Singer, 1990: 74). Of particular concern here is that developing countries are increasingly investing in cattle production primarily for export. This has had the effect of reducing the amount of crops for local consumption, as well as causing environmental problems, since deforestation is often required to create more and more land for grazing (Moore Lapper, 1971). It would be simplistic to claim that the focus on raising and killing animals for food is the only, or even the most important, cause of food shortages in the world. Famine is not a unicausal problem and is caused by, for instance, distribution problems as much as anything else. Nevertheless, the obsession with animal-derived protein undoubtedly contributes to world food problems.

Benefits of animal agriculture

Having examined the cost side, we are now in a position to look at the benefits to humans of animal agriculture in general, and factory farming in particular. It is undoubtedly the case that meat and fish are one, although by no means the most exclusive, source of protein and other nutrients. In this sense, factory farming, at least superficially, provides economic benefits to the consumer. Intensive farming was introduced precisely because it offered the prospect of a plentiful supply of cheap food. Despite the costs noted above, it has largely delivered on this front. At one time in Britain, for instance, chicken was a luxury which many families could not afford at any meal other than on special occasions. Factory farming has made it commonplace. Similarly, battery eggs are cheaper than free-range alternatives.

Producers have obviously benefited too. We saw earlier how big a part of the economy animal agriculture has become. The evolution of intensive animal agriculture has created a whole new set of economic beneficiaries. Traditional actors such as farmers and veterinarians are now a tiny cog in a very large agribusiness wheel. This includes the various input industries – the animal feed industry, suppliers of farm equipment, and the increasingly important role played by the pharmaceutical and chemical industries – those concerned with transporting animals and animal products, slaughtering and rendering them, the food processing and manufacturing industries, and those with a stake in advertising animal products. To end animal agriculture would, at least in the short term, produce job losses in general and create significant problems for areas dependent on its continuation.

A number of pro-animal philosophers, I think, have underestimated the economic benefits of factory farming in particular, and animal agriculture in general. For example, DeGrazia (2002: 73) remarks that 'We cannot plausibly regard any of the harms caused to' factory farmed animals 'as necessary'. Rowlands (2002: 111), likewise, suggests that the consequences for humans of the abolition of factory farming results, at worst, in the loss of 'certain pleasures of the palate'. This is because it will result in more expensive food which may mean, for some, having to give up eating meat. Rowlands wants to go even further by suggesting that the abolition of even free-range farming systems is justified because the loss to humans of so acting, judged to be limited to pleasures of the palate, is no match for the loss of animal lives, however good their lives have been (2002: 117–19).

There is no mention here of possible economic costs, which are ignored completely by Francione (2000). Rowlands (2002: 122) mentions them but quickly dismisses them on the grounds, first, that they can be mitigated by economic opportunities in other areas of agriculture, and, second, that 'practices that are morally wrong cannot be justified by appeal to economic considerations'. This latter argument, while open to a contractarian like Rowlands, is not, of course, open to a utilitarian since what is moral depends upon an examination of factors such as economic ones that contribute towards pleasure and the satisfaction of preferences.[4] The former argument probably underestimates the economic dislocation likely to be caused by the end of animal agriculture.

Both Regan (1984: 221–2) and Frey (1983: 197–206) do not underestimate these costs, the latter in particular providing an impressive list of the consequences of an end to animal agriculture, thereby disputing Singer's assertion that the utility involved in abolishing animal agriculture outweighs the disutility. This list includes the impact on livestock and poultry farmers, government meat inspectors, those in the food industry who depend upon meat production, animal feed manufacturers, road and rail haulage firms, the refrigeration industry, fast food retailers and restaurants, the pet food and pharmaceutical industry, university staff involved in animal-related departments such as veterinary science, publishing businesses responsible for titles relating to animal agriculture, the advertising industry, the leather and wool industries. And all of this is not to mention the impact on tax revenues generally as well as the more nebulous impact on social life where, as Frey (1983: 200) points out, 'meat permeates our lives and our relations with others to an extraordinary degree'.

The moral orthodoxy and animal agriculture

So, what should our conclusions be about the desirability, on animal welfare grounds, of animal agriculture? The first point to make is that the complete abolition of animal agriculture is not justified by the moral orthodoxy. There are too many human benefits at stake here. Moreover, it is possible, I think, to envisage a form of animal agriculture in which the suffering inflicted on animals is minimized to the extent that it is not problematic. Remember that, from an animal welfare perspective, the painless death of farm animals does not raise any moral issues. Eating free-range meat and eggs is, from this perspective, much more morally commendable behaviour than eating meat or eggs from animals that have been intensively reared.

But what of factory farming? It is impossible to be precise here (see below) but the case for prohibiting aspects of intensive animal agriculture from the perspective of the moral orthodoxy is strong. From the consumer perspective, the extra cost of purchasing free-range meat and eggs is not prohibitive, at least for most people in developed countries. In any case, eating meat and eggs regularly cannot be regarded as a significant human interest, particularly when it is weighed against the denial of interests that are of enormous significance to animals. From the perspective of the producer the position is less clear-cut, but animal agriculture will still exist and there will still be a considerable role for many of the agribusiness interests, and not a substantial loss of profit if the extra costs are passed on to consumers. The clinching argument, I think, is that there are also human benefits to be had from the ending of factory farming. Our health and our environment will be improved as a consequence.

The need for action against factory farming is accepted by most of those philosophers who do not want to morally prohibit meat eating in general (Frey, 1983: 207; Scruton, 2000: 139–45). More significantly, the need for reform is also being increasingly accepted by governments in Europe. Britain has already prohibited individual veal-calf crates, and sow stalls and tethers. Now the European Union has also decided to phase out battery cages – although a larger enriched cage will still be permitted – sow stalls and tethers, individual veal-calf crates once the animal reaches eight weeks old, and beak trimming. Much, however, remains to be done and, for the moment at least, the dominant form of animal agriculture is incompatible with the moral orthodoxy.

Beyond the moral orthodoxy

From the perspective of those who argue that to all intents and purposes humans and animals ought to be regarded as morally equal, the animal welfare or moral orthodoxy approach is, of course, painfully inadequate. There is no justification for exploiting animals, treating them as a means to an end, in order to provide a human source of food, and this would apply irrespective of the nature of the human gains. We have not yet established whether it is appropriate to attach rights to farm animals, or indeed to the humans who eat them. So the caveat to the previous argument is that all of it holds, unless we are prepared to treat humans in the same way, as sources of food for other humans and animals.

What, though, if we apply the sentiency view to the raising and killing of animals for food? This position, the reader will remember, holds that humans are full persons but animals are not and, as a consequence, human lives are worth more than animal lives. At the same time, unlike the moral orthodoxy, the position also holds that it is difficult to deny that animals have an equal interest in not suffering. Here, it seems to me that the conflict – between a human's interest in living and an animal's interest in avoiding pain and suffering – does not necessarily emerge in the case of animal agriculture, but would depend upon the methods used. As we saw, most humans do not need to eat animals to survive and, even if they did, humane methods of killing animals exist. Inflicting suffering in the course of producing animals for food, therefore, does remain illegitimate, and this would rule out most modern forms of factory farming which in a variety of ways cause animals to suffer. As with the moral orthodoxy, free-range farming in which animals lead good lives and have painless deaths is not such a moral problem from the perspective of the sentiency view.

This conclusion we have just reached from the perspective of the sentiency view, of course, is not acceptable to those, like Singer or

Regan, who want to see a complete end to animal agriculture and vegetarianism become compulsory. For those, such as Regan, who hold that animals have a right to life, it is possible to say categorically that eating animals is morally illegitimate, however the animals are raised and whatever the economic benefits that derive from raising and killing them for food (Regan, 1984: 330–49). Animal agriculture, he remarks, 'violates the rights of' farm animals. He continues:

> As such, no one, neither those directly involved in the meat industry nor those who would be affected by its collapse, has a right to be protected against being harmed by allowing that industry to continue. In this sense and for these reasons, the rights view implies that justice *must* be done, though the (economic) heavens fall. (Regan, 1984: 346–7)

There are two problems relating to the consistency of Regan's claim that meat eating is morally wrong. In the first place, as we saw in chapter 5, Regan weakens his position by denying that humans and animals have lives of equal value. The consequence of this position is that in a hypothetical 'lifeboat' situation, where the choice is either to save a human or an animal life, we must always choose the human. Tailoring this lifeboat example to the issue of meat eating, Regan (1984: 351–2) agrees that in the event of a food shortage where the five occupants will die of starvation if one of them is not killed and eaten, it should always be the dog that is eaten on the grounds that 'the harm that death is in the case of that animal is not as great a harm as the harm that death would be in the case of any of these humans'. In such a lifeboat situation, then, vegetarianism can be jettisoned.

Regan responds to allegations of inconsistency by rightly pointing out that the real world is very different from the situation pertaining in the lifeboat. Crucially, we do not need to eat meat in order to stay alive. Of course, there may be human communities who, in the past and currently, do need to eat animal flesh in order to survive. The vast majority of us, however, can prosper on a non-animal diet, and many millions do so. For Regan, the death of a farm animal, although not as great as the death of a human, causes harm and therefore infringes a right-to-life. It is therefore morally impermissible to kill animals for food, whatever the circumstances of their lives and the nature of their death. While the lifeboat example cited above has no impact on Regan's case for vegetarianism, it may have important implications for the validity of Regan's case against animal experimentation. We will therefore return to this question in chapter 8.

The second problem with Regan's case for vegetarianism is that he thinks that in all probability some animals – chickens, turkeys, frogs, for instance – lack the necessary characteristics to be accorded the status of subjects-of-a-life (Regan, 1984: 349). The implication is that these animals do not have rights and therefore that eating them, or subjecting them to scientific experimentation, is not wrong as it is for those animals who are subjects-of-a-life. Regan responds in a number of ways to this, none of which are entirely satisfactory. Part of his response is to argue that it is difficult to know where to draw the line between those entities which are subjects-of-a-life and those which are not, and therefore chickens (and turkeys and frogs) probably ought to be given the benefit of the doubt (1984: 366–7, 391). The lack of precision in this statement, however, reduces its credibility as a moral guide.

Second, even more problematic is Regan's further claim that we should treat animals that are not subjects-of-a-life as if they were on the grounds that if humans are encouraged to exploit animals that are not subjects-of-a-life they are more likely to exploit animals who are (Regan, 1984: 368, 391). This adaptation of the indirect duty view towards animals is subject to all of the problems we identified in chapter 3. Most notably, it is an empirical claim that may or may not be true. It is somewhat ironic that Regan, regarded as the premier animal rights philosopher, finds himself dependent on a device utilized by those philosophers, such as Kant, who deny moral standing to animals.

The obvious response to the exclusion of some animals from inherent value and therefore rights is the employment of the argument from marginal cases. Applied to non-self-conscious farm animals, this would amount to saying that if we are prepared to eat such animals then we should also be prepared to eat marginal humans with a similar level of mental complexity, a not too appetizing prospect. More palatably, the categorical version of the argument from marginal cases would hold that, since we were not prepared to eat such marginal humans, we should not be prepared to eat animals lacking inherent value either. In his earlier work Regan (1975) was reliant on the argument from marginal cases. If, he argued, rights are granted to 'marginal' humans they ought to be granted to many animals as well since there are no morally relevant differences between them. In his later work, however, Regan eschews this approach in favour of the argument that a high proportion of humans and animals do have the characteristics necessary for inherent value. As Regan admits, though, some don't, and he has difficulty incorporating such animals within his theory. As a result, another arguably artificial boundary has been created, not this time between humans and animals but between animals and humans that are subjects-of-a-life and humans and animals who are not.

It is Singer's contention (1993: 63) that eating animals is illegitimate from a utilitarian perspective on the grounds that it represents 'a situation in which a relatively minor human interest must be balanced against the lives and welfare of the animals involved'. But can utilitarianism really condemn meat eating so rapidly and effortlessly, particularly since others such as Frey and Regan, as we saw above, do not seek to minimize the costs of ending animal agriculture? Regan, for one, doubts whether utilitarianism can even demonstrate beyond all doubt that intensive animal agriculture is ruled out. As he suggests (1984: 223): 'it is not *obviously* true that the aggregated consequences for everyone affected would be better, all considered, if intensive rearing methods were abandoned and we all (or most of us) became (all at once or gradually) vegetarians.'

As we saw above, a careful analysis of the costs and benefits of animal agriculture reveals that, while the worst excesses of factory farming are not justified, it seems that eating meat by itself is not morally condemned. How, if at all, does the utilitarianism of Singer differ from this judgement? Not much, it would seem. In the first place, since apparently the deaths of animals are not problematic from a classical utilitarian perspective, there is the distinct possibility that, shorn of the worst excesses of factory farming and where slaughterhouses are made more humane, farming animals for food would not be a problem. As Singer (1993: 133) admits, the 'killing of non-self-conscious animals may not be wrong' in circumstances 'when animals lead pleasant lives, are killed painlessly, their deaths do not cause suffering to other animals, and the killing of one animal makes possible its replacement by another who would not otherwise have lived.' Of course, the argument about the unproblematic nature of taking animal lives is dependent on, and only applies to, those animals that are not self-conscious. The interests of those animals who are self-conscious would have to be factored into the utilitarian equation, but even then their lives would count for less than human lives. Singer seems to think, and I wouldn't dissent, that, since they seem to lack self-consciousness, this would justify raising chickens for their meat in free-range conditions where their deaths were painless, and where the birds would not exist unless we ate them (ibid: 133).

It is true that Singer and other pro-animal philosophers do underestimate the economic impact of ending factory farming. To be fair to Singer, it might be noted here, Frey is equally guilty in that he implies that the only benefit from the abandonment of intensive animal agriculture would be the elimination of farm animal suffering whereas, as we have seen, there are other anthropocentric benefits of so doing. In addition, Singer counters the suggestion that his utilitarian position seems to justify meat eating providing that factory farming methods are not used by arguing that, in reality, it would not be practical to produce enough meat to feed the human population using free-range methods. He may be right. As we saw, the rationale for agricultural intensification was to produce a cheaper supply of readily available food. Once the system is abandoned, there is every reason to think that meat would be in shorter supply, and therefore much more expensive. However, this is not a satisfactory answer to those who currently eat free-range meat and would insist that they are morally entitled to do so. They would seem to have a case, particularly from a utilitarian perspective.

Moreover, as we saw above, it is also necessary to factor in the economic costs of ending factory farming or even extensive animal agriculture. Singer fails to do this adequately as do a number of pro-animal philosophers. Adding these costs clearly makes the utilitarian case for meat eating even stronger, although it would not necessarily justify intensive animal agriculture. For one thing, the costs of the economic losses experienced by those industries dependent upon factory farming has to be balanced against the fact that more traditional free-range forms of farming are more labour intensive and would create more agricultural employment (Carruthers, 1992: 64). For another, as DeGrazia (2002: 76) points out, 'the negative costs of ending factory farming would have to be borne only once, whereas perpetuating this institution entails that the costs to animals continue indefinitely'.

The problem with the utilitarian approach, as we revealed in chapter 6, is that the calculations necessary are difficult, if not impossible, to make, and this makes a definitive utilitarian judgement on an issue like meat eating problematic. All we can conclude is that, given the animal and human costs of animal agriculture, there is a strong case for saying that intensive forms of animal agriculture should be prohibited. However, this cannot be a precise moral judgement. In particular, it is difficult to say exactly at what point meat eating becomes morally acceptable. For an animal rights advocate such as Regan, of course, even this conclusion is unsatisfactory because meat eating is not completely ruled out.

Conclusion

The overriding conclusion deriving from this chapter is that by accepting the moral orthodoxy, as most people profess to do, much of what we do to animals in the pursuit of food is morally illegitimate. Indeed, there wouldn't seem to be a great deal of difference between the prescriptions mandated by the moral orthodoxy, the sentiency argument and Singer's utilitarianism. Only the view that animals have a right-to-life can make the eating of animals under the vast majority of circumstances morally wrong. To establish this position absolutely requires an acceptance of the argument from marginal cases. In terms of persuading the general public it may be a step too far. What we can say is that there is little moral justification for factory farming and there ought to be a consensus that it be ended or reformed significantly as soon as possible.

8

To Vivisect or Not to Vivisect?

In a committee room in the Palace of Westminster, the following exchange was heard during an inquiry into animal experimentation by a House of Lords select committee (HOL, 2002).

> *Earl of Onslow* (asking a question to the representatives from the National Antivivisection Society – NAVS): I am slightly of the impression . . . that what you are trying to do is make animal experimentation unnecessary rather than stop it per se . . .
> *Tim Phillips* (NAVS): The National Antivivisection Society is opposed to all animal experiments.
> *Earl of Onslow*: And would stop it now irrespective of the consequences?
> *Tim Phillips*: We believe there is no need for animal experimentation.
> *Earl of Onslow*: With respect, that is a different point of view. Irrespective of medical consequences you would like to see an end to vivisection now?
> *Tim Phillips*: Yes. We believe that animal experiments are wrong and we oppose them on those grounds. We also believe they are unnecessary . . .
> *Jan Creamer* (Director of NAVS): The way we view it is that we would like to see all animal experiments abolished . . .
> *Earl of Onslow*: Irrespective of the benefit to humanity and medical science . . . ?
> *Jan Creamer*: Yes, we would like to stop all experiments now.
> *Earl of Onslow*: Irrespective of the benefit it produces?
> *Jan Creamer*: We do not believe . . .
> *Earl of Onslow*: That is not, with respect, . . .

This exchange reveals a key distinction in the modern debate about animal experimentation, and illustrates the two-pronged strategy of the anti-vivisection movement. On the one hand, animal experimentation is condemned either because it doesn't produce the benefits to humans claimed for it, or because these benefits do exist but are trivial ones. On the other hand, the pincer action is maintained by a second claim that, in any case, animal experimentation is illegitimate, irrespective of its consequences for humans. It is no surprise that anti-vivisectionists have tended to focus, not so much on this second strand – the ethical validity of animal research – but on its utility (see, for instance, Ryder, 1975; Sharpe, 1988). A moral assessment of animal experimentation, however, involves a consideration of both of those claims.

Benefits and costs

Animal experimentation, or vivisection as it is often called, has occasioned the most heated debates of all animal issues. It is not difficult to understand the reasons why. It is, theoretically at least, possible to raise and kill animals for food with the minimum of suffering. As we saw in the previous chapter, there are a number of quite radical reforming steps that one can take short of prohibiting the raising and killing of animals for food. Indeed, the abolition of factory farming might, by making meat eating more acceptable morally, actually damage the case for vegetarianism. With animal experimentation, by contrast, there is much less room for compromise and reform. The very purpose of at least some animal experimentation is to inflict pain and suffering on animals and, indeed, it is often an inherent part of scientific procedures without which the work would not have a chance of achieving its objectives.

It is worth pausing a moment and reflecting on the content of that last sentence. We are rightly horrified at examples of torture inflicted on humans throughout the world, the details of which are often graphically displayed by groups such as Amnesty International. Leaving aside the reasons why we might do it for a moment, it is no exaggeration to state that animal experimentation does involve, at least some of the time, the torturing of animals. An example might help here. Recently, an anti-vivisection group in Britain publicized leaked reports of the suffering inflicted on primates in the course of xenotransplantation (animal to human transplant) experiments conducted by the Imutran company. An *Observer* report (20 April 2003) published descriptions of monkeys and baboons suffering from fits of vomiting and diarrhoea as they died. They also suffered from violent spasms and bloody discharges. Their behaviour expressed their pain, with grinding of teeth and manic eye movements. Some animals had completely withdrawn, lying in their cages apathetically.[1] As well as the infliction of pain, the use of animals in the laboratory includes the infliction of other forms of suffering. Not least is the potential psychological impact of keeping intelligent and social animals such as primates in isolation in barren cages.

The suffering inflicted on animals described in the last paragraph is difficult to stomach, and there is much more than space permits here. The debate about the moral validity of animal experimentation, however, is heated not just because of the severe nature of the suffering that can be inflicted on animals but also because of the significant nature of the benefits that it is claimed derive from them. So the suffering described above in the Imutran experiments has to be weighed against the enormous financial and medical benefits that would result from the successful development of animal-to-human transplants.

Vivisection in practice

To use the label vivisection as a description of what is done to animals in the laboratory is something of a misnomer. Vivisection, properly defined, refers to cutting and opening. Although some procedures using animals do involve cutting, many do not. Equally, we should not necessarily regard vivisection, narrowly defined, as the most morally problematic form of laboratory procedure, not least because it may be conducted on an animal under anaesthetic and not allowed to recover, whereas severe pain and suffering may be caused by a non-invasive procedure such as the testing of a household product on the eyes of a rabbit. Nevertheless, for the purposes of this chapter, the terms vivisection, animal experimentation and animal procedure will be used interchangeably.

Animal experimentation has a long history, dating back to ancient Greece, but it was only in the twentieth century, and particularly after 1945, that the number of animals used began to increase markedly. In Britain, where the Home Office collects annual statistics – originally under the 1876 Cruelty to Animals Act and since 1986 under the Animals (Scientific Procedures) Act – the number of animals used every year reached 5.5 million in the 1970s before declining. In 2002, there was a slight rise for the first time since the 1970s to 2.7 million, the rise explained entirely by the increasing use of genetically modified animals (HMSO, 2003).

Few other countries keep accurate and comprehensive statistics of the number of animals used, so it is difficult to calculate with any accuracy the total number of animals used worldwide. In the United States, for instance, federal government agencies reveal that around 1.5 million animals per year are used for scientific purposes. However, this figure does not include a number of species, including rats and mice, which constitute the vast majority of the animals used. A total of 20 million then would not be too far out. Worldwide, anything from 50–150 million animals has been cited.

A typology of animal experimentation requires us to identify the species being used, the nature of the procedure and its purpose. The bulk of animals used in the laboratory – customarily over 80 per cent in Britain – are rodents and particularly mice. The use of other mammals, and particularly non-human primates, is rarer but ethically more problematic. This is particularly the case where, as in many countries including the United States, the animals are not purpose bred, but taken from the wild or from pounds.

A bewildering array of procedures are carried out on animals. Some, such as the taking of blood, are relatively benign, whereas sometimes severe suffering is inflicted on animals, either as the deliberate intention of the procedure or – as in the example cited above – the unintended by-product of a particular procedure. For obvious reasons, the anti-vivisection movement tends to focus on the most severe examples of animal suffering. Before reciting some of these, it is important to distinguish between the procedures themselves and examples of suffering being inflicted on animals that is incidental to these procedures. For example, the anti-vivisection movement gained considerable publicity for revealing cruelties inflicted on primates during experiments conducted at the head injury laboratory at the University of Pennsylvania (Blum, 1994: 117–21). Videos were found showing researchers laughing at and abusing severely brain-damaged primates, smoking while carrying out procedures and using implements that had been dropped on to the floor. Obviously, such cruelties are not permissible morally by those who hold that animals have any moral standing, which only the most extreme Cartesian thinkers deny.

In terms of the procedures carried out it is important to note that most research intervenes directly with the physical state of an animal. This can be through surgical means or through the application of substances to the skin or eyes as in the Draize irritancy test or the LD50 test where, in the classical version, a group of animals are force-fed various substances until 50 per cent of them die. These are examples of toxicology tests that try to determine the safety of a wide variety of therapeutic products (such as drugs) and non-therapeutic products such as shampoos and cosmetics.

In addition, there is research carried out by behavioural psychologists. The severity of such research can vary. At the extreme end are the infamous maternal and sleep deprivation experiments pioneered by American scientists such as Harry Harlow, a highly respected psychologist, and John Oren. Harlow specialized in the creation of cloth surrogate mothers which, when introduced to infant monkeys, would turn into 'monsters' by being made to rock violently or eject compressed air or sharp spikes. Oren designed sleep deprivation experiments, involving forcing cats to run on a treadmill for up to sixteen hours, and placing them on a narrow plank inside a tank of water so that they are unable to lie down to sleep for fear of overbalancing and drowning (Orlans, 1993: 188).

As hinted above, the key distinction to be made when discussing the purpose of animal experimentation is between those procedures which have therapeutic purposes and those which do not. The former, constituting the bulk of the procedures, are those which are aimed at understanding and providing remedies for medical conditions. The latter includes basic biological research – which may have therapeutic applications when the results of the research are known – the toxicity testing of non-medical products, weapons testing and space research. The toxicity testing of cosmetics, household products and food constitutes a small proportion of the total number of procedures conducted (in Britain about 200,000 out of 2.7 million procedures in 2002) (HMSO, 2003: 57).

Special, and separate, mention should be made of the creation and use of genetically modified animals. This is likely to be the big growth area in future animal experimentation. Moreover, as we saw above, included within the arena of genetic modification are some of the most severe procedures ever inflicted on animals. By contrast, it is also claimed that the use of genetically modified animals offers us the prospect of some hugely important developments benefiting humans significantly. To add an extra dimension of complexity, the use of genetically modified animals has potentially huge negative impacts on humans as well.

The purposes of genetically modifying animals are varied. It has, for instance, an agricultural function of producing animals that will generate more meat, wool, eggs and milk. For the purposes of this chapter, however, the use of genetically modified animals as a means of improving human health is more important. They are already used in basic scientific research, where human genes are added to animals in order to produce more accurate models of human diseases. In the future there is the possibility of genetically modified animals being able to produce drugs from their blood, milk or eggs.

Finally, there is the already mentioned issue of xenotransplantation, the transplantation of cells, tissues and organs from one species to another. The use of animals for this purpose is deemed necessary because of the dire shortage of human organs. The biggest technical problem is the rejection of organs by their recipients. Two solutions to this problem are ethically contentious (Holland, 2003: 30–1). First, rejection is less likely if material from a species near to us is used. But of course the use of, for example, baboons, raises severe ethical difficulties. The second solution is genetically modifying animals to be used for transplantation. The reason why xenotransplantation may not be successful ultimately is because of the risk of potentially catastrophic transmission of animal viruses to humans.

Animal welfare and vivisection

What then of the ethics of vivisection? From the perspective of the moral orthodoxy, animal experimentation is justified morally if the suffering inflicted on animals serves a necessary human purpose. Animal experimentation law in many developed countries tries to operationalize the moral orthodoxy. This is particularly the case in Britain where the 1986 Animals (Scientific Procedures) Act contains a cost-benefit clause whereby Home Office inspectors reviewing applications for animal experimentation project licences are required to weigh up the potential benefits of the procedure against the suffering that is intended to be inflicted on the animals (for more detail on the legislation see Garner, 2004: chapter 5). Measures of mild, moderate and substantial suffering are used. In addition, even if it is recognized that there is a benefit to be had from animal research, their use must only be sanctioned if it is not possible to carry out the work some other way.

The British legislative framework actually goes further than the moral orthodoxy prescribes, or at least stretches its boundaries, in the sense that there is a 'termination condition' whereby an experiment must stop – irrespective of the consequences for the research – if the suffering inflicted exceeds what is allowed for in the licence. Moreover, since 1997, government ministers – following guidelines from advisers on the Animal Procedures Committee – have taken decisions not to approve licences for the testing of cosmetics, alcohol and tobacco on the grounds that such procedures cause unnecessary suffering to animals (Radford, 2001: 301–2). By contrast, the same ministers have, under considerable pressure from the research lobby, sought to defend, against a concerted campaign by the anti-vivisection movement, what they perceive to be the vital role played by animal experimentation in medical research.

The case for animal experimentation according to the moral orthodoxy then involves a weighing up of the costs and benefits. Take the genetic modification of animals. It need not necessarily be the case that genetically modified animals suffer, and insofar as they do not the practice is morally legitimate from the perspective of the moral orthodoxy. However, it is clearly the case that many animals do suffer as a result of genetic modification, either because it is inherent to the project or where the process has gone badly wrong, as in the infamous experiments in the United States to create more productive pigs, which resulted in animals with crippling arthritis, deformed skulls and poor vision (*Guardian*, 5 March 1997). Any suffering identified has to be balanced against the benefits to humans. These could be considerable. Scientists tell us that gentically modifying animals offers the prospect of much more convincing animal models of various human diseases. In addition, xenotransplantation is seen as a way of rectifying the desperate shortage of human organs available for transplants. As we have seen, however, the benefits of increased transplant availability need to be balanced against the transfer of viruses from animals to humans which could have a devastating effect on the human population.

In general terms, there has been a sustained public debate about the necessity of animal experimentation partly at least because, as was suggested earlier, anti-vivisectionists spend a great deal of their time disputing the necessity of animal experimentation rather than denying its ethical validity whatever the benefits it produces for humans. This can be described as the *practical anti-vivisection* approach in the sense that, contrary to the supporters of vivisection, it argues that animal research should be prohibited because the human benefits are either non-existent or not worth having (Francione, 2000: 31–49; Sharpe, 1988). From the standpoint of the practical anti-vivisection position, then, the legislative framework in Britain and everywhere else does not comply with the moral orthodoxy because if it did animal experimentation would be prohibited. This practical anti-vivisection approach can be distinguished from the approach of those who advocate reforms to animal experimentation – usually couched in the language of the three Rs of refinement, reduction and replacement (Russell and Burch, 1959) – but who nevertheless think that at least some animal experimentation is necessary and therefore ethically desirable because of the benefits to humans that accrue.

The central premise of the practical anti-vivisectionist case is based on the assertion that animal experimentation does not work and where it does work it is unnecessary, either because it is trivial or because there are alternative non-animal methods of achieving the same results. We can unwrap this position even further. A number of propositions derive from the central premise. These are, first, that the increased life expectancy of our own time, and the better health that accompanies it, is largely the product of improved environmental health. Sanitation, for instance, surely played a key role in reducing the impact of the major infectious diseases of the nineteenth century – bronchitis, pneumonia, influenza, cholera, typhoid and so on. Second, a related point is that no ultimately effective treatments have been developed for the modern killer diseases of heart disease and cancer. Most cases of cancer and heart disease, it may be claimed, are, in any case, preventable through better diet and giving up tobacco and alcohol.

Third, while animals have been used, and are virtually always used, in the development of new drugs or medical procedures, that is very different from saying that this use was fundamental for the key medical breakthroughs. Indeed, practical anti-vivisectionists argue that a mixture of clinical observation and pure chance has been more important. Moreover, it is suggested that on occasions the reliance on animals inhibits medical research breakthroughs. This is because, it is argued, animal models make very poor models of human conditions. Finally, animals are used unnecessarily, either because the drugs being developed and tested are so-called 'me too' drugs already produced by other companies or because the toxicity testing of animals for yet another household product or cosmetic is trivial.

It is beyond the scope of this chapter to examine the claims of the practical anti-vivisectionists in detail (see Garner, 2004: chapter 5 for a fuller analysis). A number of observations will suffice. In the first place, while it is ostensibly the case that these claims are subject to empirical validation, it is important to note that the debate between exponents and opponents of vivisection is also coloured by prior ethical assumptions. Three examples will illustrate this. Take, first, the issue of the need for drugs. Here, much depends on what we mean by a real need and in the vivisection debate the different sides have very different answers. For the practical anti-vivisectionist, the moral status of animals is set so highly that only those drugs which have life-saving potential should be included as a real need. Advocates of vivisection, by contrast, would draw the line much lower and sanction the production of drugs which have important medicinal properties, even if they are not absolutely essential. Indeed, advocates of vivisection might also regard the toxicity testing of cosmetic and household products as necessary, either because of the economic benefits ensuing or because of the benefits humans get from being able to use cosmetics.

Of course, practical anti-vivisectionists also argue that the use of animals is not the most decisive factor in the development of medicine. Determining the exact role that animals have played in medical discoveries is difficult, not least because of the problem of identifying the key point where a breakthrough has been made. It is undoubtedly the case, though, that animal experimentation has made a contribution to medical research, and to take away this option for scientists is to deprive them of one possible strand of enquiry that may be important. For the pro-vivisectionist, the possibility that the use of animals might produce important developments in medicine is enough to justify it. For the practical anti-vivisectionist, by contrast, a great deal more certainty that the use of animals is crucial is necessary before their use becomes justified.

The third illustration relates to the issue of personal responsibility. Many practical anti-vivisectionists argue that animals should not be used to try to find solutions to human ailments that are predominantly caused by individual lifestyle choices. Thus, it is asked, why should animals be asked to suffer so that there might one day be a cure for, say, lung cancer or heart disease when these diseases are the product, more often than not, of human choices to smoke and/or eat inappropriate foods. 'It's high time we started taking responsibility for the choices we make,' Rowlands (2002: 149) tells us in a classical example of this view, 'and not expecting someone or something else to suffer for those choices.'

There may be a lot of force in the choice argument described above. What it does reveal, however, is that for practical anti-vivisectionists the moral status of animals is such that they should only be used when absolutely necessary, and this does not include cases where humans have brought problems on themselves. For advocates of vivisection, on the other hand, the importance attached to human interests and the corresponding belief in the minimal nature of the moral status of animals, leads to the view that it would be morally illegitimate not to try to help those humans with life-threatening conditions, even where the condition was preventable. Finally, of course, not all cases of cancer or heart disease or HIV/AIDS occur because humans have chosen to put themselves at risk. Are we to say to them we can't help them because others have the diseases because of their lifestyle choices?

In a purely empirical, as opposed to normative, sense, it can be said that some animal experimentation for the reasons explored above is illegitimate even from the perspective of the moral orthodoxy. As we saw, it is becoming increasingly recognized that some experiments – such as for the toxicity testing of cosmetics – are illegitimate because they are regarded as unnecessary. Some medical research fits into the same category. For example, the sleep and maternal deprivation experiments described above would seem to be ruled out because of their severity and because there is the option of examining those (many) humans who have been subject to various kinds of childhood neglect. The scientists conducting the maternal deprivation experiments with monkeys found that maternal deprivation impacts profoundly negatively on the subject. Isn't this obvious, one might ask?

Equally, it has to be accepted that, although the benefits of animal experimentation may have been exaggerated, it does at least sometimes have beneficial consequences. Many pro-animal philosophers are prepared to admit this much. Singer (1990: 91) concedes, for instance, that: 'No doubt there have been some advances in knowledge which would not have been attained as easily without using animals' (see also Rowlands, 2002: 144). Francione too (2000: 42), despite adopting a practical anti-vivisection position, does not dispute that humans have learnt something from animal experimentation, and only wants to challenge the vivisection community's view that 'all animal use is concerned with finding cures for human diseases or improving human health'. We can readily agree that Francione is right without giving up the central point that at least some vivisection does produce human benefits that are substantial.

Accepting that some animal experiments have produced results is very different from accepting such benefits as morally acceptable ones. However, if we want to advocate a complete prohibition on vivisection we have to look to other ethical positions that prohibit the use of animals whatever the benefits of such use for us. As Singer (1990: 92) remarks, rather oddly for a utilitarian, the 'ethical question of the justifiability of animal experimentation cannot be settled by pointing to its benefits for us'.

The sentiency view and vivisection

It is by no means clear that what happens in Britain, let alone in other countries, is consistent with the moral orthodoxy, not least because of the difficulties of enforcing effectively the animal experimentation legislation that is in place (Garner, 1998: 198–200; 223–7). If we move beyond the moral orthodoxy, it is crystal clear that there is a gap between the 'is' and the 'ought'. Take the sentiency view. Insofar as research using animals can be shown to contribute to the longevity of human life and involves no pain being inflicted on animals, from the perspective of the sentiency view, it is morally legitimate. This is because, the reader will remember, the sentiency view holds that the infliction of pain on humans and animals is, all things being equal, morally equivalent but human life is superior to animal life.

Much depends here, of course, upon the empirical validity of the claims made by researchers, not, as we have seen, an easy thing to evaluate. The research on animals that has no prospect of contributing to the longevity of human life, on the other hand, remains illegitimate. The key point here is the infliction of pain. All of the research that causes animals anything more than minor pain ought to be prohibited according to the sentiency view, a position, of course, which puts it at odds with the moral orthodoxy and the actual current practice. Research, even of an extremely invasive kind, however, is legitimate according to the sentiency view providing that the animal is anaesthetized and is either not allowed to recover or provided with enough pain-killers to experience nothing but the mildest discomfort.

Rights and animal experimentation

As with the eating of animals, the only way of morally prohibiting the use of animals in the laboratory out of hand is to accord to them a right-to-life. Thus, just as it is illegitimate to use humans for experiments that might produce benefits, it is equally illegitimate to use animals as a means to an end, whatever the level of suffering inflicted on them in the process. From an animal rights perspective, for instance, the genetic alteration of animals is unacceptable because it infringes their fundamental rights. This position can be described as *ethical anti-vivisection* to distinguish it from the *practical anti-vivisection* we encountered earlier. Both positions reach the conclusion that animal experimentation is morally illegitimate but from different routes, the former ruling it out irrespective of the benefits that might accrue, and the latter ruling it out because the benefits are regarded as either non-existent or not worth having.

Regan (1984: 363–94) very clearly adopts a version of ethical anti-vivisection. Since at least some animals are subjects-of-a-life, for reasons that we explored in an earlier chapter, all laboratory uses of such animals should be prohibited since they violate rights. To use animals in the laboratory is to treat them 'as if their value was reducible to their possible utility relative to our interests' and since animals 'have a value of their own, logically independently of their utility for others it is morally wrong to do so' (ibid.: 384–5). This, then, explicitly rules out the use of animals even if substantial benefits are likely to accrue. As Regan (ibid.: 393) insists, 'the harm done to animals in pursuit of scientific purposes is wrong. The benefits derived are real enough; but some gains are ill-gotten, and all gains are ill-gotten when secured unjustly.'

A consistent application of Regan's theory in its entirety, however, raises doubts about its claim to justify the complete abolition of animal experimentation. As we saw in chapter 5, Regan – seemingly in order to comply with what he perceives to be our moral intuition – wants to argue that human lives are more important than animal lives, so that in a lifeboat example if we have to choose between a human and an animal we should always choose the human, providing that the human is adult and healthy. Indeed, he goes further by suggesting that a human life is worth any number of animal lives.

Now, as was pointed out in chapter 7, Regan's valuation of human and animal lives has no bearing on his claim that vegetarianism is morally compulsory because most of us do not need to eat meat in order to stay alive. In vivisection, however, the comparable value of human and animal lives does come into play. This is because advocates of vivisection do claim that using animals in scientific procedures does, in a way that no alternative could, contribute to the longevity of human life. So, it seems, Regan cannot hold at one and the same time the positions that animal lives can be sacrificed to save human lives and that all animal experimentation is morally prohibited.

Regan denies the conclusion that animal experimentation is justified even though human lives are more valuable than animal lives. This is, he argues, because there is a distinct difference between the lifeboat example cited above and the situation regarding animal experimentation. The difference is that the lifeboat example depicts a situation where all of those on board would die if nothing is done. In the case of vivisection this is not so because the animals used will not die if they are not used in the laboratory. In this situation, where one party is not threatened by inaction, to harm them is illegitimate because it is to treat them as a means to an end.

Regan provides us with another lifeboat scenario to illustrate animal experimentation (1984: 385). In this example, the lifeboat is well stocked so there is no question of starvation if someone is not sacrificed. Rather, in this example the lifeboat contains four adults, all with a degenerative brain disease, and a healthy dog. Regan then supposes that also on board is a medicine that may provide the cure to the disease and also the means to give the same degenerative disease to the dog. In this situation, he asks, would it be permissible to administer the drug to the dog to test its properties? The answer for Regan (1984: 385) is no because:

> Animals are not to be treated as if their value were reducible *merely* to their possible utility relative to human interests, which is what the survivors would be doing if they made the healthy animal (who, after all, stands to gain nothing and lose everything) run their risks in their stead.

While Regan is correct to note the difference between his original lifeboat example and the situation pertaining in the case of a choice whether or not to use animals in the laboratory, it is by no means clear this gets him off the hook. This is because, while it is true that in his revised lifeboat example the dog would come to no harm if a decision was made not to administer the drug, there still remains a choice to be made. This choice in general terms is whether we decide to use animals with the objective of saving human and/or animal lives in the future. And since Regan admits that human lives are worth more than animal lives, aren't we still duty bound to use animals so as to save human lives? If this experimentation involves little pain and suffering, although it does mean death, then the case for going ahead seems even stronger.

If we do not accept Regan's answer to the inconsistency charge, there would seem to be a number of ways that his anti-vivisectionism can still be rescued. One way would be for him to drop the insistence that human lives are more valuable. This principle seems to derive from Regan's desire to remain close to what he perceives to be moral intuition. But why, it might be asked, should intuition always be right and why should an animal rights advocate such as Regan be concerned with following it so avidly?

The second way that Regan's anti-vivisectionism can be rescued is by invoking the argument from marginal cases. Those who accept the validity of the argument from marginal cases would have to conclude that, unless we also consider using marginal humans in the laboratory, we should not use animals either, irrespective of the fact that their lives are less valuable than those of normal adult humans. Most of us would probably want to accept the categorical version of the argument from marginal cases – that because we do not feel it is right to use marginal humans, we should not use animals. There is some philosophical support, however, for the biconditional version, which leaves open the possibility of using marginal humans and thereby being able to use animals. If this is accepted then the argument from marginal cases no longer rescues Regan.

The notion that we might actually consider using marginal humans for experimental purposes has come, as we saw in chapter 4, principally from Frey (1983: 111–15; 2002). As a utilitarian, Frey recognizes that benefits can occur through animal experimentation. But he also recognizes that the justification for using animals, on the grounds that humans unlike animals have full-personhood, breaks down if we insist on treating marginal humans, who are not full-persons, as if they were. Therefore, in order to continue getting the benefits of animal experimentation while remaining morally correct we must also be prepared to use marginal humans.

As discussed in chapter 4, it is not necessarily counter-intuitive to argue for the differential treatment of normal and marginal humans. To some degree, it happens in practice as in the allocation of scarce medical resources. Of course, as we also indicated in chapter 4, there is quite a difference between withdrawing medical treatment from a marginal human and using him or her in a scientific experiment which involves the deliberate infliction of pain or other harm. Even the use of marginal humans to benefit the health of others is not entirely counter-intuitive. Holland (2003: 46), to give one example, discusses the possibility of using the organs of anencephalic babies for transplant. The utilization of such humans with little if no capacity for consciousness is significantly different, however, from the infliction of pain and suffering on a thinking, feeling human. Few, if any, would really countenance that as morally acceptable in anything but the most exceptional circumstances.

Utilitarianism and vivisection

Singer, writing from a utilitarian perspective, also wants to claim that animal experimentation is morally wrong. The application of the equal consideration of interests principle, he argues, 'would mean the end of the vast industry of animal experimentation as we know it today' (Singer, 1990: 87). However, as with the issue of eating animals discussed in the last chapter, it is not clear that a utilitarian can say, at least not without a great deal of empirical research, that all animal experimentation is illegitimate. A classical utilitarian would have to accept non-painful experiments as morally unproblematic. For the others, the costs and benefits of inflicting pain and suffering on animals would have to be examined. Indeed, the use of animals in the laboratory would seem to be the classic example of an issue where aggregating interests is most appropriate. Who would argue against the sacrifice of a few individuals if the end result is a cure for cancer or some other terrible affliction? Singer actually seems to concur. He writes (1993: 67): 'if one, or even a dozen animals had to suffer experiments in order to save thousands, I would think it right and in accordance with equal consideration of interests that they should do so.' The problem here is that utilitarianism is not so selective and would sanction the use of animals in experiments even if the benefits were only marginally greater than the costs. As Regan (1984: 392) accurately comments, for a utilitarian: 'If the consequences that result from harming animals would produce the best aggregate balance of good over evil, then harmful experimentation is permissible.'

This scenario would be unacceptable to Singer. Indeed, as we saw, he wants to claim that his preference utilitarianism would, on balance, prohibit the vast majority of animal experimentation, if not all. To justify this claim Singer has to show that the use of animals in the laboratory does not produce the claims made for it, either because animal experiments do not work or because they are unnecessary. As we have seen, he has a reasonably strong case here, but it is not credible to say that no animal experiments have in the past or will in the future provide important benefits for humans and, indeed, other animals. Moreover, Singer would have to take the interests of everyone into account. Thus, as well as the interests of the animals and the possible future benefits that might accrue to humans and animals, a utilitarian would also have to take into account 'the interests of those who do the tests or conduct the research, their employers, the dependants of these persons, the retailers and wholesalers of cages, animal breeders', to name but a few of those with a stake in animal experimentation (Regan, 1984: 393).

Singer has a fall back position here which was not available to him in the case of agricultural animals. Singer adopts a non-speciesist version of utilitarianism, and this is where his position differs from the moral orthodoxy. This non-speciesist version holds that, unlike the moral orthodoxy which adopts what Singer would regard as a speciesist version of utilitarianism, human interests in not suffering must, all things being equal, count the same as the equivalent interests of animals. He is entitled to ask, therefore, whether there is a case for sacrificing the interests of humans in animal experiments. The equivalent argument was not really available to him in the context of eating animals because the vast majority of humans would balk at the prospect of eating other members of their species.

Most humans, too, would be deeply opposed, of course, at the thought of using members of their own species in painful and possibly fatal experiments.[2] Like the employment of the categorical version of the argument from marginal cases, maybe Singer relies on this opposition to illustrate why we should not use animals either in such experiments. Intuitively, I suspect, most of us would concur with the view that it is repugnant to use humans as experimental objects. As a utilitarian, however, this route is not open to Singer – except perhaps if he was an advocate of a version of rule utilitarianism (which he is not). As a result, Singer would have to consider the possibility of using humans in animal experimentation. Given the problems we encountered earlier, of animals being poor models for human ailments, it may be that, on a purely technical basis, there is a strong case for using humans rather than animals to find cures for human conditions.

Conclusion

This chapter has revealed that there is a strong case, even from the perspective of the moral orthodoxy, for reforming animal experimentation. Too often, the uses of animals are unnecessary either because trivial or because they do not produce the benefits claimed. Although it is a clever tactic for anti-vivisectionists to focus increasingly on the utility of using animals in the laboratory, it would be inaccurate to claim that the use of animals produces no benefits. Indeed, sometimes these benefits are considerable. To rule out animal experimentation in most circumstances, then, requires us to adopt an animal rights position. A middle-way position, which I believe could generate a great deal of public support, is provided by the application of the sentiency view. Here, animals can be used in the laboratory but only when there is an expectation of substantial benefit accruing, and only when the pain inflicted on animals is minimized or, even better, eliminated.

9

Zoos, Pets and Wild Animals

In addition to being eaten and experimented on, animals are used in a variety of other ways. This chapter serves as a home for a discussion of these, sometimes disparate, uses. Basically, we can divide these remaining animal issues into two broad categories. The first I would label entertainment. This includes the ethics of domesticating animals as pets, and their use in circuses and zoos. In addition, other forms of entertainment using animals, which constraints of space prevent us from considering, include bull-fighting, rodeos, greyhound racing, and horse-racing. Second, there is the broad category of wild animals. There is some overlap here, in the sense that wild caught animals are kept in zoos, circuses and as pets. For the purposes of this chapter, however, once wild animals are caught they are included within the category of domesticated animals. In this chapter I want to consider the ethics of our behaviour towards non-domesticated wild animals in general, and this will be achieved largely through a discussion of the ethics of hunting them.

Superficially at least, the issues raised in this chapter do not seem to be as morally problematic as the raising and killing of animals for food and their use in the laboratory. This is partly because fewer animals are involved here than in animal agriculture, and the level of deliberate infliction of suffering is not equal to that occurring in vivisection, and partly because some of the uses to be discussed in this chapter are morally unproblematic, either because they are clearly morally legitimate or because they are quite clearly, under any but the most Cartesian outlook, morally illegitimate. As a result, the issues to be raised in this chapter have not produced the same kind of fundamental moral conflict as the use of animals for food and in the laboratory. To be sure, hunting, particularly in Britain, has been an issue of considerable political conflict. This chapter will attempt to show, however, that the moral case for hunting is weak even from the perspective of the moral orthodoxy.

Companion animals

As well as being sources of food and medical advance, animals have also been a source of entertainment for humans. In the past, this has produced what would now be regarded as morally unacceptable levels of suffering undertaken merely for human amusement. The classic example of this total disregard for the interests of animals was the slaughter of millions of animals in Roman amphitheatres. In Britain, cock- and dog-fighting and bear-baiting were common activities. It was not until the nineteenth century in Britain that legislative action was forthcoming and a more enlightened moral climate developed.[1]

The legislation governing the treatment of domesticated animals kept as pet or companion animals remains, in Britain, the Protection of Animals Act 1911, an amalgam of various nineteenth-century statutes. This legislation sets out a classic animal welfare position, replicated in many countries in the world, whereby the law is transgressed if substantial suffering is inflicted on an animal unnecessarily.

From the perspective of the moral orthodoxy, the keeping of companion animals is, by itself, morally unproblematic. Many of the millions of animals kept by humans as their companions are well cared for and few, if any, welfare problems arise. Moreover, the humane killing of companion animals raises no moral issues from the animal welfare perspective. Indeed, the willingness of veterinarians and the owners of animals to have sick animals with no realistic chance of recovery humanely destroyed should be applauded ethically. Surprisingly high numbers of companion animals are, however, deliberately harmed or, as is most common, neglected to the point where severe suffering ensues. There are, for instance, commonly 2–3,000 cruelty convictions in Britain per year, and many cases of cruelty where the RSPCA issues cautions and advice for better treatment (*Guardian*, 28 June 2001).

In the case of companion animals, where there is no perceived benefit from exploitation as in the case of food and laboratory animals, the infliction of suffering is usually unnecessary and therefore falls foul of the moral orthodoxy and the law in most developed countries. Since the infliction of suffering is not an inherent part of pet-keeping, however, the institution is not condemned as a result of the actions of the relatively few who abuse companion animals. That is not to say that, even from the perspective of the moral orthodoxy, some reforms are not necessary. Tougher sentences for cruelty would be welcomed as would the blanket introduction of measures preventing those guilty of cruelty from owning animals again. Some animals make unsuitable pets, and others, such as birds and small mammals, should not really be kept confined in isolation in small cages. The often brutal trade in exotic wild birds should be prohibited and the laws designed to protect endangered species of birds properly enforced.

If we go beyond the moral orthodoxy, the moral acceptability of keeping animals as pets becomes less clear. From a utilitarian perspective, it is necessary to weigh up any suffering that might be inflicted on companion animals with the benefits to humans of the practice. This must include not just the benefits, often psychological, of pet ownership but also other interested parties such as the breeders and pet shops, the pet food industry, the veterinary profession, and the pharmaceutical companies.

There are those who, arguing from an animal rights position, insist that the keeping of companion animals infringes their rights. John Bryant, a long-time British animal rights activist, for instance, writes that 'I have not the slightest hesitation in saying that pet animals should be completely phased out of existence.' This is because, for Bryant, pets are 'slaves and prisoners' and the fact that they may be well-fed, loved and not in pain is irrelevant just as it would be if we were discussing human slaves (Bryant, 1990: 9–10).

It is not clear to me that Bryant is correct here, but since his critique can also apply to the keeping of wild animals in captivity – in zoos and circuses – I will consider it in detail later in the chapter after the ways in which humans domesticate wild animals have been examined. For now, it should be noted that the destruction of healthy animals is illegitimate from the rights perspective. The existence of large numbers of strays is a perennial problem for public authorities and those agencies responsible for dealing with the issue. In the United States, in particular, many millions of healthy cats and dogs are destroyed every year merely because their owners abandoned them. Many agencies, such as the RSPCA in Britain and countless shelters in the United States, operate a policy of the humane destruction of unwanted pets.

While justified ethically by the moral orthodoxy, even animal welfarists are increasingly concerned that by killing large numbers of animals they are unwittingly preventing the introduction of a viable solution to the problem of strays – such as greater penalties for abandoning animals and a dog registration scheme so that owners can be traced. From the perspective of the rights view, the destruction of healthy animals is morally prohibited and, if it becomes clear that the institution of pet-keeping cannot be divorced from the production of huge numbers of unwanted animals, then the moral validity of the whole institution is brought into question by the rights perspective.

Domesticated wild animals

The human species has long sought to capture and display wild animals. The keeping of animal collections dates back to Ancient Egypt, but the first modern zoos were created from the late eighteenth century and became hugely popular institutions in nineteenth-century Britain, not least because many of the animals came from far-flung parts of the British Empire and their capture symbolized British dominion (Ritvo, 1987: 205–42). As well as being kept in zoos, wild animals are used in circuses and marine mammal displays. These latter two institutions are much more ethically problematic than zoos because their major purpose is to entertain the public, whereas zoos claim a broader array of benefits. As a result, relatively trivial benefits can be easily outweighed by the undoubted suffering that takes place. The case against circuses, even from the perspective of the moral orthodoxy, is made stronger by the fact that they can prosper without the use of animals.

Animal suffering in circuses has been increasingly recognized. Sometimes this is deliberately inflicted cruelty as a result of the training methods adopted (Johnson, 1990: 96–112). More often than not the suffering occurs as a consequence of the need to keep animals – such as tigers, lions and elephants – confined and moved from one location to another. 'Limitations of space, loss of social structure, and abnormal behaviour help chart the dimensions of animal suffering in circuses' (Regan, 2004: 126). As we shall see with zoos, it is difficult to generalize about circuses since the degree to which they rely on animal 'acts' differs. Moreover, the degree of regulatory supervision also varies from country to country, non-existent in Spain and Portugal but quite thorough in Finland, Sweden and Norway (Johnson, 1990: 318). It is well nigh impossible, however, to avoid inflicting suffering on wild animals in circuses.

The use of dolphins – and other marine mammals such as orcas, seals and sea lions – as a source of entertainment can be equally condemned because of the level of suffering involved (Johnson, 1990: 165–313; Regan, 2004: 134–9). Dolphins are extremely intelligent mammals, and they are not only harmed by their removal from the wild but their captivity has been shown to cause enormous suffering, as the animals try to cope with a barren environment shorn of social life and space. Life expectancy and breeding rates of captive dolphins are much lower than in the wild and signs of abnormal behaviour, the kind that we noticed in the case of factory farmed animals, have been noted too. Against this, marine mammal displays provide limited conservation and education functions. Entertainment remains by far the most important rationale, and of course with entertainment comes money for the owners. In Britain, unlike the United States, marine mammal parks no longer exist, not because they are illegal but because people have recognized their ethically problematic nature, and are no longer prepared to patronize them.

It is estimated that, worldwide, some 5 million animals are kept in about 10,000 zoos, which have become the most important means of domesticating wild animals. From a strict animal rights perspective, zoos (as well as marine mammal displays and circuses) might be regarded as morally illegitimate because captivity deprives animals of the crucial right to freedom or autonomy, although below I will dispute this blanket condemnation. If we reject an animal rights or Cartesian perspective, morally assessing zoos is difficult. This is partly because they differ markedly in quality, partly because the level of suffering inflicted depends crucially on species, and partly because the benefits claimed for at least some zoos are much more varied than circuses.

The very best zoos provide environments that maximize the chances of animals being able to perform their natural behaviour. The very worst ones provide such poor conditions for the animals that they are condemned even by the moral orthodoxy. Even in Britain, which has in the region of 400 zoos, standards are variable not least because those insisted upon by the regulatory mechanism are pretty minimal. Stereotypical behaviour of the type described in chapter 7 – including excessive grooming, pacing, and self-mutilation – is common among the animals in the poorest quality zoos, and difficulties with conceiving and rearing offspring is another indicator of stress. Even the very best zoos find it difficult to cater for the largest, most complex mammals. The polar bear provides the paradigmatic example of an animal whose natural behaviour patterns are impossible to replicate in captivity and, as a consequence, very few reputable zoos will now countenance exhibiting them. There is increasing evidence that elephants and big cats suffer from captivity too (*Guardian*, 23 October 2002). The needs of other, usually smaller, species, however, are much easier to meet, and relatively minor adjustments to their environments can greatly improve the quality of their lives.

Clearly, unless zoos provide a very good environment for the animals and no species are kept which are difficult to cater for, then the moral orthodoxy would prohibit zoos if the only purpose of their existence was the amusement and entertainment of paying customers. Unlike circuses and marine mammal displays, however, zoos claim a variety of different functions, and in terms of both utilitarianism and the moral orthodoxy, these claims need to be examined before a reasoned conclusion on the morality of zoos can be arrived at. In addition to entertainment, zoos claim to provide an educative function, a research function and a conservation function. It must be questioned whether even those zoos which make an effort in this direction can provide much of educational value. This is particularly the case now that natural history television programmes show the lives of wild animals in their natural habitats, not in small cages! As Rowlands (2002: 155) points out: 'The complete failure of zoos to succeed in their supposedly educational mission seems to stem in part from the fact that many of them make no real effort at education, but also, in part, from the apathetic and unappreciative character of the majority of the zoo-going public.'

Research undertaken by zoos is either field research, where animals are studied in their natural habitat, or research on animals confined in zoos (Rowlands, 2002: 156–7). It is not clear why zoos are required to fund field research, and most do not anyway. Very few zoos do research on their own animals, not least because what can be done to them is limited by the need to continue to exhibit them. Research can be limited to behavioural studies, as opposed to invasive anatomical work, but then what can we learn from animals artificially confined, except maybe that confinement damages them? Again, studies of animals in the wild would seem to be a much more preferable alternative and most of this work is not funded by zoos.

It is the conservation function that has been emphasized by zoo authorities in recent years (Tudge, 1992). Here, the claim is that captive breeding programmes have made a substantial contribution to the problem of threatened and endangered species. Indeed, some species, such as the tamarin monkey and the European bison, would be extinct now if it wasn't for zoos. Moreover, the creation of gene banks may be vital in future reintroductions.

There are a number of weaknesses with the conservation argument, however. In the first place, whereas some zoos, such as London

Zoo, do useful conservation work, many do little or no such work. Most zoo animals are, in fact, not endangered anyway. Second, even though the survival of particular species may serve certain human interests – such as aesthetics or economics – it is not an animal welfare issue. Indeed, it may be better to destroy humanely animals who struggle to cope with captivity, irrespective of the fact that they are members of an endangered species. Third, zoo conservation programmes are irrelevant to the extent that the biggest threat to wild animals is loss of habitat. Breeding them in zoos, therefore, does not address the habitat problem so that, in many cases, even if breeding programmes are successful there is not the remotest chance that the animals can be reintroduced into the wild. It is not clear anyway why breeding programmes have to be undertaken in zoos, as opposed to specialist breeding centres.

Zoos, companion animals and the rights view

We saw earlier that it has been suggested keeping animals as pets infringes their rights. The argument, by Bryant, applies equally well to captive wild animals, although he does not make the link. An animal rights critique of the zoo therefore would be that, however good the environment provided for the animals, it is a morally illegitimate institution because it infringes their right to freedom. Now, clearly, where animals are confined *and* their interests are harmed it makes sense to talk about their rights being infringed. In many cases this happens in zoos and, insofar as it does, that particular zoo is illegitimate from the rights perspective because it infringes the rights of the animals kept captive. Similarly, it makes sense to say that if a companion animal loses his or her freedom in such a way that it causes harm then that, too, is an illegitimate infringement of rights.

If, however, the right to liberty is theoretically infringed because an animal is held captive, but little or no harm to the animal results, then it does not seem sensible to say that this captivity is morally illegitimate, either in the case of zoos or companion animals. To make this claim of moral illegitimacy, it seems to me, is equivalent to saying that denying animals a right to vote or a right to worship is a genuine deprivation. Clearly it isn't. Rachels (1990: 121–3) is right to point out that it only makes sense to grant rights in accordance with the harms that are likely to accrue if those rights were to be infringed. Depriving animals of a right to vote or worship is not to harm them. DeGrazia (2002: 82–4) makes a similar point when he distinguishes between '*captivity*, which restricts one's liberty, and *confinement* in our specific sense: restricting liberty in a way that significantly inter-feres with one's ability to live well'. Only the latter case is morally illegitimate, because 'only confinement entails harm'.

To summarize, then, although keeping animals as companions or in zoos is nominally tantamount to infringing their right to liberty, it only becomes morally relevant when this infringement causes harm. For some pro-animal philosophers, this loss of autonomy always causes harm. Rowlands (2002: 153), for instance, comments that 'confinement in a zoo is, almost certainly, a thwarting of one of the most vital interests of an animal' (see also Francione, 2000: 23–5). I am less clear that this is so. It will depend upon the nature of the zoo and the species. Well-resourced and organized zoos which provide environmental enrichment are, therefore, better than cramped and barren zoos. Similarly, well-cared-for companion animals which, for at least some of the time, are provided with appropriate exercise and the ability to socialize with members of their species are better off than animals confined in isolation.

In other words, what is being claimed here is that in the case of companion animals and zoos the degree to which captivity harms animals will be a matter of empirical examination. For example, those animals – such as polar bears – who are prevented by captivity from performing their natural behaviour clearly have their rights infringed. Likewise, 'when you have a wolf in a Spanish zoo confined, in iso-lation, in a small, sterile, concrete run, then it does not take much intelligence or imagination to realize that the life of that unfortunate creature is going to be one of overwhelming misery' (Rowlands, 2002: 153). As a result their captivity is morally illegitimate from the rights perspective. Many zoo animals, however, are not affected in the same way and their captivity is therefore not, or less, morally illegitimate.

Wild animals

The dominant ways of thinking about wild animals do not sit easily with the theories that have preoccupied us in this book. This is pri-marily because the dominant mode of conservationism is holistic in nature. That is, attention, in theory and practice, is directed towards the protection of species or ecosystems and not to the protection and well-being of individual animals. It is therefore permissible in the case of a holistic conservation ethic to sacrifice the interests of indi-vidual animals if by so doing the integrity of a species or ecosystem is maintained.

There are two main types of conservation, an anthropocentric and an ecocentric version. Much wildlife conservation in practice is anthropocentric in nature. That is, the major purpose of protecting wild animals lies in the value they provide for us (Moore,1987; Passmore, 1974). In other words, it is a version of the indirect duty view we encountered in chapter 3. Humans may wish to preserve wild animals for a variety of reasons, from the aesthetic pleasure they gain from their existence to medicinal or economic benefit that might accrue. Virtually all international wildlife treaties emphasize the benefits to humans of conservation. To take one classical example, the treaty set up to protect whales in the 1940s (The International Convention for the Regulation of Whaling) was designed not to protect whales for their own sake but so as to ensure that enough whale stocks were left to continue catching them. In more recent years, non-whaling nations, with very different ethical positions, have come to predominate in the treaty and, as a result, it has proven difficult for the whaling nations to insist that whaling continues when it is deemed stocks are large enough to avoid extinction (Cherfas, 1988; Garner, 1994).

The ecocentric version of wildlife conservation is equally holistic (Fox, 1984; Leopold, 1949; Naess, 1973). By contrast with the anthropocentric version, however, it regards not just wild animals as having moral standing but also nature as a whole. That is, wild animals and other living and inanimate parts of nature are regarded as having value independently of the value they have for humans. This position, sometimes described as a genuine environmental ethic, does not necessarily regard all parts of nature – sentient and non-sentient, human and non-human – as of equal value. However, it does open the prospect of sacrificing the interests of humans if by so doing the ecological balance can be maintained.

It is important to recognize that two versions of holism can be identified here. The first version of holism holds that value lies in the whole ecosystem and not in individuals who can be sacrificed to maintain the integrity of the whole. In other words, it is being claimed that ecosystems 'have a good independent of that of their component individuals, and as such have their own moral standing' (Attfield, 2003: 11). This kind of approach is associated, above all, with Aldo Leopold, a founding father of environmental ethics, who wrote in a famous – or infamous depending on your point of view – passage that: 'A thing is right when it tends to preserve the integrity, stability and beauty of the biotic community. It is wrong when it tends otherwise' (1949: 217). A relevant corollary of this position is that extreme holistic environmentalists tend to regard domesticated animals as of little worth and, in some cases, a blight on the land-scape (Callicot, 1995: 50).

An alternative version of holism is less extreme in the sense that although ecosystems have value, this value, in Attfield's words (2003: 10), 'arises . . . from the way that ecosystems facilitate the lives and the flourishing of the numerous individual creatures that comprise them or depend on them'. In other words, individuals have value but it is recognized that the only way in which wildlife can survive is if they have a sustainable environment. It follows that in order to main-tain a sustainable environment it may be necessary, from time to time, to sacrifice individual animals. This is not to be done because ulti-mate value rests with the whole, but because this is the only way that the vast majority of the animals can survive.

The holistic nature of both anthropocentric and ecocentric versions of conservation tends to result in a focus on the plight of endangered species. There is also a preoccupation with endangered species in international wildlife treaties, where one of the most important is the Convention on International Trade In Endangered Species of Wild Fauna and Flora (CITES), a treaty designed to prevent trade in those species deemed to be endangered or threatened. At the national level too, it is invariably endangered species or those species that have some particular value to humans which are privileged legislatively. In Britain, for instance, it is only relatively recently that a general anti-cruelty statute has applied to non-captive wild animals. In the meantime, other wild animals, such as badgers and otters, are comprehensively protected (Radford, 2001: 213).

This perceived need to protect endangered species has led to some potential confusions which a thorough account of animal ethics must clear up. The CITES treaty demands that trade in those species deemed to be endangered is prohibited. Controversy has particularly centred on the African elephant. Sought for their valuable ivory, elephants were hunted almost to extinction before the trade was banned. In many African countries, and particularly Kenya, the elephant was protected by the state to the point where poachers were shot on sight. The fact that the attacking of elephants by humans was to be eliminated – coupled with the fact that the inter-ests of the elephants appeared to be given greater weight than the interests of local people who were damaged by their existence – might lead us to suppose that this is a practical application of animal rights. Indeed, so much had the balance switched towards the elephants that a strong, and partly successful, campaign has been mounted over the past few years (principally by Southern African states) for an alternative sustainable use policy which allows for the need to cull some elephants to provide economic benefits from their ivory and meat.

The protection of elephants, however, is not an example of animal rights against which the advocates of sustainable use are arrayed. Rather, it is an example of competing anthropocentric motives (Garner, 1994). On the one side are those in favour of exploiting the elephant for its ivory and other products. On the other are those who see the elephant as a source of income from tourism. This includes Western governments and conservation organizations, with no vested interest in the killing of elephants for economic gain, who are keen for the elephant to survive so that its beauty and splendour can still exist.

The focus on endangered species, by anthropocentric and ecocentric versions of conservationism, is understandable since extinctions can alter the balance of a particular ecosystem as well as ending the human benefit – whether aesthetic, medicinal or economic – that members of the extinct species provided. Moreover, the disappearance of many species provides a startling illustration of the way in which the interests of wild animals have been sacrificed by humans. The evidence suggests that humans are causing extinctions to occur at many times more than the natural rate would otherwise have done (*Guardian*, 29 September 2000). We have identified and catalogued a small proportion of the total number of species living on the earth – about $1\frac{1}{2}$ million out of between 5 and 30 million (Regenstein, 1985: 119). From an anthropocentric perspective, this level of extinction may have prevented us from discovering hugely important new medicines as well as denying us economic opportunities.

Animal welfare and wildlife conservation

Because of the dominant role played by holism in wildlife conservation, little role has been found for advocates of animal welfare. Wildlife conservation has not been an arena where issues of animal cruelty have been much mentioned, partly at least, I suspect, because nature is regarded as red in tooth and claw anyway, whatever humans do to wildlife. Moreover, the biggest threat to wild animals has come, not from deliberate acts of cruelty, but from loss of habitat caused by human encroachment. There are exceptions, though. There has been, for instance, an animal welfare dimension to whaling, with some claiming that it is not the killing of whales per se that is the problem but the *way* it is done (a harpoon carrying an explosive charge is detonated inside the whale's body).

Moreover, successful campaigns by animal protection groups such as the International Fund for Animal Welfare have been based upon highlighting cruelty to seals clubbed to death in Canada and animals caught in painful leg-hold traps. Something in the region of 30 million animals are trapped in the wild for their fur and a further 40 million are raised and killed on fur farms (Ryder, 1989: 235). In addition, it has been estimated that in the United States alone, some 134 million animals are hunted and killed annually, some in so-called 'canned hunts' where animals, usually exotic ones, are presented in enclosed areas for members of the public who pay for the privilege to take pot shots at them (Regan, 2004: 142–50).

From an animal welfare perspective, the – undoubtedly severe – suffering inflicted on many wild animals is only justified if it can be shown to be necessary. A full answer to this question requires a case by case analysis of each practice. The issue of hunting is discussed in more detail below. It is doubtful, with the exception of some subsistence hunting perhaps, whether whaling is necessary since it is now more concerned with issues of national pride rather than economic or dietary necessity. This benefit would not seem to outweigh the suffering caused to the whales.

Similarly, the case for ending the fur trade would seem to be strong from the perspective of the moral orthodoxy. The level of suffering inflicted on wild-caught animals is intense. The major fur producers in countries in Eastern Europe and North America still use the steel-jawed trap which causes enormous suffering to the animals unlucky enough to be caught in them. It is also indiscriminate, with many non-targeted animals such as squirrels, dogs and cats caught in them too. The fact that the industry describes these non-target animals as 'trash' animals reveals starkly their utter contempt for all non-human animal life. Society, in return, ought to show its utter contempt for this disregard by morally condemning and politically organizing a ban on such trapping.

Animals may be left for days in traps in chronic pain before being put out of their misery, or they might gnaw off a leg in order to escape. If found by a trapper they will often be stomped on until they suffocate, shooting or beating them being a less attractive option because of the damage that would cause to the pelt. Animals suffer other indignities in fur farms. Trapped in small cages, animals such as minks and Arctic foxes – used to travelling huge distances in the wild – are eventually killed, either by having their necks broken, asphyxiation or electrocution, which involves the application of electrodes to the mouth and anus of the animals (Regan, 2004: 109–10).

This suffering would not seem to be outweighed by the benefits of fur, which, in the West at least, is an item of fashion rather than a necessity. As Regan (2004: 112) computes, 'a forty-inch fur coat made from coyotes, for example, equals sixteen dead coyotes, *plus* an unknown number of dead non-target animals, *plus* more than two hundred hours of animal suffering'. There are, of course, economic benefits to be had from the fur trade. Having said that, though, the market for fur substitutes should more than make up for the loss of income from a ban on the fur trade. The British government, at least, recognized the case against fur when it became the first government in the world to ban fur farming in 2003. Britain is, however, a small player in the international fur trade. Moreover, the EU has banned the use of the leg-hold trap in member states, and its attempts to ban the import of fur products from countries still allowing the trap to be used has been a source of sustained political conflict (see Garner, 2004: chapter 7).

Animal rights and wildlife conservation

From an animal rights perspective, three general principles are elaborated. First, the vast majority of pro-animal philosophers, including Singer and, although with less certainty, Regan, want to rule out granting moral standing to non-sentient entities. Their arguments were explored in chapter 3 and there is no need to rehearse them again here. Second, the general recommendation from the animal rights perspective is that wild animals should, as far as possible, be left alone. 'Being neither the accountants nor managers of felicity in nature', Regan (1984: 357) writes, 'wildlife managers should be principally concerned with *letting animals be*, keeping human predators out of their affairs, allowing these "other nations" to carve out their own destiny.'

Third, no special status should be accorded to animals that are part of an endangered species. Indeed, if there is a choice between saving a few members of an endangered species or many more of a common species, the fact that some animals are members of an endangered species is, for Regan, irrelevant, so that in the event of a moral conflict as described above, the choice must be to save the more populous group since by so doing more individual rights are being protected (Regan, 1984: 359–61). Protecting members of endangered species is not unimportant for Regan, but they should be protected not because they are endangered but because they are subjects-of-a-life with equal inherent value.

This critique of the conservationist's emphasis on endangered species is part of a devastating attack by Regan on the holistic nature of environmentalism. For Regan (1984: 361–2), Leopold's statement of the holistic position, cited above, amounts to a form of 'environmental fascism' because it would seem to require the sacrifice of individuals in order to maintain the 'integrity of the biotic community'. Even the less extreme version of holism is problematic from an animal rights perspective, since it is still justifiable to sacrifice the interests of some animals providing that this is necessary to ensure the survival of the vast majority.

This attack on holism by pro-animal philosophers, and their unwillingness to sanction the culling of wild animals in order to preserve habitats, has been criticized as environmentally naive and overly emotional by environmental ethicists (Callicott, 1995). Moreover, this conflict between holism and individualism has been the source of some conflict between the environmental and animal protection movements (Garner, 2005: chapter 6). It is possible to identify two distinct criticisms of the animal rights position here. The first is that leaving wild animals alone is not a viable option since in the long run it will damage either humans or wild animals, or both. The second line of criticism is that an animal rights position cannot sanction leaving wild animals alone since it is obliged to protect animals being attacked and killed by other animals.

We can deal with the second criticism speedily here since the arguments were explored in chapter 5. Regan's assertion that animals are not moral agents goes a long way, if not all the way, towards answering the charge that an acceptance of animal rights leads to the absurd conclusion that we should intervene to prevent the wolf from killing the sheep or the lion the wildebeest. The first criticism is more difficult to answer. In the first place, it has been suggested that if we do not intervene to manage wild animals, which will usually involve some element of culling, then ultimately wild animal populations, and individual animals with them, will be damaged. To put it crudely, it may be a choice between killing a few animals or letting many others suffer a long, lingering death from starvation.

It is true, of course, that the best chance for the survival of wild animals is to ensure protection of their habitats. To take one classic example, over half of all the species so far identified can be found in the tropical rainforests. There is obviously little hope for these animals unless the rainforest is protected. Sometimes, moreover, it has to be admitted, the survival of a particular habitat or ecosystem necessitates sacrificing the interests of individual animals. In response, though, Regan and other animal rights advocates would no doubt

say the number of habitats upon which wild animals can rely is dwin-
dling because of human exploitation of the natural environment.
Moreover, the surge in population of a particular species is often
caused by the eradication – usually by humans – of a prey animal's
natural predator. The slaughter of wolves in the United States at the
turn of the twentieth century, to give one example, led to a massive
rise in deer numbers (Rowlands, 2002: 167). The consequence of
killing wolves was known in 1900 since the very aim of the exercise
was, at least partly, to produce more deer for humans to shoot! We
are back, then, at square one with Regan's clarion call 'leave them
alone' resonating in our ears.

The second criticism of the 'leave wild animals to their own
devices' view is provided, amongst others, by Warren (1997: 78–84;
116–17). In what she describes as the 'comparable interests dilemma',
Warren argues that the granting of rights to wild animals would
require so much protection of animal interests that human survival
would become difficult if not impossible. Instances where human
interests would be damaged if they did not act against the interests
of animals include crop cultivation (which Warren thinks would have
to be stopped because it involves the killing of wild animals) and the
killing of rodents whose 'very existence and mode of life' threatens
human beings.

Although Warren's critique is directed principally at Singer's preference utilitarianism it is equally applicable to the animal rights view.
There are at least three ways in which this charge against the animal
rights position might be answered. In the first place, Warren focuses
on the harm that befalls many invertebrates as a result of necessary
human activities such as food production. But no one writing from
an animal rights perspective would be prepared to grant equal moral
status to such animals. Second, as regards sentient mammals that
might be harmed by humans, we might want to say that no one
claimed the adoption of an animal rights position would be easy and
cost-free. Indeed, since its very purpose is to remove humans from a
position of moral superiority then we can expect that humans are
going to have to make some sacrifices.

Third, however, it is not really necessary to go this far since Regan,
whom Warren is particularly targeting, would deny her premise that
humans would have to make sacrifices. Since humans need to eat to
survive, and since rodents threaten human life as carriers of disease,
then humans can act against animals in these cases as a matter of self-
defence. Moreover, as we have seen, Regan is prepared to accept that
human lives are of greater value than animal lives and, since Warren's
examples are equivalent to a lifeboat scenario, it is quite acceptable,

for Regan at least, to sacrifice the interests of the animals in these cases. Of course, finally, a recognition of the moral importance of animals necessitates that humans take due care to ensure that any animals that are to lose out do so in the most humane way possible.

Hunting and animal rights

The conflict between the holism of environmentalism and the individualism of animal rights emerges with particular venom over the issue of hunting. Regan is adamant that hunting animals infringes their rights and therefore should be morally prohibited. Irrespective of the suffering caused by death from starvation, which may or may not be worse than death from hunting, he argues that: 'No approach to wildlife can be morally acceptable if it assumes that policy decisions should be made on the basis of aggregating harms and benefits ... Policies that lessen the total amount of harm at the cost of violating the rights of individuals ... are wrong' (Regan, 1984: 356). Singer, likewise, argues that the pleasures received by those who hunt animals are trivial set against the suffering of individual hunted animals (Singer, 1993: 133–4).

There has been at least one attempt, however, to reconcile both Regan (and Singer) to a case for hunting. Varner (1998) argues that hunting is consistent with animal rights and liberation pro-animal philosophers in some circumstances. In the first place, it has to be hunting which is 'designed to secure the aggregate welfare of the target species, the integrity or health of its ecosystem, or both'. In other words, it is justified where the deaths of some animals results in other animals from the same species prospering (so-called 'therapeutic' hunting). Second, the species hunted must be one whose population size regularly becomes too great for its allotted habitat. This rules out hunting merely for sport which, he argues, holistic environmentalists, along with pro-animal philosophers, reject anyway.

Varner's analysis does little to bridge the gap between an animal rights ethic and a holistic environmentalism. In the first place, relatively little hunting is of the therapeutic variety anyway, and so Varner would agree with Regan and Singer that hunting merely for 'sport' is ruled out of court by an animal rights ethic. In addition, the attempt to reconcile Regan to therapeutic hunting is not successful. Varner suggests (1998: 113) that Regan's miniride principle, discussed in chapter 6, allows for therapeutic hunting on the grounds that in the event of a conflict between the interests of the few and the interests of the many, where if we do not sacrifice the few we will have to sacrifice the many, it is justifiable to take the former option. This is exactly the scenario with therapeutic hunting. If we fail to allow hunting then more animals will suffer and die than it will be necessary to kill by hunting.

It is by no means clear, however, that hunting represents the kind of choice situation that Regan has in mind for his miniride principle. There is a choice. Leave the animals alone is Regan's mantra. We do not need to act. Of course, as was indicated above, the real problem for wildlife is that their habitats have been persistently destroyed, leaving less and less space. More often than not, wild animals exceed the carrying capacity of their habitats precisely *because* of human intervention. Hunting then becomes a solution to a problem largely created by humans in the first place. Moreover, the kind of animals that therapeutic hunting necessitates killing are those – the old, the injured and the sick – which are most likely to succumb to hard winters and food shortages. Yet these are exactly the kind of animals that are not attractive to hunters because it is too easy to kill them (Regan, 2004: 148–9).

Although Varner does little to bridge the gap between animal rights and environmental holists, he might have a better chance of reconciling a pro-hunting position with Singer's animal liberation. He notes (1998: 103–11) that Singer, as a utilitarian, can justify therapeutic hunting on the grounds that it involves less pain than letting nature take its course. As with eating animals or experimenting on them, what utilitarianism will morally allow will depend upon an empirical examination. Varner's case, as he himself recognizes, in part depends on the impracticality of using, as Singer suggests, non-lethal methods of population control. In addition, a utilitarian would have to consider all of the costs and benefits of hunting, including the pleasure that those doing the hunting derive from it. Needless to say, a utilitarian's response to hunting is likely to vary depending on the circumstances. For example, subsistence hunting is much more likely to be accepted on utilitarian grounds than hunting merely for sport.

Animal welfare and fox-hunting

We have seen that, despite the best efforts of Varner, hunting, even of the therapeutic variety, is not consistent with an animal rights ethic. It might even be suggested that most forms of hunting are not even justified by the moral orthodoxy. To see that this is so take the example of fox-hunting. The hunting of foxes – as well as the hunting

of deer and the coursing of hares – has been an intermittently important political issue in Britain, culminating in the decision by the
House of Commons in November 2004 to force through a hunting
ban in the teeth of opposition from the House of Lords and the
hunting community. The hunting ban came into force on 18 February 2005. It is estimated that 20–25,000 foxes are killed by hunts
every year (*Guardian*, 13 June 2000). Even the Countryside Alliance
– avowed opponents of the anti-hunting lobby – would have to admit
that for a long time a high proportion of the British people have
opposed hunting. Clearly, this is not because a majority think that
foxes have rights. Rather, it appears that, for many, fox-hunting is
illegitimate because it causes unnecessary suffering.[2]

The first question to ask is the degree to which hunting causes
foxes to suffer. The hunting community deny that foxes suffer, or at
least suffer any more than they would if any other method of control
was used or, indeed, if they were left to die naturally. There must be
doubts about this claim. Foxes, for one thing, are not natural prey
animals and so therefore are totally unprepared for the stress involved
in the chase. Even if we left out of account the fact that some foxes
are ripped apart by a pack of hounds before the hunters reach them,
the chase itself, as stated in the Burns Report – the report of a committee set up by the British government to examine the issue – 'seriously compromises the welfare of the fox' (*Guardian*, 13 June 2000).
Even if it is necessary to cull foxes – an assertion that can be disputed
– then there is a strong case for saying there are alternative, more
humane, ways of doing it.

The fact that foxes do suffer in the course of being hunted means
we need to ask whether this suffering can be deemed to be necessary.
Clearly, sport or entertainment alone is not an adequate enough
reason to justify inflicting suffering on foxes from the perspective of
the moral orthodoxy. The hunting community has recognized this
and has put forward a variety of justifications for the continuation
of hunting. These have included the claim that the fox is a pest that
needs eradicating, the claim that hunting has a conservation function,
the claim there will be significant economic costs of abolishing
hunting, and finally the claim that abolition is an infringement of
minority rights.

A number of observations about these claims are pertinent. First,
there is, of course, a conflict between the first and second justifications. The hunting community cannot, while remaining consistent,
hold both that foxes are a pest that must be eradicated and that
hunting provides an incentive to preserve the habitat that foxes rely
on. If foxes are a pest then the logical thing to do would be to destroy

their habitat. The second, conservation, function is much more convincing than the first since evidence suggests that the fox causes less damage to animal agriculture than was originally thought. The notion that hunts control fox numbers can be challenged too. Research undertaken during the temporary cessation of hunting during the foot-and-mouth crisis in 2001 revealed no significant rise in fox numbers (*Guardian*, 5 September 2002). By contrast with the pest argument the conservation case for hunting would appear to be stronger. However, the protection of the species is not an animal welfare issue. According to the moral orthodoxy, if the choice was between the eradication of the species and pain and suffering inflicted on a significant number of foxes then we must choose the former.

The second observation is that the economic losses sustained if fox-hunting was to be abolished should not be exaggerated. The hunting community have suggested that whole swathes of the rural economy will be devastated by a ban on hunting. The Burns Report, however, suggested a much more tolerable impact with only 700 job losses of those directly employed by the hunt and up to 8,000 indirect jobs threatened, significantly less than those claimed by the hunting lobby and all of which would be offset within a ten-year period (*Guardian*, 13 June 2000).

Finally, the hunting community's increasing reliance on minority rights is somewhat bogus, albeit relatively popular. At the time of writing legal action is being initiated by pro-hunting supporters on the grounds that the legislation banning hunting infringes the Human Rights Act. In practice, this may or may not be the case. What is clear, however, is that consideration of moral issues cannot be constrained merely because those whose activities are being scrutinized are in the minority. Such a position would protect any behaviour undertaken by individuals in the minority, however morally abhorrent, from being questioned and prohibited. No doubt a minority would still like to engage in bear-baiting, dog- and cock-fighting and so on. Yet society has regarded such activities as morally reprehensible because they cause unnecessary suffering. In reality then, moral evaluation is not dependent upon the number of people who engage in a particular practice. As a result, the minority rights argument for the continuation of hunting fails.

Conclusion

From the material presented in this chapter we can develop a manifesto based on alternative ethical positions. It has been argued that animal circuses and dolphinaria, hunting and the fur trade are morally illegitimate institutions, *even from* the perspective of the moral orthodoxy. To seek the end of these practices, then, animal protection organizations do not have to go beyond the moral orthodoxy. No claims of rights for animals are necessary, although of course the application of an animal rights ethic renders these activities as morally illegitimate too. As we will see in the last chapter, the fact that it is not necessary to go beyond the moral orthodoxy has an important bearing on the political praxis of animal ethics.

The issue of companion animals and zoos is less clear-cut. Much of the cruelty inflicted on companion animals is morally illegitimate from the perspective of the moral orthodoxy and some zoos are so poor that the suffering inflicted on the animals kept is unnecessary, particularly if no viable claims are made for education and conservation roles. There are those who argue that keeping animals as pets or as captive animals in zoos, whatever the environment provided, is illegitimate because it infringes rights. In this chapter, I sought to argue against this view on the grounds that a right to liberty only becomes relevant when to deprive animals of their freedom causes them harm. The extent to which it does so in the case of companion animals and zoos will depend upon empirical examination. Finally, the destruction of millions of healthy abandoned animals is anathema from the rights perspective. In so far as this destruction is an inevitable consequence of the keeping of animals as pets then the moral validity of the whole institution, from a rights view at least, is put in doubt.

10

Political Agency and Animal Rights

Peter Singer (1993: 317) suggests that 'a distinguishing feature of ethics is that ethical judgements are universable', so 'ethics requires us to go beyond our own personal point of view to a standpoint like that of the impartial spectator who takes a universal point of view'. The ethics of the pro-animal philosophers, however, require us to go much further in the altruism stakes. Indeed, the animal rights and radical ecology movements are unique for being the only social movements whose aim is to benefit non-humans, *even when* the consequence of doing so is to damage the interests of humans. Not only is this extremely altruistic, it also raises crucial interrelated issues of agency and, more broadly, strategy. Who exactly is best placed to achieve the goals of the animal rights/liberation movement? What is the most appropriate strategy for animal advocates to adopt? And which ideological position is most functional for achieving animal rights/liberation goals? Attempting to provide answers to these questions is the subject matter of this final chapter.

Strategies

Animal protection groups adopt a variety of strategies to achieve their aims (see Garner, 2004: chapters 7 and 8). For the most part, the animal protection movement has focused on the traditional tactics of a protest movement, lobbying politicians and officials, organizing demonstrations and the distribution of literature. Two debates about the utility of animal protection strategies have arisen. The first, which I will not consider in detail here, asks whether animal advocates should become 'insiders', taking opportunities to negotiate with politicians and officials, or whether they should remain in principled opposition, refusing to 'muddy their hands' with the kind of compromise and respectability that is thought to be required for insider status. I have argued elsewhere (Garner, 1998; 2004: chapter 7) that animal advocates should adopt the former approach, not least because where they have done so important advances in the well-being of animals have been achieved. The second debate asks whether animal advocates should participate in, or support, direct action in defence of animals. It is this second debate that I want to focus on in this section.

The validity of direct action will depend on an examination of a number of factors. First, what kind of direct action has been utilized? Second, does this direct action achieve its goals? Third, is direct action politically justified? And, finally, is direct action ethically justified? Direct action is often associated in the public mind with illegality and violence. However, it need involve neither. For example, one of the most common activities of an animal advocate – which might be classified as a form of direct action since it eschews the indirect approach of seeking action from political decision makers – is a lifestyle choice. The animal issue is particularly suited to such an approach. One can choose to be a vegetarian, refuse to wear fur and leather, refuse to attend zoos and circuses, and refuse to buy products tested on animals.

Although of symbolic importance, a lifestyle strategy, by itself, will probably fail to make much of an impact. It is extremely unlikely that enough people will opt for the animal rights option. As a result, legislative change promoted by a political elite whereby choice is eroded is probably a more worthwhile objective for the animal rights movement. It is for this reason that Frey (1983: 207–16) disputes Singer's assertion that becoming a vegetarian is not merely a symbolic gesture but also has an impact on the meat industry. Such is the scale of the meat industry that my decision to give up eating meat will have absolutely no impact on the amount of meat produced. It requires similar action from many, many others at levels that have, up to now, not been achieved. So, even though it is regularly claimed that up to 10 per cent of British people are vegetarians, there is little evidence that the meat industry has been harmed. Indeed, production of at least some forms of meat, especially poultry, has soared as vegetarianism has increased.

Most direct action in defence of animals is not violent, at least in the sense of violence aimed at people. Some of it can be defined as civil disobedience. This includes sit-ins and vigils of various kinds.

The tactic of breaking into laboratories (causing the minimum of damage) in order to gather information and release the animals is one example as was the attempt, during the live-export dispute in Britain in the mid-1990s, to prevent the export of live animals by sitting in front of transporters. The work of hunt saboteurs in trespassing on private land to disrupt hunts is another example. Civil disobedience, despite involving breaking the law, has an honourable tradition in political protest. It is widely recognized that, providing the participants accept the consequences of their actions, then such action is justified in a democracy.

From the 1980s in Britain, though, action, primarily carried out in the name of the Animal Liberation Front (ALF), was increasingly targeted against the property of animal exploiters. For example, the windows of butchers' and furriers' premises were targeted, and research labs trashed. More recently, the property of the companies involved in building new animal research establishments has been targeted. In one recent instance, property belonging to a construction company providing concrete for a new research laboratory at Oxford University was severely damaged (*Guardian*, 19 July 2004).

The ALF, versions of which now exist in many countries, has repeatedly stated that it does not entertain action that is designed to threaten the physical or psychological integrity of humans. Yet since the 1980s some animal rights activists, whether associated with the ALF or not, have undertaken such activity, either through the use of incendiary devices or, more rarely, the use of high explosives, or through, as explained below, the use of intimidation and harassment. The nature of animal rights direct action has changed in Britain since the early 1990s in the sense that activists now tend to engage in concerted campaigns against a small number of targets. The classic example here is the direct action targeted against the Huntingdon Life Sciences company, owner of the largest contract research laboratory in Europe situated in the east of England. Following this on-going campaign, activists have also targeted plans to build animal research establishments, first at the University of Cambridge and more recently at Oxford.

There have been law-abiding elements to the campaigns against these institutions, in the form, for instance, of Stop Huntingdon Animal Cruelty (SHAC), which denies any involvement in direct action aimed at intimidating humans. However, there have been some activists who have been prepared to engage in such activities, commonly including intimidatory communication with individual scientists or those, or the families of those, who work for companies which engage in, or fund, animal research. This has been through threatening phone calls and e-mails as well as the targeting of the homes of those involved, however peripherally, in animal research. By 2004, the media was littered with scare stories of a transatlantic network of dangerous animal rights extremists moving freely between Britain and the United States (*Observer*, 25 July 2004; 1 August 2004; *Guardian*, 2 August 2004).

As a result of the increasing propensity of violent direct action, or at least the perception of it, the British Government has taken action to prevent the targeting of the homes of those involved in animal research as well as increasing penalties for sending hate mail (*Guardian*, 22 February 2001; 30 July 2004). Similar legislation has existed in the United States for some years. Such is the climate in Britain at the time of writing that it was said that the government actively considered using the army to protect animal research establishments.

Clearly, the case for direct action aimed at harming humans is much more difficult to sustain. It should be pointed out at this stage, though, that such acts represent a tiny proportion of the total amount of animal rights direct action, which in turn represents a tiny proportion of the total amount of animal rights activism. Most of the mainstream animal rights groups condemn activists who engage in violence and threatening behaviour. Moreover, although this does not justify what some animal rights activists do, those who exploit animals sometimes engage in violence against animal rights activists. In addition, although quite legal in most cases, animal exploiters engage in violence against animals in the course of raising and killing them for food and cutting, burning, starving, shooting, crushing and drowning them in laboratories.

Three justifications for animal rights activism that targets humans might be considered. First is the utility argument that animal rights direct action works. It is undoubtedly true that many forms of animal rights direct action do seem to work. First, civil disobedience is generally respected by the general public and animal issues receive valuable publicity in the process. Second, a great deal of the information used in campaigns against vivisection has come from illegal laboratory break-ins. The secrecy surrounding vivisection means that, in Britain at least, there is little other way to find out what is going on in laboratories. Sometimes, as in the infamous Pennsylvania University head injury laboratory, mentioned in chapter 8, animal rights activists uncover evidence of appalling animal cruelty.

Third, the fact that animals are sometimes released in raids on laboratories and factory farms is usually also a generally positive outcome from an animal rights perspective. Finally, mention should also be made of the added costs of security that those engaging in animal experimentation have to undergo as a result of the threat of direct action. There is absolutely no doubt that the more recent campaigns against HLS and the proposed research facility at Cambridge, which have included an element of direct action – some legal, some not – have been very effective. HLS was brought to its knees, and despite winning the planning application on appeal, Cambridge decided not to go ahead with their project, not least because of the on-going potential for animal rights activism. In the case of Oxford, the project has quickly run into difficulty with the main contractor being forced to pull out because of a fall in its share price (*Guardian*, 20 July 2004).

Against this positive verdict, there is the argument that direct action that threatens or uses violence alienates public opinion. Only a small minority of activists may be prepared to harm animal users but the whole animal movement is discredited by it, and the direct action itself becomes the issue rather than animal exploitation. No one involved in animal exploitation has been killed as a result of direct action, but this is down to chance rather than design. The point is that if someone is killed, the animal rights movement's case would undoubtedly be damaged. Finally, here, it should be noted that even if public opinion is not alienated, there is no substitute for legislative action to ban vivisection and hunting, since activists can only 'rescue' a tiny proportion of laboratory and hunted animals.

The second justification for the most extreme forms of animal rights direct action is that it is politically justified. Clearly, the nature of the political system within which decisions are taken will impact on the legitimacy of the tactics used by social movements. Put simply, direct action would seem to be more justified in a dictatorship than a democracy. In a democracy, it might be argued that sufficient means are available for a social movement to achieve its aims. If it cannot persuade a majority to adopt its objectives then it should not impose its minority views on to society as a whole.

Democracy has been defined here, as it often is, in terms of majority rule. But how far does majority rule exist in practice in so-called 'democracies'? (See the discussion in Garner, 2004: chapter 8; Singer, 1993: 298–305.) The first point to make here is that in a representative democracy it is not always the case that the majority view of the electorate will be adequately represented. Elections are not referendums on one particular issue. Moreover, it is often an intensely expressed minority view that gets noticed and acted upon. Indeed, such is the dominance of minorities in modern politics that one notable American political scientist, Robert Dahl (1956), recommends that we drop the term democracy in favour of what he calls 'polyarchy', or rule by minorities. There is a pertinent example here from an animal issue. In Britain, fox-hunting survived for many years at least partly because of an extremely enthusiastic campaign by an intense minority of those opposed to abolition. Indeed, as was indicated in chapter 9, the fox-hunting community specifically now uses the argument that a minority should not be persecuted for following what they have chosen as their way of life.

It may also be the case that a decision is not a genuine reflection of majority opinion. It could be, for instance, that the public are not aware of a materially important piece of information. It would then, arguably, be justified to undertake direct action in order to inform the majority. Relatively mild forms of civil disobedience could be justified on these grounds, as an 'attempt to restore, rather than frustrate, the process of democratic decision making' (Singer, 1993: 303). One of the regular complaints of the animal rights movement is that the public is not aware of what goes on in laboratories, and once informed of this – through the help of information retrieved by laboratory break-ins – public opinion might move towards the protesters' position. This has happened in some cases. The revelations of the cruelties inflicted on animals by researchers in the United States, for instance, had a considerable impact on public opinion, providing the impetus necessary for federal legislation in 1985 (Garner, 1998: 202–9). Of course, this end does not justify the means of violence against people.

On this theme, of the degree to which majority rule exists in practice, it has also been suggested that, in the context of a small number of extremely powerful interests, the notion that decisions are taken by a majority is in any case a chimera. The usual candidate for dominant interest status is business, which some hold to have a privileged position in liberal democracies (Lindblom, 1977), although others have suggested the existence of a number of different elite groups drawn from different sections of society (Mills, 1956). In terms of our present concern, it might be argued that improvements to the way animals are treated are regularly obstructed by those – agribusiness or pharmaceutical interests – who have a vested interest in being able to continue exploiting animals. An examination of this claim is beyond the scope of this book. My own research indicates, though, that the reality is a mixed picture with some sectors of policy-making more open to general influence than others (Garner, 1998). What is clear is that if it can be established that majority opinion is being thwarted in this way then direct action becomes more justifiable. Whether it makes it politically justified to harm humans is a moot point, and it is equally unclear at what point we can say that the animal rights movement has exhausted all non-violent means.

Direct action and ethics

There is also an ethical case for direct action, which supersedes the tactical and political justifications. Put simply, if one believes that the exploitation of animals is fundamentally wrong, then the fact that a majority are prepared to accept it is an irrelevant consideration. As Rowlands (2002: 184) points out: 'The laws that permit our current treatment of animals are incompatible with absolutely central components of our moral tradition. These laws are, therefore, as unjust as any laws can be. And we are, therefore, under no overriding obligation to obey them.' This moral case is particularly relevant when we are talking about the use of violence, either against property or against people. There are those who suggest that it is morally impermissible to infringe the rights of those who themselves infringe the rights of animals, since to do so is to 'undermine the animal movement's ethical basis' which is that sentiency matters morally and humans, like animals, are sentient (Singer, 2004).

An alternative view would be that it is legitimate to infringe the rights of those who are infringing the rights of animals. The argument here is that not to do so would lead us to the counter-intuitive conclusion that, say, it would have been morally illegitimate to physically harm a concentration camp guard in order to free the inmates. What is shocking about this statement, should the reader find anything shocking, is not the conclusion about concentration camp guards but the fact that I am drawing parallels with animals. All I am claiming here, though, is that *if* animals have rights, and particularly a right-to-life, then this conclusion follows. The dispute then is over whether animals have rights, not over what follows if we accept that they do. Of course, the moral condemnation will vary, so that someone who works for a company supplying an animal research facility with equipment, say, is clearly not implicated anywhere near as much as a scientist who actually inflicts suffering on an animal. Likewise, what constitutes appropriate violence in this case is a moot point. The use of force designed to stop vivisection would seem to be appropriate here, although what that is will be a matter of empirical examination.

Accepting the arguments in the previous paragraph is by no means the last word on the matter since other reasons for condemning violence in defence of animals might be adopted. It might be argued that violence in defence of animals is wrong on the grounds that violence is always wrong. But this absolute rule, adopted by pacifists, is open to the objection that those who desist from using violence against someone who is inflicting violence and/or death on others, are then responsible for failing to prevent this future violence and/or killing by not using violence to end it (Singer, 1993: 308). As a result, most people would probably accept that violence against other humans, including killing other humans, is justified on the grounds of self-defence, or in order to save an innocent third party, or in the case of war (Rowlands, 2002: 190).

Alternatively, we might object to violence on the grounds that its consequences are undesirable (Singer, 1993: 310–13). One consequence might be that it has a hardening effect on its perpetrator, so that violence becomes easier to commit in the future. However, it is unlikely that someone who commits violence in a genuine attempt to liberate animals is any more likely than anyone else to commit violence for other goals in the future. At the very least this contention must be shown, empirically, to be true. Another consequence might be that accepting that violence is legitimate does 'damage to the fabric of civil society' since it sets a precedent whereby anyone who feels that his moral view is being frustrated, such as an anti-abortionist, is entitled to use violence in pursuit of his/her objectives (Singer, 2004). Such a situation presages social instability if not anarchy.

Finally, we might object to violence in defence of animals on the grounds that we can never be entirely sure that it will produce the ends desired for it or that these ends could not have been reached by other means. This particularly applies to the use of indiscriminate violence which threatens 'innocent' people. There is a great deal of truth in this objection. It is undoubtedly true, for instance, that the use of bombs in the pursuit of animal liberation is much more difficult to justify than more targeted violence, precisely because of its indiscriminate character. Moreover, it is also true that any examination of the use of violence should involve a consideration of its utility. Does it work better than an alternative tactic? As we noted above, in some cases violence, particularly if it is directed at property, does work, but violence directed at people, particularly if it involves serious physical harm, is unlikely to be sustainable.

The importance of agency

Much attention, both within and outside the animal rights movement, has been focused on the issue of direct action. In my view, though, of greater importance in discussing the prospects of the animal rights movement achieving its aims, or some of them, is the issue of agency. Agency focuses not so much on what has to be done to achieve the objectives of animal advocates as on who is to do it. The animal protection movement has not done enough thinking about agency. More often than not there is an assumption that all the animal protection movement has to do is to publicize its issues and once fellow humans come to see the rational case for animal rights they will adopt it without question. Regan, to give one example, argues that the future success of animal rights depends upon the conversion of what he calls the 'Muddlers' (Regan, 2004: 181–96), those who are open to the animal rights message but are, for a variety of reasons, reluctant to take the final step. Muddlers are resistant to animal rights, Regan argues, because the animal rights movement is seen as negative, or outlandish, or too conservative, or too unrealistic, or because it courts too many celebrity endorsements, or because its campaigns are sometimes tasteless, or self-righteous, or violent, or because Muddlers themselves don't feel they can contribute anything worthwhile.

There is little doubt that all of the factors Regan raises as obstacles to someone somewhere becoming an animal rights advocate are important ones. Indeed, I have argued myself (Garner, 2004: chapter 7) that the self-righteous moral purity exhibited by some in the animal rights movement undoubtedly alienates those who might otherwise become supportive of animal rights goals. Focusing exclusively upon the factors that might alienate potential converts, however, only takes us so far. The issue of agency requires us to look more fundamentally at the issue of interests. The history of social reform movements suggests that it is not enough to hope that ideas will attract public support and, somehow miraculously, be converted into legislative goals and social conventions. Rather, the ideas that tend to predominate are those which are associated with important social groupings. Liberalism and socialism emerged as important nineteenth-century ideologies precisely because they were associated with the middle and working classes created by the Industrial Revolution. Feminism, likewise, is a hugely important social movement for the obvious reason that it appealed to a new female consciousness produced by wider social forces.

Electoral politics are, similarly, not so much about isolated individuals voting independently of others but are about group loyalties transformed into voter choices. In between elections, too, it is the voice of organized groups that governments listen and respond to. By definition, the larger the group or coalition of groups, the greater likelihood that the group will achieve its objectives. Likewise, being able to attract and mobilize as high a proportion of a group's potential support as possible is another important resource.

Animal protection organizations are, of course, classic examples of cause or promotional concerns. As a result, the animal protection movement does not have the common geographical or occupational location associated with interest groups. The fact that most of the animal protection movement's opponents are interest groups with an assured membership and source of income puts it at a competitive disadvantage. I have argued elsewhere (Garner, 1998: chapter 3) that the animal protection movement has, in the past, compensated for this by developing a group identity, usually based on animal rights ideology, and by relying on 'entrepreneurs' to set up groups and mobilize others to join. In this sense, elites have been very important in creating and sustaining the animal protection movement.

In addition, as indicated in the introduction to this chapter, the animal rights movement is also disadvantaged because the achievement of its objectives may well require human interests to be sacrificed. This, of course, is why campaigns designed to show that the exploitation of animals is unnecessary are attractive. If, for example, we can show that animal experimentation does not work, or that we do not need to eat meat and that meat is bad for your health and the environment, then the chances of the animal rights movement achieving its objectives are greater. This is, of course, because all traces of species conflict disappear. If, on the other hand, we persist in saying that animal interests ought to be protected, irrespective of the cost to humans, then whatever the moral merits of so doing, it is clearly going to be more difficult to persuade humans to accept it. And, of course, the problem is compounded because animals – unlike blacks, women and the working class – are not able to liberate themselves. They require humans, who may have to sacrifice some of their own interests in the process, to do it for them.

All that has been said so far in this chapter reinforces the importance for the animal protection movement of allying itself with important social groupings and ideological traditions. Dobson (2000: 147), in the context of the ecology movement, sets out the problem and the opportunity thus: 'Radical greens must abandon their Utopian, universalistic strategy, and instead identify and organize a group of people in society whose immediate interests lie in living the dark-green life, with all that that implies.' Translated into more appropriate language for the subject matter of this book, animal advocates should abandon the view that everyone can be persuaded of the case for animal rights if only they understand the issues. Rather, they should look for a social grouping and ideological tradition that can justify or, even better, require the incorporation of animal interests.

The parallels with the ecology movement only take us so far here. It is doubtful if there is much mileage in seeking to embrace individuals with an interest in animal rights, in the sense that their lives would be materially or physically better if the interests of animals were protected. There is some scope for this. Those living with the pollution, noise and stench of factory farms and abattoirs would have better lives if the factory farms and abattoirs did not exist. Similarly, as we saw in chapter 7, intensive animal agriculture harms the interests of small farmers, and the food produced from factory farms is generally of a lower quality than free-range produce and is associated with human health problems. Likewise, those who have been the victims of a drug previously tested on animals but still found to be dangerous for humans to consume might be another group who animal advocates could try to mobilize.

There is some truth in the assertion by Rowlands (2002: 196) that: 'It is impossible to view the world and everything in it primarily as a resource without this infecting the way we view each other.' The negative impact on humans of factory farming is the major illustration of this that Rowlands provides. There are at least two problems with this argument. In the first place, it only applies to the end of factory farming and not all animal agriculture and all eating of animals. Second, factory farming has undoubtedly had some positive impact on humans. Indeed, it has largely achieved its original function which was to ensure a plentiful, cost-effective and regular supply of food. Therefore in some, probably the majority of, cases the direct interests of humans are not necessarily served by an end to animal exploitation.

The parallel argument, of course, is that relatively few humans will have their direct physical or financial interests furthered by the protection of animals. We can get round this problem, however, if we broaden the notion of interests. In other words, as well as identifying those human interests that are directly furthered by the protection of animals, we can also identify those interests that humans have in common with animals. To do this, we have to ask to what degree can social groupings and the ideologies that bind them together identify with the interests of animals?

Ideologies and animals

The obvious starting point in a quest to find the most appropriate ideological location for animal protection is liberalism. Liberalism is not only the predominant ideological tradition in the West, but it is also the basis of most of the attempts to secure a higher moral status for animals. Rights, utilitarianism and contractarian approaches to animal ethics derive from the liberal tradition. Not only does liberalism occupy a central place in Western societies but it also has some other essential attributes, at least from an animal protection perspective. For one thing, it is individualistic. For another, it is a universal ideology, proclaiming to apply everywhere unlike, for instance, the more relativistic and particularistic character of communitarianism, one of liberalism's major rivals these days (Garner, 2005: chapter 4). The advantage is that liberalism does predominate in contemporary Western society. All that is required is its extension across the species boundary.

This extension is easy to write about, but much more difficult to achieve. Questions about agency still remain. Who exactly is going to ensure that animals become the beneficiaries of rights and utilitarian calculations? Surveys do seem to suggest that the animal rights movement is predominantly white and middle-class, like many other social movements (Greanville and Moss, 1985). Most white middle-class people, however, are not animal advocates and some working-class people are.

It is also important to note that the consequences of not achieving the granting of rights status for animals within liberal thought can be extremely detrimental to their interests. Some have suggested, for instance, that there is little hope for achieving even the most basic welfarist reforms to the way animals are treated if they continue to be treated as our property (Francione, 1995). Even if one rejects this view, which I do (Garner, 2005: chapter 2), liberalism is still problematic. In particular, as we saw in chapter 6, there is a tendency in liberal political thought and practice to exclude animals from a theory of justice (Rawls, 1972). As a result, animals are subject to a wider realm of morality.

Few, if any, contemporary liberal political theorists hold that we owe no obligations to animals, most adopting a version of the moral orthodoxy. The problem is that even the most basic protection of animal interests, way short of what the granting of rights would give them, conflicts with the important liberal principle of moral pluralism. This is the view, derived initially from Mill (1972), that the state has no right to intervene in the moral beliefs of its citizens providing that they are not harming other humans in the process. This moral pluralism has become an important part of political practice in liberal democratic societies, particularly as a consequence of greater multiculturalism. It has impacted on the welfare of animals too, most notably in the issues of ritual slaughter in many countries and fox-hunting in Britain. Thus, despite the fact that there is strong evidence that ritual slaughter causes suffering for animals because it denies the use of a stunning device prior to death, governments throughout the liberal world have failed to act for fear of infringing the sacrosanct principle of moral pluralism. As we saw in chapter 9, too, the British hunting community has, with some success, used the impeccably liberal argument that to ban hunting would be an intolerable intrusion into the moral choices of a minority.

If not liberalism, though, where do we go instead for the most appropriate location for the protection of animal interests? At least three possibilities present themselves. First, there is socialism. Socialism offers animal advocates a distinct social grouping – the industrial working class – and a distinct identity of interests. Like the working class, the argument goes, animals are an exploited group. Although not necessarily capitalist, the corporate targets of the animal protection movement – the large agribusiness and pharmaceutical companies – are familiar to the left. Moreover, animal exploitation does take place principally in the private sector with a substantial amount of capital investment, and the major motivation for it is profit. Where free market liberalism is practised, the sanctity of private property makes it even more difficult to justify intervening to protect the interests of animals.

Historically, in Britain at least, there have been links between the socialist movement and animal protection. Left of centre legislators, too, appear to be more supportive of animal issues than others in both Britain and the United States (Garner, 1999). Also, opposition to hunting is very much an issue associated with the left in Britain, with Labour MPs, almost without exception, voting in favour of abolition. There has been an attempt to theorize the link between animal rights and the left in the work of the British social theorist Ted Benton (1993), who adopts a Marxist theory of justice based on needs which is much more appropriate for animals than theories based on desert.

There would seem, therefore, to be some mileage associating animal protection with socialism. In particular, there is some scope, as recognized by the late American animal rights campaigner Henry Spira, in seeking to mobilize those working in the animal industry – notably slaughterhouses, and factory farms – because they are undoubtedly an exploited part of the labour force. There are limitations, too, in associating animal protection with socialism. It is, first, very much an oppositional ideology, particularly in the United States. In addition, with some exceptions, the left has not been particularly interested in animal issues and has remained anthropocentric in outlook. Benton's theoretical attempt, while ingenious, has its limitations too (Garner, 2005: chapter 5). There is little to suggest that a change in economic ownership alone will alter public perceptions of animals, and state-controlled factory farming and animal experimentation is a likely eventuality of a socialist society.

Feminism too offers animal advocates a distinct social grouping, women, and a distinct identity of interests. It is very noticeable that women constitute the bulk of the membership of the animal protection movement. A number of feminists have attempted to draw parallels between the position of animals and those of women. Two distinct arguments have been forthcoming. The first is that women and animals represent groups exploited by men, and as a result women should be able to empathize with the plight of animals (Adams, 1990, 1994). The second suggests that those values associated with females such as compassion, empathy, sympathy and context are particularly suited to human relationships with animals. By contrast, so-called 'masculine' language, emphasizing rationalism, logic and universalism are particularly unsuited to animal protection. This leads some feminists to abandon theories based on rights – associated with masculine values – in favour of an ethic of care associated above all with Gilligan (1982).

It might be thought that feminism represents the most fruitful ideological location for the protection of animal interests, and the animal protection movement should look more closely at forging alliances with the women's movement. This may be the case. Before we get too carried away, however, it is important to note some problems with this potential alliance. First is the empirical point, equally applicable to socialism, that while the vast majority of animal advocates are women, the vast majority of women are not members and do not adopt an animal rights lifestyle, eating meat and buying products tested on animals.

There are theoretical problems with associating feminism with the protection of animals too. The oppression argument only takes us so far, not least because violence against women and sexism in general is frowned upon and legislatively proscribed in the developed world, whereas violence against animals in the course of food production and research is not. In terms of the values approach, the juxtaposition between so-called female values of caring and compassion on the one hand, and rights on the other, can be challenged. Rights theory emphasizes the need to protect individuals, surely not a cold and calculating objective, and the work of major, male, figures in animal ethics – such as Regan and Singer – is replete with references to the caring and compassionate side of their life's work.

Moreover, rights theory still offers us, in my view and – it should be added – the bulk of feminists, a better guide to action than an ethic of care. It is not clear from an ethic of care, for instance, whether meat eating is wrong per se or whether the care stops at the point of slaughter. Likewise, care can include humans too, of course, so what happens in the event of a conflict between the interests of humans and animals such as in medical research? By contrast, rights offers us much more definite answers to these questions.

Finally, there is the case for associating the protection of animals with the environmental movement. Again, the links here are obvious. Most notably, of course, both movements are concerned with protecting the non-human world. Moreover, the radical dark-green part of the movement, furnished with an ecocentric ethic, seeks to dethrone humans from the moral pedestal, and therefore seeks to protect the interests of the non-human world independently of those of humans.

Again, there are limits to the viability of the links between environmentalists and animal advocates. The two movements have tended to treat each other with suspicion and, particularly in the United States, with some hostility. This reflects ideological conflicts that were explored in chapter 9. Much of the environmental movement is anthropocentric in nature. That is, the interests of animals are only considered when it suits human interests to do so for aesthetic, economic or medicinal reasons. When it doesn't suit human interests, then animals have no worth and can be sacrificed. There is conflict too between dark-green environmentalists and animal advocates. For one thing, an ecocentric ethic seeks to accord moral standing to the whole of nature and not just to sentient beings. Animal advocates, as we have seen, tend to be pretty strict about limiting moral standing to sentiency. In addition, environmentalists of both anthropocentric and ecocentric hues adopt a holistic position whereby it is justified to sacrifice the interests of individual animals if by so doing the ecosystem is preserved. This, as we saw, is incompatible with the individualistic character of animal rights.

An embellished liberalism

Socialism, feminism or environmentalism, then, do not offer us a completely satisfactory natural home for animal advocates. Liberalism, it seems, still offers the best hope, not least because it is, unlike its competitors, a mainstream ideology in Western societies. The task for animal advocates is to formulate a revised version of liberalism that deals with some of its present weaknesses and recognizes that other ideological traditions may also have something to offer. This will involve including animals within a liberal theory of justice. In addition, it should be recognized that unfettered, free-market liberalism, with its emphasis on the maximization of profits and the sanctity of private property, makes it much more difficult to reform the infrastructure of animal exploitation. Animal advocates, too, ought to be in the forefront of campaigns for greater equality between humans, since it is difficult to justify greater equality between humans and animals if there are major class or gender inequalities.

The issue of agency for animal protection remains to be fully worked out but the preceding discussion has identified a number of fruitful avenues worth exploring. There is no reason why animal advocates cannot take a multi-dimensional approach in the absence of one obvious ally. Those living near factory farms and abattoirs, those who have been put out of business by factory farms, those who have been victims of animal experimentation, those who work with poor pay and conditions in animal enterprises, those who might be able to identify in general with the parallels between human and animal exploitation – on the grounds of class or gender or race – should be the animal protection movement's allies. All can be focused on the achievement of a left-leaning liberalism, advocated traditionally by the Democrats in the United States and the Labour Party in Britain, which incorporates animals into a liberal theory of justice and which seeks to reduce inequalities between human beings and between humans and animals.

One should not underestimate the difficulties of achieving greater equality between humans, let alone extending it beyond the species barrier. The latter objective requires a paradigm shift in liberal moral and political thought. Yet there is some evidence that, at the level of ideas at least, human dominion is weakening its grasp. The fact that there is now a market for a book like this illustrates the point. Moreover, in the last twenty years or so we have witnessed the emergence of a more enlightened anthropocentrism that has begun to improve the welfare of the animals with whom we share the planet. There are many noble men and women who work hard and tirelessly to achieve a better life for animals. I, for one, hope they succeed.

Notes

Chapter 1   Introduction

1   Brigid Brophy's article for the *Sunday Times* (1965) is credited as one of the first attempts to put animal rights on the agenda in the modern period. Almost a decade later, in 1973, three Oxford philosophers – Roslind and Stanley Godlovitch and John Harris – edited a set of articles collectively published as *Animals, Men and Morals*, which included contributions from Brophy and Ryder. After reviewing this volume, Peter Singer – an Australian moral philosopher – wrote *Animal Liberation* in 1975. Singer's utilitarian defence of animals (the second edition of which was published in 1990) was followed by a number of accounts which sought to accord rights to animals. This included work by Andrew Linzey (1976; 1987), Stephen Clark (1984) and Ryder (1975) who wrote, among other things, one of the first animal rights-based attacks on animal experimentation. In the meantime, the American philosopher Tom Regan began to develop, in a series of articles (1982), a rights-based critique of the moral orthodoxy. This culminated in *The Case for Animal Rights* (1984).

2   The 'second wave' includes Rowlands (1998 and 2002) on contractarianism, Francione (1995) and Wise (2000), both of whom examine the legal constraints on the well-being of animals, and DeGrazia (1996 and 2002) and Pluhar (1995) who concentrate primarily on particular aspects of the debate, the mental complexity of animals and the so-called 'argument from marginal cases' respectively. In addition, there have been attempts to define where animal ethics stands ideologically. A general account is provided by Garner (2005), while there have also been attempts to ground animal ethics in socialism (Benton, 1993) and feminism (Donovan and Adams, 1996). The 'backlash' to the animal rights/liberation literature has come in the form of a number of book-

length defences of the moral inferiority of animals by, most notably, Leahy (1991), Carruthers (1992) and Scruton (2000).

Chapter 2   Animals and the Equal Consideration of Interests

1   Having said all this, Sapontzis (1993: 274) correctly raises the possibility that although animals do not take an interest in voting they have an interest in it on the grounds that whoever is elected can have a considerable impact on their well-being. As a consequence, animals might 'need the right to vote – through a concerned, informed guardian – in order to protect their interests in life, liberty and the pursuit of happiness'.

Chapter 3   Are Animals Worth Anything?

1   A full assessment of environmental ethics is beyond the scope of this book (see Attfield, 2003; Dobson, 2000). For the record, I'm with Singer and the others on this one. As Frey (1983: 154–5) astutely remarks, while it makes sense to say that we can harm non-sentient entities such as a river or a mountain or a tree, it does not seem to make sense to say that we can wrong them. Of course, the river, mountain and tree may have some value but this value is extrinsic in the sense of their usefulness to other, sentient, elements that rely on them. While denying that non-sentient parts of nature lack moral standing, most environmental ethicists would not deny that those possessing sentiency have greater moral significance. As Fox (1984: 199) memorably wrote: 'Cows do scream louder than carrots', and by virtue of this do have greater moral significance. Attfield (2003: 44–6) develops such an hierarchical ethical system whereby humans, animals and living – but non-sentient – parts of nature all have moral standing but decreasing amounts of moral significance.
2   Discussion of the issue of animal sentiency can be found in DeGrazia (1996: 108–12); DeGrazia (2002: 41–5); Rodd (1990); Rowlands (2002: 5–9).
3   The importance of language for beliefs is a view held by a number of philosophers including, most notably, Davidson (1985) and Stich (1983).
4   See Hobbes (1992: 97), Locke (1988: 271), Kant (1965: 345–6) and Descartes (1912: 43–6), to name but a few.

Chapter 4   Why Shouldn't Animals Be Equal?

1   The reader is advised to consult the reviews in DeGrazia, 1996: chapters 4–7; Griffin, 1992; Pluhar, 1995: 46–55; Regan, 1984: chapters 1 and 2; Regan and Singer, 1990: Part Two; Rodd, 1990: 79–86; Rowlands, 2002: 12–25; Singer, 1993: 110–17; Wise, 2000: 119–62.

2 Research on the capabilities of non-human primates is reviewed by Wise (2000: 217–30). For a discussion of the teaching of sign language to apes see Fouts and Fouts (1993) and Singer (1993: 111–12). Examples of animal moral agency are discussed in Pluhar (1995: 55–6) and Singer (1981: 6–7).

3 This is the basis, for instance, of the so-called Great Ape Project (Cavalieri and Singer, 1993), a worldwide campaign that seeks to argue the case for the attachment of legal rights to creatures closest to us.

4 I am indebted to an anonymous reader for this point.

Chapter 5 Questions of Life and Death

1 Representative statements of this position are provided by McCloskey (1979) and Townsend (1979).

2 Rowlands (2002: 95–7), for instance, argues that Regan's assertion can be challenged by the application of a contractarian approach (see chapter 6). To put it simply, Rowlands imagines a hypothetical pre-social situation where we are unaware whether we are to turn out to be humans or animals. In such a situation, it is inconceivable that rational individuals would choose a principle that allowed millions of animals to die in order to save the life of one human since the odds are stacked in favour of them being one of the dogs rather than a human.

Chapter 6 Rights, Utility, Contractarianism and Animals

1 Three articles, by Pritchard and Robinson (1981), Singer (1988) and Vandeveer (1979) set out the pro-animal critique of Rawls. The most sustained and sophisticated version has been the book-length studies by Rowlands (1998; 2002).

2 Key contemporary advocates of rights are Dworkin (1978), Nozick (1974) and Rawls (1972).

Chapter 7 Should We Eat Animals?

1 For a detailed account of the stress caused by factory farming, see the evidence provided by Fraser and Broom (1990: 267–8, 318–28, 307–17).

2 For details of ritual slaughter, see reports by the British Farm Animal Welfare Council (FAWC, 1985; 2003). On problems in British slaughterhouses, see FAWC reports (1982, 1984) and newspaper articles in the *Guardian* (8 March 1989) and the *Sunday Times* (9 July 1989). For an American perspective, see Scully (2002: 282–4) and Eisnitz (1997).

3 Details of the contribution meat eating makes to health problems is covered by Frey (1983: 6–16), and Mason and Singer (1990: 52–69). The

environmental consequences are discussed by Singer (1990: 166–9) and Mason and Singer (1990: 72–127).

4   As Rowlands (1998: 147–57) is able to show convincingly, a contractarian approach is able to justify vegetarianism without recourse to a costs and benefits analysis involving economic factors. As he points out (1998: 151):

> Once it is allowed that knowledge of one's species should be one of those things excluded by the veil of ignorance, it would be just as irrational to opt for a system that permitted harmful or injurious treatment of non-humans as it would be to opt for a system that permitted the same sort of treatment for humans.

As a result: 'Given that you don't know whether you will be human or non-human, eater or eaten . . . it is fairly clear that to opt for the . . . world without an animal husbandry industry . . . would be the rational choice.' Since this harm includes not just suffering but also death, the contractarian approach rules out all forms of animal agriculture and not just intensive forms which cause more suffering.

The reason for relegating this insight to a note is that, as we saw in chapter 6, the contractarian approach, in my view, is not entirely separate from the rights and utilitarian positions but relies on some of the arguments – such as the argument from marginal cases – commonly found in pro-animal philosophy.

Chapter 8   To Vivisect or Not to Vivisect?

1   The publicity given to these experiments by the Uncaged Campaign group led to considerable controversy, with the Home Office inspectorate being criticized for granting project licences for them. A subsequent investigation by the inspectorate backed the original decision and found no evidence of wrong-doing by those conducting the research. Some argued that this investigation was seriously flawed and disguised significant problems, but, whether or not this is true, the severe nature of the suffering of the animals, coupled with doubts about the viability of xenotransplantation, make it unlikely that any future projects of this kind will be licensed in Britain.

2   Except perhaps the suggestion that convicted criminals could be used, which seems to be a popular view amongst some segments of the public. Leahy (1991: 235) suggests, with all seriousness apparently, that criminals ought to be offered the chance to participate in medical experiments on the understanding that, if they survive, their sentences should be reduced or commuted. This proposition, I would say, is counter-intuitive. It certainly differs from the proposition that we should use marginal humans in experiments. The use of marginal humans is justified on the grounds that they are unlikely to suffer as much as 'normal' humans. No

such justification is open when discussing the use of criminals. What seems to be coming into play, instead, is a principle based on desert whereby criminals are not as deserving as those who have not committed an offence. Of course, too, at least in Leahy's plan, the decision to participate remains voluntary.

Chapter 9   Zoos, Pets and Wild Animals

1   For historical accounts of our treatment of animals see Ritvo (1987), Ryder (1989) and Turner (1964).
2   I am not considering here the hunting of deer, the coursing of hares, the shooting of game birds and fishing. These issues raise questions that space prevents us from considering. As with fox-hunting, though, an assessment of the moral legitimacy of these practices from the perspective of the moral orthodoxy requires us to weigh up the suffering inflicted on the animals with the benefits deriving from exploiting them.

References

Adams, C. (1990) *The Sexual Politics of Meat: A Feminist Vegetarian Critical Theory*, New York: Continuum.

Adams, C. (1994) *Neither Man Nor Beast: Feminism and the Defence of Animals*, New York: Continuum.

Aglionby, J. (2000) 'Blood on the Beaches', *Guardian*, 24 November.

Arneson, R. (2000) 'The Priority of the Right Over the Good Rides Again', in P. Kelly (ed.), *Impartiality, Neutrality and Justice. Re-reading Brian Barry's Justice as Impartiality*, Edinburgh: Edinburgh University Press, 60–86.

Attfield, R. (2003) *Environmental Ethics*, Cambridge: Polity.

Ayer, A. J. (1936) *Language, Truth and Logic*, London: Gollancz.

Barry, B. (1995) *Justice as Impartiality*, Oxford: Clarendon Press.

Bauston, G. (2002) 'For a Mouthful of Flesh', in K. Stallwood (ed.), *A Primer on Animal Rights*, New York: Lantern, 171–82.

Bell, L. (2001) 'Abusing Children – Abusing Animals', *Journal of Social Work*, 1 (2): 223–34.

Bentham, J. (1948) *An Introduction to the Principles of Morals and Legislation*, New York: Hafner Press.

Benton, T. (1993) *Natural Relations: Ecology, Social Justice and Animal Rights*, London: Verso.

Blum, D. (1994) *The Monkey Wars*, Oxford: Oxford University Press.

Brandt, R. (1992) *Morality, Utilitarianism, and Rights*, Cambridge: Cambridge University Press.

Brophy, B. (1965) 'The Rights of Animals', *Sunday Times*, 10 October.

Browne, P (2002) 'Ten Weeks to Live', *Guardian*, 10 March.

Bryant, J. (1990) *Fettered Kingdoms*, Winchester: Fox Press.

Callicott, J. (1995) 'Animal Liberation: A Triangular Affair', in R. Elliot (ed.), *Environmental Ethics*, Oxford: Oxford University Press, 29–59.

Carruthers, P. (1989) 'Brute Experience', *The Journal of Philosophy*, 86 (5): 258–69.

Carruthers, P. (1992) *The Animals Issue*, Cambridge: Cambridge University Press.

Cavalieri, P. (2001) *The Animal Question: Why Nonhuman Animals Deserve Human Rights*, Oxford: Oxford University Press.

Cavalieri, P. and Singer, P. (eds) (1993) *The Great Ape Project: Equality Beyond Humanity*, London: Fourth Estate.

Cherfas, J. (1988) *The Hunting of the Whale*, London: The Bodley Head.

Clark, S. (1984) *The Moral Status of Animals*, Oxford: Clarendon Press.

Clarke, P. and Linzey, A. (1990) *Political Theory and Animal Rights*, London: Pluto Press.

Coetzee, J. (1999) *The Lives of Animals*, Princeton: Princeton University Press.

Cohen, C. (1986) 'The Case for the Use of Animals in Biomedical Research', *New England Journal of Medicine*, 315 (14): 865–70.

Dahl, R. (1956) *Preface to Democratic Theory*, Chicago: University of Chicago Press.

Davidson, D. (1985) 'Rational Animals', in E. LePore and B. McLaughlin (eds), *Actions and Events: Perspectives on the Philosophy of Donald Davidson*, Oxford: Blackwell, 473–80.

Dawkins, M. (1980) *Animal Suffering: The Science of Animal Welfare*, London: Chapman and Hall.

Dawkins, R. (1993) 'Gaps in the Mind', in P. Cavalieri and P. Singer (eds), *Great Ape Project*, 80–7.

DeGrazia, D. (1996) *Taking Animals Seriously: Mental Life and Moral Status*, Cambridge: Cambridge University Press.

DeGrazia, D. (2002) *Animal Rights: A Very Short Introduction*, Oxford: Oxford University Press.

Dennett, D. (1976) 'Conditions of Personhood', in A. Rorty (ed.), *The Identities of Persons*, Berkeley: University of California Press, 175–96.

Descartes, R. (1912) 'Discourse V', in J. Veitch (ed.), *Rene Descartes: A Discourse on Method*, London: Dent.

Dobson, A. (2000) *Green Political Thought*, London: Unwin Hyman, 3rd edn.

Dombrowski, D. (1997) *Babies and Beasts: The Argument from Marginal Cases*, Chicago: University of Illinois Press.

Donovan, J. and Adams, C. (eds) (1996) *Beyond Animal Rights: A Feminist Caring Ethic for the Treatment of Animals*, New York: Continuum.

Duran, J. (1994) 'Commentary', *Between the Species*, Winter and Spring: 8–9.

Dworkin, R. (1978) *Taking Rights Seriously*, London: Duckworth.

Eisnitz, G. (1997) *Slaughterhouse*, Amherst: Prometheus.

FAWC (1982) *Report on the Welfare of Poultry at the Time of Slaughter*, London.

FAWC (1984) *Report on the Welfare of Livestock (Red Meat Animals) at the Time of Slaughter*, London.

FAWC (1985) *Report on the Welfare of Livestock When Slaughtered by Religious Methods*, London.

FAWC (2003) *Report on the Welfare of Farmed Animals at Slaughter or Killing*, London.

Feinberg, J. (1986) 'Abortion', in T. Regan (ed.), *Matters of Life and Death*, New York: Random House, 256–93.

Fort, M. (2001) 'Yes, Our Food is Cheap – and so is Our Talk', *Observer*, 11 March.

Fouts, R. and Fouts, D. (1993) 'Chimpanzees' Use of Sign Language', in P. Cavalieri and P. Singer (eds), *Great Ape Project*, 28–41.

Fox, W. (1984) 'Deep Ecology: A New Philosophy of Our Times', *The Ecologist*, 14 (5): 199–200.

Francione, G. (1995) *Animals, Property and the Law*, Philadelphia: Temple University Press.

Francione, G. (2000) *Introduction to Animal Rights: Your Child or the Dog*, Philadelphia: Temple University Press.

Fraser, A. and Broom, D. (1990) *Farm Animal Behaviour and Welfare*, London.

Frey, R. (1980) *Interests and Rights: The Case Against Animals*, Oxford: Oxford University Press.

Frey, R. (1983) *Rights, Killing and Suffering*, Oxford: Clarendon Press.

Frey, R. (1987) 'Autonomy and the Value of Animal Life', *Monist*, 70 (1): 50–63.

Frey, R. (2002) 'Ethics, Animals and Scientific Inquiry', in P. Gluck et al., *Applied Ethics*, 13–24.

Garner, R. (1994) 'Wildlife Conservation and the Moral Status of Animals', *Environmental Politics*, 3 (1): 114–29.

Garner, R. (1998) *Political Animals: Animal Protection Politics in Britain and the United States*, Basingstoke: Macmillan.

Garner, R. (1999) 'Animal Protection and Legislators in Britain and the United States', *Journal of Legislative Studies*, 5 (2): 92–114.

Garner, R. (2003) 'Animals, Politics and Justice: Rawlsian Liberalism and the Plight of Non-Humans', *Environmental Politics*, 12 (2): 3–22.

Garner, R. (2004) *Animals, Politics and Morality*, Manchester: Manchester University Press, 2nd edn.

Garner, R. (2005) *The Political Theory of Animal Rights*, Manchester: Manchester University Press.

Gilligan, C. (1982) *In a Different Voice*, Cambridge, Mass.: Harvard University Press.

Gluck, J., DiPasquale, T. and Orlans, F. B. (2002) *Applied Ethics in Animal Research*, Indiana: Purdue University Press.

Godlovitch, S., Godlovitch, R. and Harris, J. (eds) (1973) *Animals, Men and Morals*, New York: Taplinger.

Goodin, R. and Reeve, A. (eds) (1989) *Liberal Neutrality*, London: Routledge.

Greanville, P. and Moss, D. (1985) 'The Emerging Face of the Movement', *Animals' Agenda*, March–April: 36.

Griffin, D. (1992) *Animal Minds*, Chicago: University of Chicago Press.

Guerrini, A. (2002) 'The Rhetorics of Animal Rights', in J. Gluck et al., *Applied Ethics*, 55–76.

Harrison, G. (1979) 'Relativism and Tolerance', in P. Laslett and J. Fishkin (eds), *Philosophy, Politics and Society*, Fifth Series, Oxford: Blackwell, 273–90.

Harrison, R. (1964) *Animal Machines*, London: Vincent Stuart.

Hegel, G. W. F. (1942) *Philosophy of Right*, Oxford: Oxford University Press.

HMSO (1965) *Report of the Technical Committee to Enquire into the Welfare of Animals Kept under Intensive Livestock Husbandry Systems (the Brambell Report)*, Cmnd. 2836.

HMSO (2003) *Statistics of Scientific Procedures on Living Animals 2002*, Cmnd. 5886.

Hobbes, T. (1992) *Leviathan*. Cambridge: Cambridge University Press.

Holland, A. (1984) 'On Behalf of a Moderate Speciesism', *Journal of Applied Philosophy*, 1 (2): 281–91.

Holland, S. (2003) *Bioethics. A Philosophical Introduction*, Cambridge: Polity.

House of Lords (2002) *Select Committee on Animals in Scientific Procedures*, Minutes of Evidence, 17 July 2001.

Hutton, J. (1981) 'Animal Abuse as a Diagnostic Approach in Social Work: A Pilot Study', *Paper presented at the International Conference on the Human/Companion Animal Bond*, Philadelphia, PA.

Jamieson, D. (1985) 'Against Zoos', in P. Singer, *In Defence of Animals*.

Johnson, A. (1991) *Factory Farming*, Oxford: Blackwell.

Johnson, W. (1990) *The Rose Tinted Menagerie*, Oxford: Blackwell.

Jones, P. (1994) *Rights*, Basingstoke: Macmillan.

Kant, I. (1965) *Metaphysics of Morals*, New York: Bobbs Merrill.

Kuhse, H. and Singer, P. (1985) *Should the Baby Live: The Problems of Handicapped Babies*, Oxford: Oxford University Press.

Kymlicka, W. (2002) *Contemporary Political Philosophy*, Oxford: Oxford University Press, 2nd edn.

Leahy, M. (1991) *Against Liberation: Putting Animals into Perspective*, London: Routledge.

Leopold, A. (1949) *A Sand County Almanac*, Oxford: Oxford University Press.

Lindblom, C. (1977) *Politics and Markets*, New York: Basic Books.

Linzey, A. (1976) *Animal Rights: A Christian Assessment of Man's Treatment of Animals*, London: SCM Press.

Linzey, A. (1987) *Christianity and the Rights of Animals*, London: Crossroad.

Locke, J. (1988) *Two Treatises of Government*. Cambridge: Cambridge University Press.

Locke, J. (1997) *An Essay Concerning Human Understanding*, Harmondsworth: Penguin.

Lodge, R. (1951) *Appled Philosophy*, London: Macmillan.

Lukes, S. (1974) *Power: A Radical View*, London: Macmillan.

Lynch, J. (1994) 'Is Animal Pain Conscious?', *Between the Species*, Winter and Spring: 1–7.

Lyons, D. (1965) *Forms and Limits of Utilitarianism*, Oxford: Oxford University Press.

McCloskey, H. (1979) 'Moral Rights and Animals', *Inquiry*, 22: 23–54.

McGinn, C. (1992) *Moral Literacy*, London: Duckworth.

Marquis, D. (1989) 'Why Abortion is Immoral', *Journal of Philosophy*, 86 (4): 183–202.

Mason, J. (2002) 'Making a Killing', in K. Stallwood (ed.), *A Primer on Animal Rights*, New York: Lantern, 199–209.

Mason, J. and Singer, P. (1990) *Animal Factories*, New York: Harmony Books.

Midgley, M. (1983) *Animals and Why They Matter*, Harmondsworth: Penguin.

Mill, J. S. (1969) 'Three Essays on Religion', in J. M. Robson (ed.), *John Stuart Mill: Essays on Ethics, Religion and Society*, London: Routledge and Kegan Paul.

Mill, J. S. (1972) *Utilitarianism, On Liberty, and Considerations on Representative Government*, London: Dent.

Mills, C. Wright (1956), *The Power Elite*, New York: Oxford University Press.

Moore Lapper, F. (1971) *Diet for a Small Planet*, London: Ballantine.

Moore, N. (1987) *The Bird of Time: The Science and Politics of Nature Conservation*, Cambridge: Cambridge University Press.

Naess (1973) 'The Shallow and the Deep, Long Range Ecology Movement. A Summary', *Inquiry*, 16: 95–100.

Nagel, T. (1974) 'What Is It Like To Be a Bat?', *Philosophical Review*, 83 (4): 435–50.

Nagel, T. (1987) 'Moral Conflict and Political Legitimacy', *Philosophy and Public Affairs*, 16 (3): 215–40.

Narveson, J. (1977) 'Animal Rights', *Canadian Journal of Philosophy*, 7 (2): 161–78.

Narveson, J. (1987) 'On a Case for Animal Rights', *Monist*, 70 (1): 21–49.

Nozick, R. (1974) *Anarchy, State and Utopia*, Oxford: Blackwell.

Orlans, F. B. (1993) *In the Name of Science: Issues in Responsible Animal Experimentation*, New York: Oxford University Press.

Passmore, J. (1974) *Man's Responsibility for Nature*, London: Duckworth.

Patterson, F. and Gordon, W. (1993) 'The Case for the Personhood of Gorillas', in P. Cavalieri and P. Singer (eds), *Great Ape Project*, 58–77.

Piper, H. (2003) 'The Linkage of Animal Abuse with Interpersonal Violence. A Sheep in Wolf's Clothing', *Journal of Social Work*, 3 (2): 161–77.

Pluhar, E. (1995) *Beyond Prejudice: The Moral Significance of Human and Nonhuman Animals*, Durham: Duke University Press.

Pojman, L. (1993) 'Do Animal Rights Entail Moral Nihilism?', *Public Affairs Quarterly*, 7 (2): 165–85.

Poole, R. (1996) 'On Being a Person', *Australasian Journal of Philosophy*, 74 (1): 38–56.

Pritchard, M. and Robinson, W. (1981) 'Justice and the Treatment of Animals: A Critique of Rawls', *Environmental Ethics*, 3: 55–61.

Rachels, J. (1983) 'Do Animals Have a Right to Life?' in Miller and Williams (eds) *Ethics and Animals*, 275–84.

Rachels, J. (1990) *Created From Animals*, Oxford: Oxford University Press.

Radford, M. (2001) *Animal Welfare Law in Britain*, Oxford: Oxford University Press.

Rawls, J. (1963) 'The Sense of Justice', *The Philosophical Review*, 72 (3): 281–305.

Rawls, J. (1972) *A Theory of Justice*, Oxford: Oxford University Press.

Rawls, J. (1993) *Political Liberalism*, New York: Columbia University Press.

Regan, T. (1975) 'The Moral Basis of Vegetarianism', *Canadian Journal of Philosophy*, 5 (2): 181–214.

Regan, T. (1982) *All That Dwell Therein*, Berkeley: University of California Press.

Regan, T. (1984) *The Case for Animal Rights*, London: Routledge.

Regan, T. (2004) *Empty Cages. Facing the Challenge of Animal Rights*, Lanham, MD: Rowman and Littlefield.

Regan, T. and Singer, P. (1976) *Animal Rights and Human Obligations* (2nd edn, 1990), Englewood Cliffs, NJ: Prentice Hall.

Regenstein, L. (1985) 'Animal Rights, Endangered Species and Human Survival', in P. Singer, *In Defence of Animals*.

Ritvo, H. (1987) *The Animal Estate*, Cambridge, Mass.: Harvard University Press.

Rodd, R. (1990) *Biology, Ethics and Animals*, Oxford: Clarendon Press.

Rollin, B. (1981) *Animal Rights and Human Morality*, New York: Prometheus.

Rollin, B. (1989) *The Unheeded Cry: Animal Consciousness, Animal Pain and Science*, Oxford: Oxford University Press.

Rowlands, M. (1998) *Animal Rights: A Philosophical Defence*, Basingstoke: Macmillan.

Rowlands, M. (2002) *Animals Like Us*, London: Verso.

Russell, W. and Burch, R. (1959) *The Principles of Humane Experimental Technique*, London: Methuen.

Ryder, R. (1975) *Victims of Science*, London: Davis-Poynter.

Ryder, R. (1989) *Animal Revolution: Changing Attitudes Towards Speciesism*, Oxford: Blackwell.

Ryder, R. (1998) *The Political Animal: The Conquest of Speciesism*, Jefferson, NC: McFarland.

Sapontzis, S. (1987) *Morals, Reason, and Animals*, Philadelphia: Temple University Press.

Sapontzis, S. (1993) 'Aping Persons – Pro and Con', in P. Cavalieri and P. Singer (eds), *Great Ape Project*, 269–77.

Scanlon, T. (1982) 'Contracturalism and Utilitarianism', in A. Sen and B. Williams (eds), *Utilitarianism and Beyond*, Cambridge: Cambridge University Press.

Scruton, R. (2000) *Animal Rights and Wrongs*, London: Metro.

Scully, M. (2002) *Dominion: The Power of Man, the Suffering of Animals and the Call to Mercy*, New York: St Martin's Press.

Sharpe, R. (1988) *The Cruel Deception: The Use of Animals in Medical Research*, Wellingborough: Thorsons.

Sidgwick, H. (1966) *The Methods of Ethics*, New York: Dover.

Singer, B. (1988) 'An Extension of Rawls' Theory of Justice to Environmental Ethics', *Environmental Ethics*, 10: 213–32.

Singer, P. (1974) *Democracy and Disobedience*, Oxford: Oxford University Press.

Singer, P. (1981) *The Expanding Circle: Ethics and Sociobiology*, Oxford: Oxford University Press.

Singer, P. (ed.) (1985) *In Defence of Animals*, Oxford: Blackwell.

Singer, P. (1990) *Animal Liberation* (2nd edn), London: Cape.

Singer, P. (1993) *Practical Ethics*, Cambridge: Cambridge University Press, 2nd edn.

Singer, P. (1994) *Rethinking Life and Death*, Oxford: Oxford University Press.

Singer, P. (2004) 'Humans Are Sentient Too', *Guardian*, 30 July.

Smart, J. (1973) 'An Outline of a System of Utilitarian Ethics', in J. Smart and B. Williams, *Utilitarianism: For and Against*, 1–74.

Spencer, C. (1995) *The Heretic's Feast: A History of Vegetarianism*, Hanover: University Press of New England.

Stich, S. (1983) *From Folk Psychology to Cognitive Science*, Cambridge, Mass.: MIT Press.

Taylor, P. W. (1986) *Respect for Nature: A Theory of Environmental Ethics*, Princeton: Princeton University Press.

Thomas, G. (1993) *An Introduction to Ethics*, London: Duckworth.

Tooley, M. (1972) 'Abortion and Infanticide', *Philosophy and Public Affairs*, 2 (1): 37–65.

Tooley, M. (1983) *Abortion and Infanticide*, Oxford: Clarendon Press.

Townsend, A. (1979) 'Radical Vegetarians', *Australasian Journal of Philosophy*, 57 (1): 85–93.

Tudge, C. (1992) *Last Animals at the Zoo: How Mass Extinction can be Stopped*, Oxford: Oxford University Press.

Turner, E. (1964) *All Heaven in a Rage*, London: Centaur.

Vandeveer, D. (1979) 'Of Beasts, Persons and the Original Position', *The Monist*, 62 (3): 368–77.

Varner, G. (1998) *In Nature's Interests? Animal Rights and Environmental Ethics*, New York: Oxford University Press.

Waldron, J. (ed.) (1987) *'Nonsense upon Stilts: Bentham, Burke and Marx on the Rights of Man*, London: Methuen.

Waldron, J. (1989) 'Legislation and Moral Neutrality', in R. Goodin and A. Reeve (eds), *Liberal Neutrality*, London: Routledge, 61–83.

Warnock, M. (1998) *An Intelligent Person's Guide to Ethics*, London: Duckworth.

Warren, M. (1997) *Moral Status*, Oxford: Clarendon Press.

Webster, J. (1994) *Animal Welfare: A Cool Eye Towards Eden*, Oxford: Blackwell.

Wenz, P. (1988) *Environmental Justice*, Albany: State University of New York Press.

Wilkins, D. (1997) *Animal Welfare in Europe*, London: Kluwer Law International.

Wise, S. (2000) *Rattling the Cage: Toward Legal Rights to Animals*, Cambridge, Mass.: Perseus Books.

Index

Printed in the United States
140142LV00005B/32/P